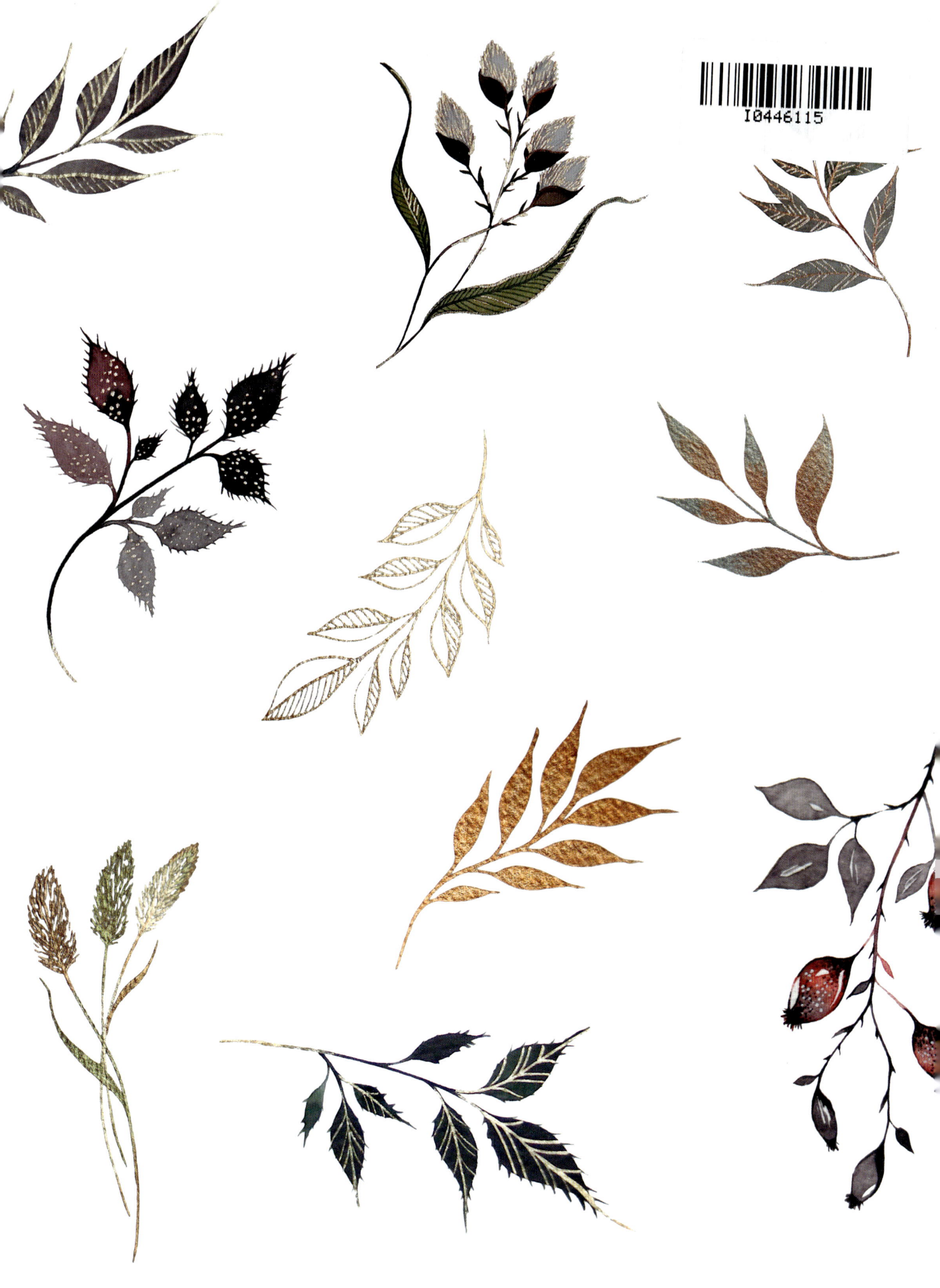

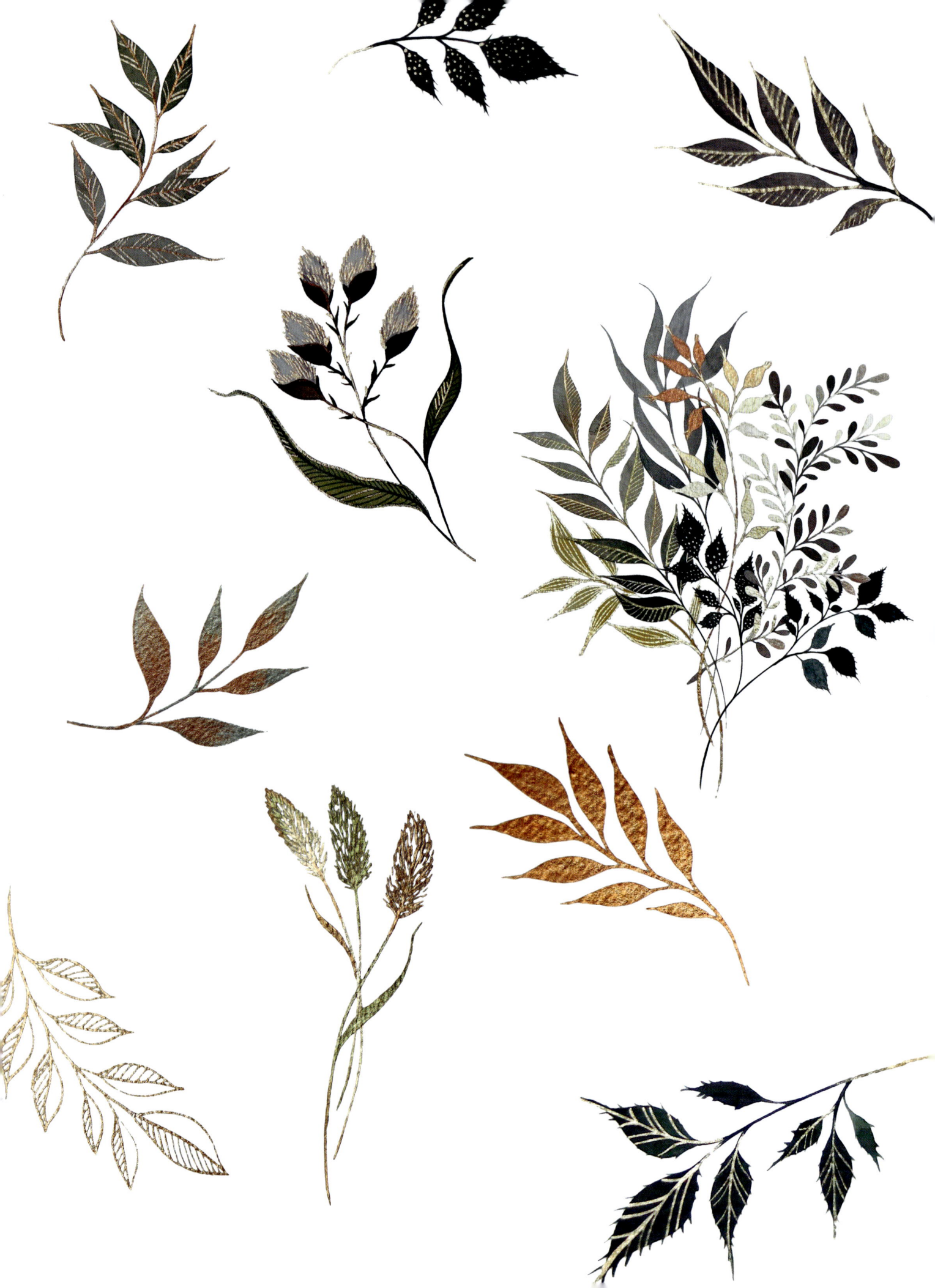

Metallic
WATERCOLOR

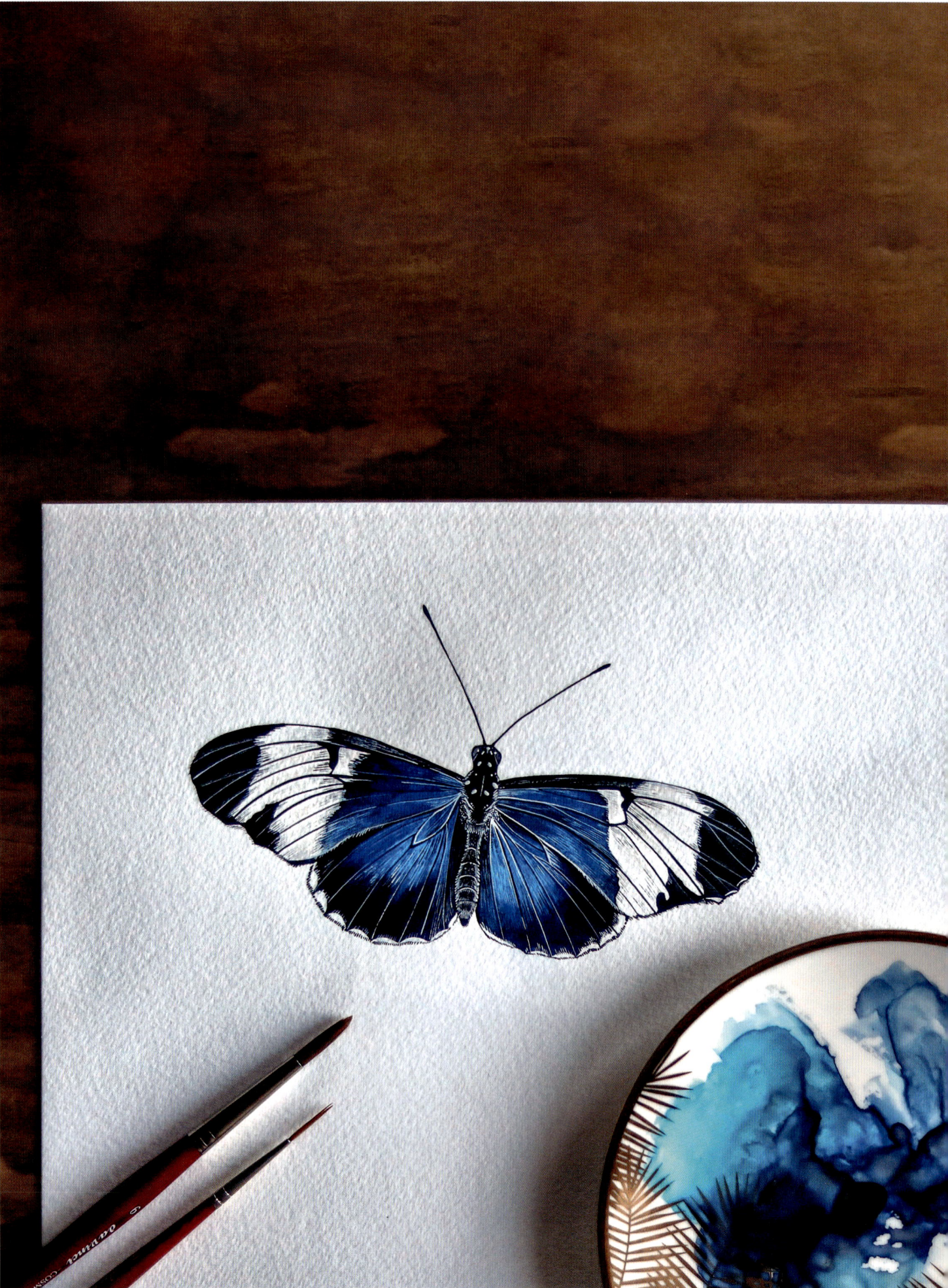

Metallic

WATERCOLOR

CREATE SHIMMERING ARTWORK WITH METALLIC PAINTS

**ELISABETH GÖTZ
@ LISILINKA**

STEP-BY-STEP
PROJECTS
FOR FLORA,
FAUNA, FEATHERS,
AND MORE

QUARRY

CONTENTS

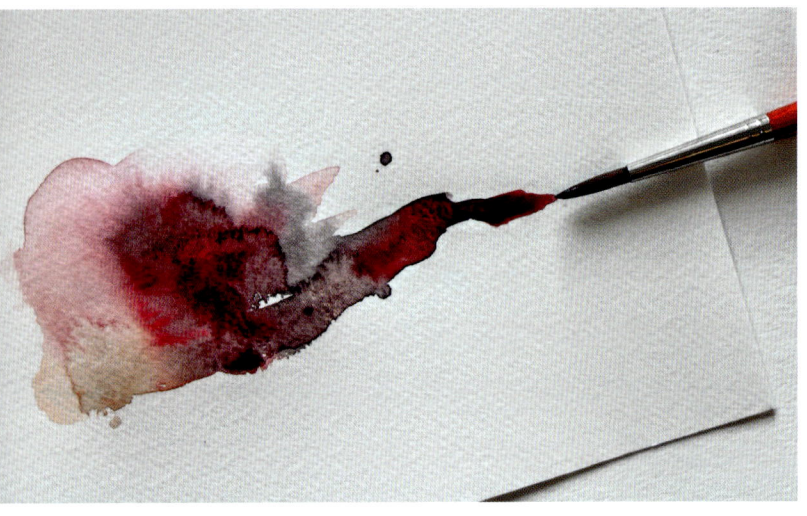

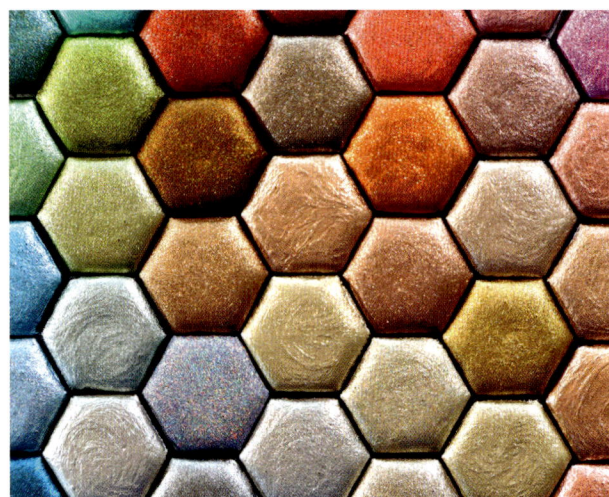

Basics

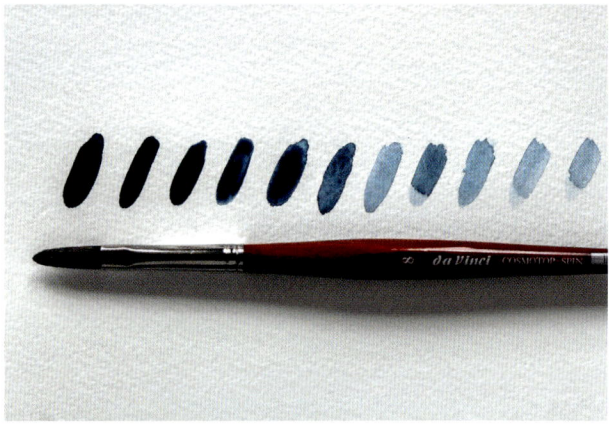

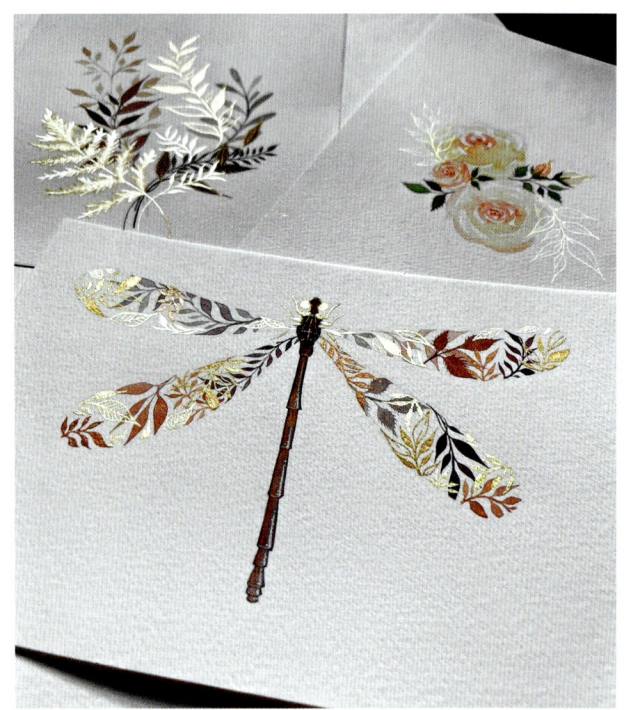

Projects

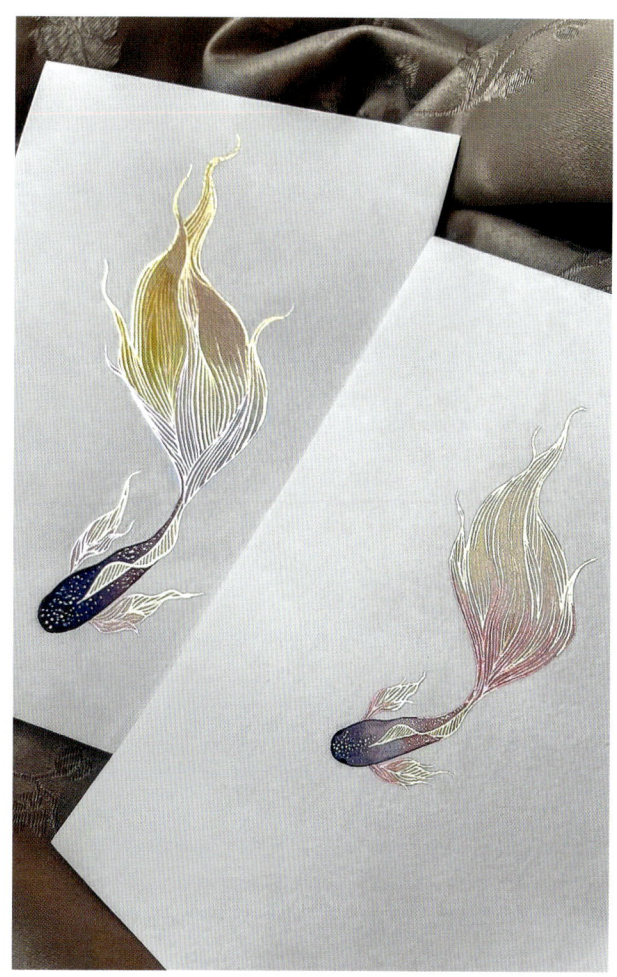

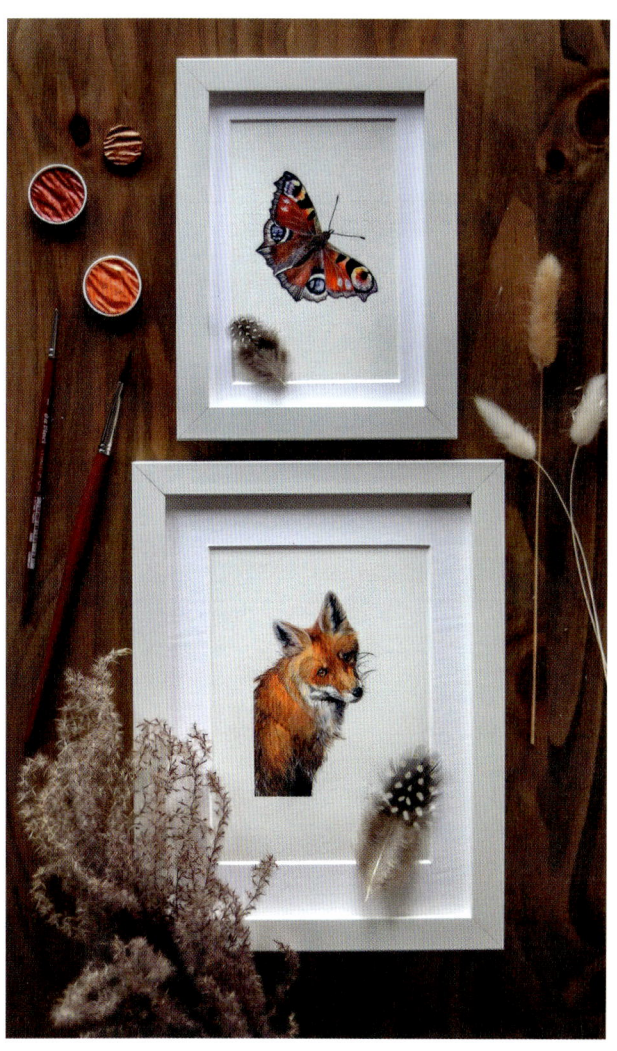

INTRODUCTION

Join me in my love of the details!

People often ask how long I've been drawing, and every time, my answer is more or less the same: ever since I've been able to think. My first pictures were made at the tender age of three. Even then, I mostly drew motifs from nature. In that respect, not much has changed. Although my drawing style has improved over the years, the world of plants and animals, with its spectrum of colors and endless details, is my greatest source of inspiration.

My parents were both math teachers, so my education was very science-focused, and I pursued a career as a psychologist. I always kept one foot in the art world, though, and used my pictures to finance my life as a student and as a creative oasis during my studies. It was at this time that I discovered my love of watercolor painting, a love that has stayed with me to this day. Watercolors offer endless possibilities and create striking effects with beautiful gradients. They can even be used to add fine details to your work and give your paintings a unique, sophisticated touch. I find that the more delicate the textures are, the more meditative the process of painting becomes.

Sparkling metallic paints really make a delicate watercolor shine. The combination of conventional watercolor paints, metallic paints, and my own filigree painting style has become my trademark as an artist.

Thanks to social media, I can now share my pictures with the world, and my Instagram profile has become my personal portfolio. It feels great to be in touch and to exchange ideas with creatives from all over the world. This platform has been the springboard for many exciting projects—and now, with this book, you can accompany me on my creative journey.

Whether you consider yourself an experienced artist or are just setting out on your creative path, let's create a space where we can pick up our paintbrushes and forget the stress of our fast-paced lives for a while.

Time to get started!

Elisabeth Götz

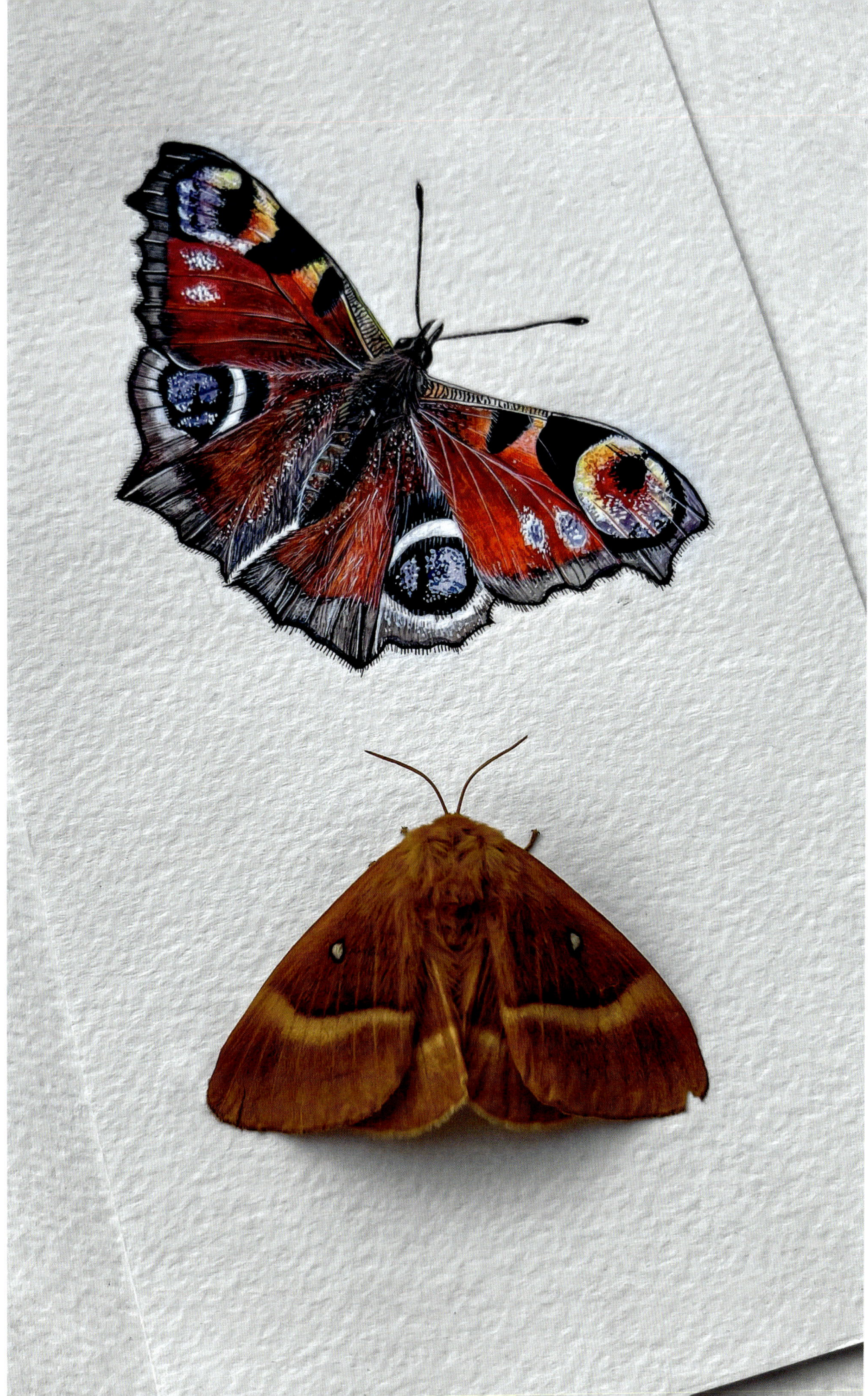

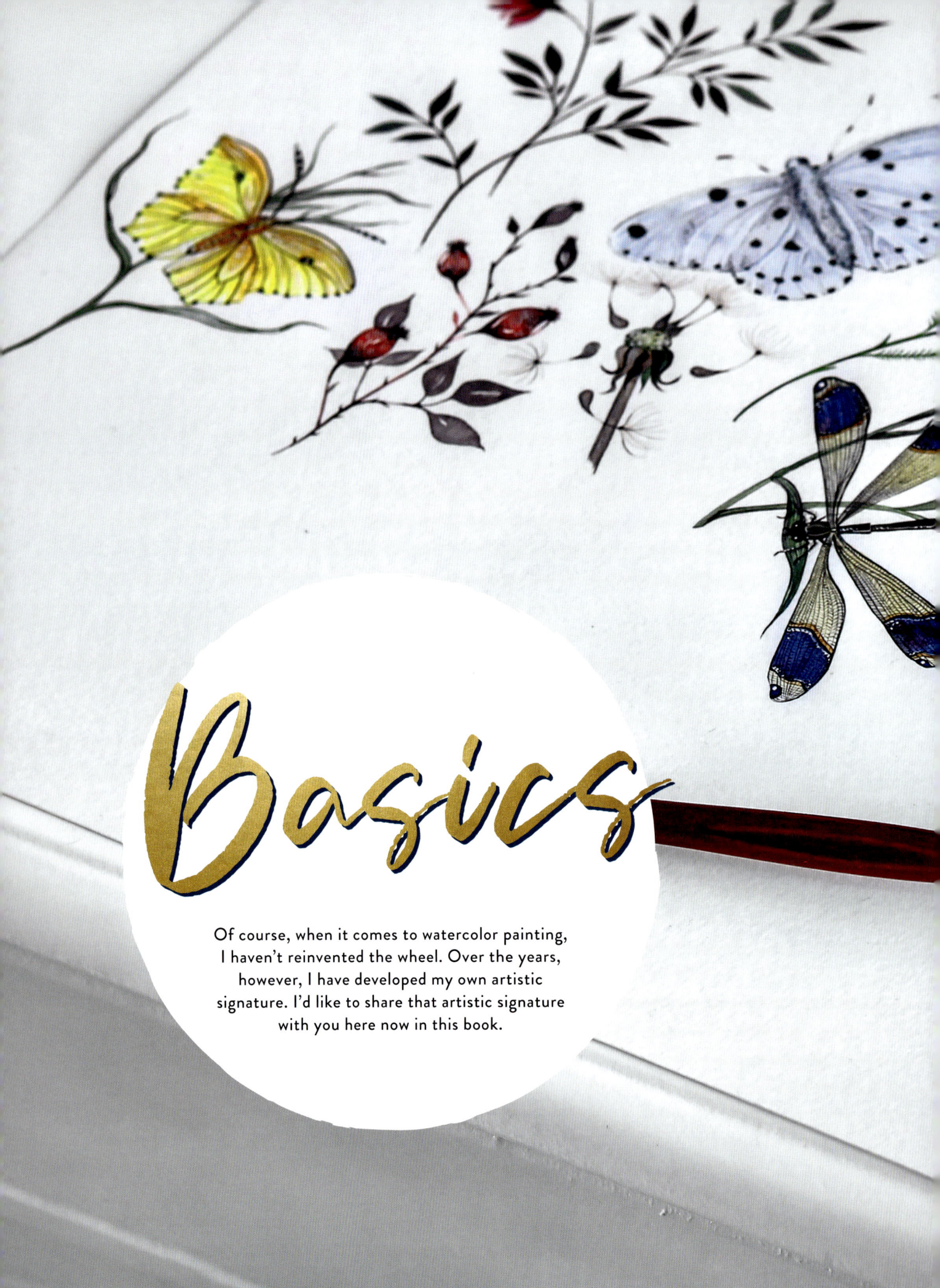

Basics

Of course, when it comes to watercolor painting, I haven't reinvented the wheel. Over the years, however, I have developed my own artistic signature. I'd like to share that artistic signature with you here now in this book.

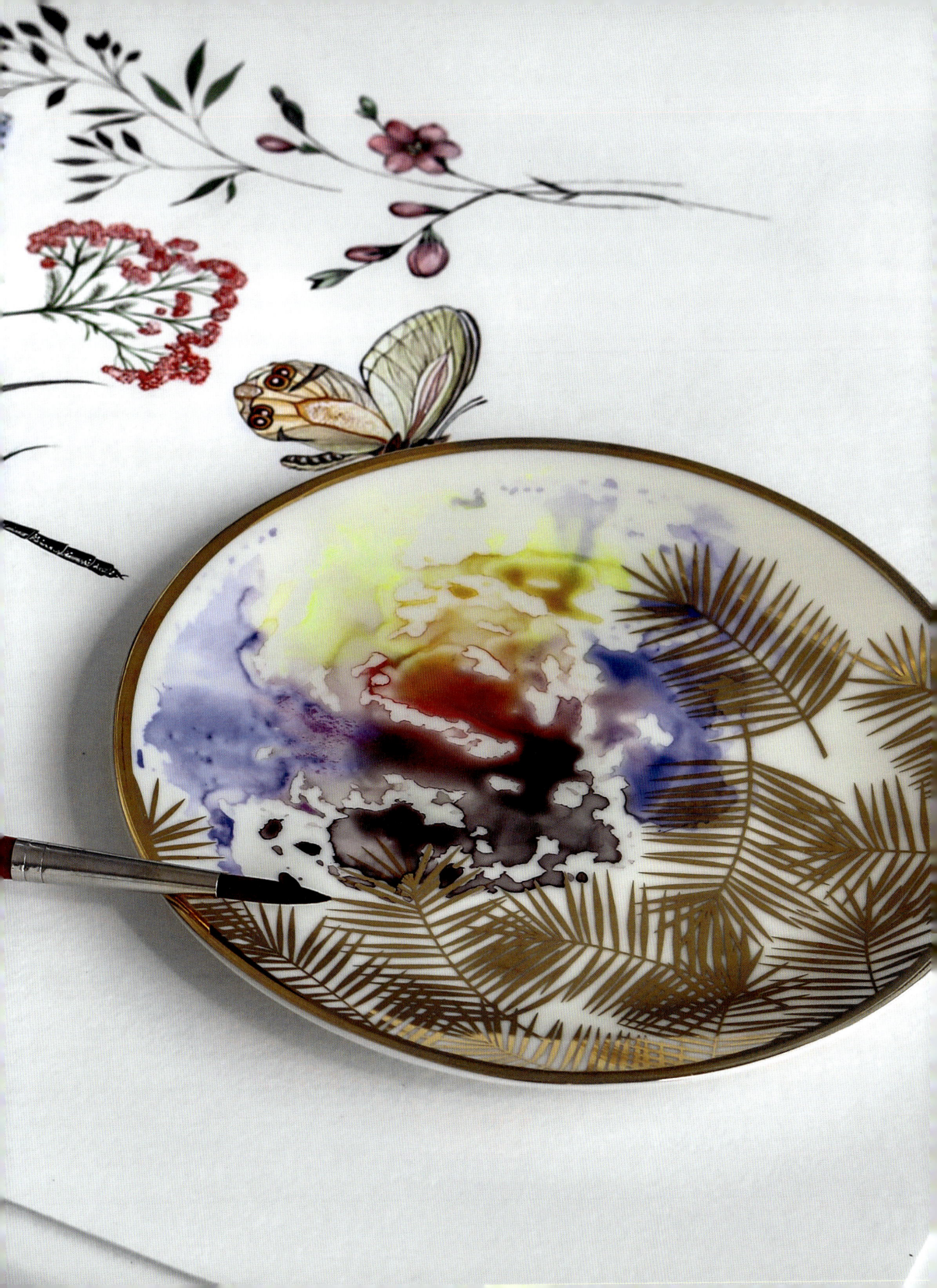

Materials

Once you become interested in watercolor painting, you'll soon find there's a large and varied range of materials for each style. For beginners in particular, this surplus of options can get overwhelming pretty fast. So the question is, what do I actually need? Over the next few pages, I'll introduce you to the materials that, over time, have become essential to my development as an artist.

QUANTITY OR QUALITY?

In general, the answer comes down to what you want to create on the page. By now, however, I'm convinced that you don't actually need that many different resources. Less is more! The combination of high-quality watercolor paints, brushes specifically designed for watercolor, and the right paper at the right weight is the foundation of every artwork.

In time you'll discover which materials work best for you and the brands you most enjoy working with. Give them a try and find out which options are best for you and your pictures. When it comes to watercolor paper in particular, I personally needed a long time to find the right one. It's all about trial and error and having the courage to make mistakes!

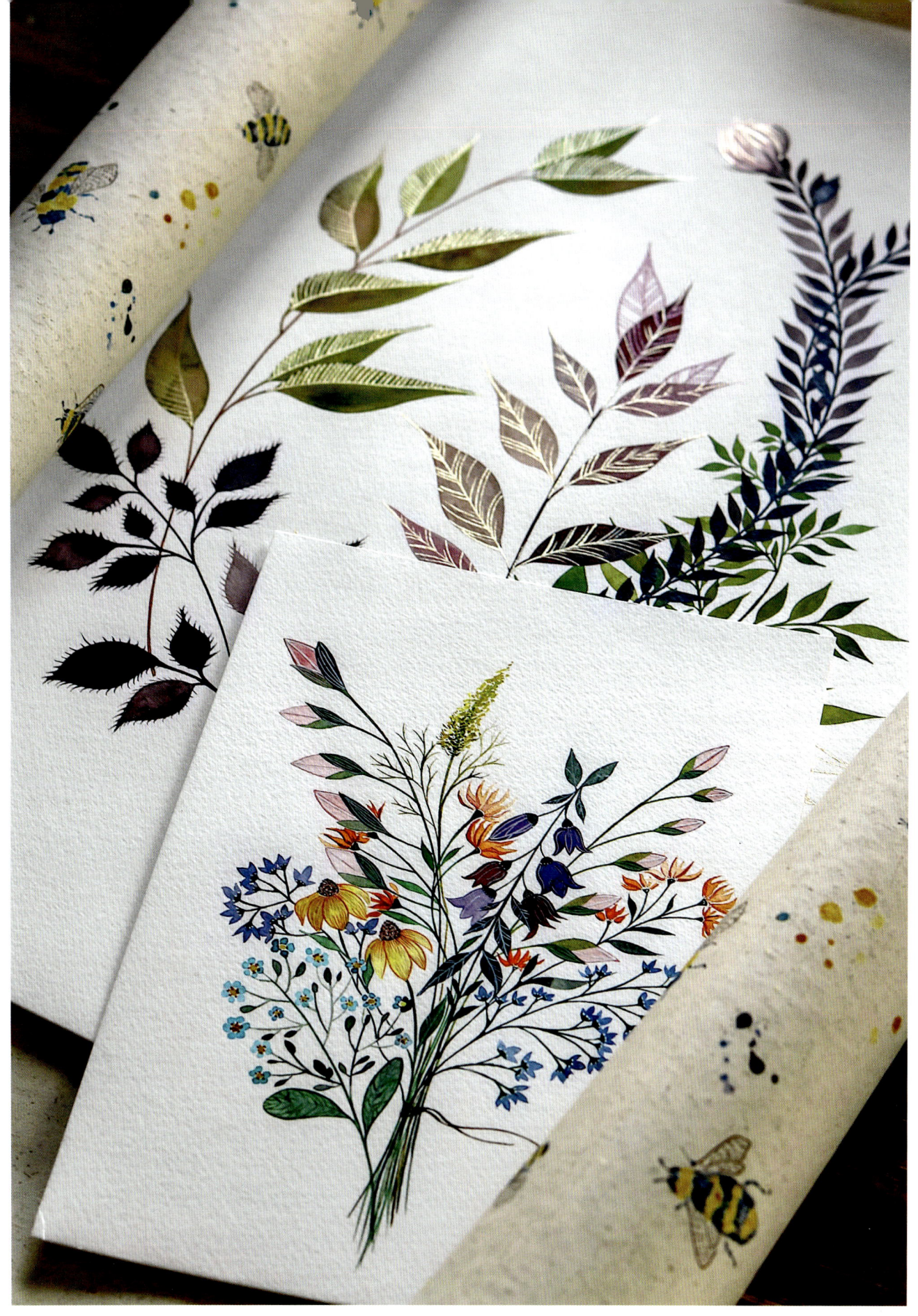

WATERCOLOR PAINTS

A luminous radiance and wonderful flowing transitions are the two things that come to mind when I think of watercolors. When I first started exploring this style of art ten years ago, I was immediately hooked. Watercolor painting is hugely addictive. Those little pans of paint really called to my artist's heart!

MORE THAN JUST WATERCOLORS

What exactly are watercolors? And how are artist-grade watercolors different from the watercolors many of us remember from our school days?

The answer lies in the amount of pigment. In student-grade watercolors, it's much lower and usually lower quality. It's the high quantity of high-quality pigments that gives watercolor paintings the intense coloration I love so much.

Another unique feature is the transparent effect created by watercolor paints when thinned with water and applied to paper with a brush. This is referred to as low coverage, meaning that the paper still shines through after the paint has been applied. Artist-grade watercolors get their texture, depth, and intensity from the application of several transparent layers of paint.

In conclusion, then, student-grade watercolors have more opacity., meaning they are less transparent and are much less intense in color.

PANS OR TUBES?

Watercolors come in liquid form in tubes and in solid form in pans. Both types can be used to achieve the same intensity of color. The difference is their consistency. When working with pans, you'll need to add a little more water. Personally, I prefer solid watercolors, so I only use pans. I'll describe them in a bit more detail later.

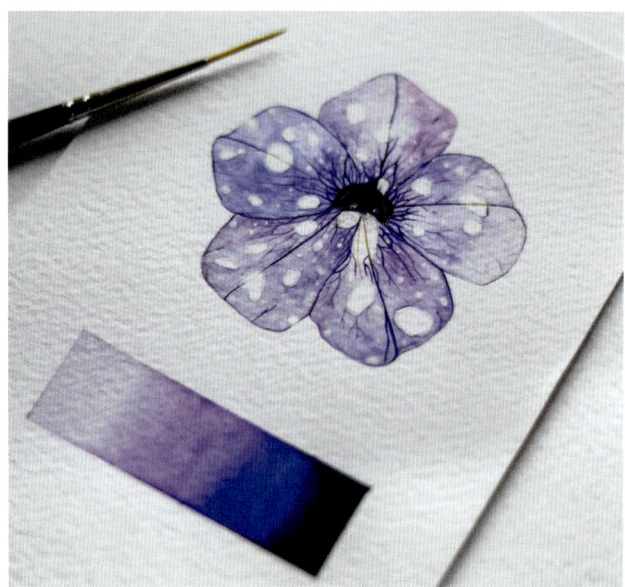

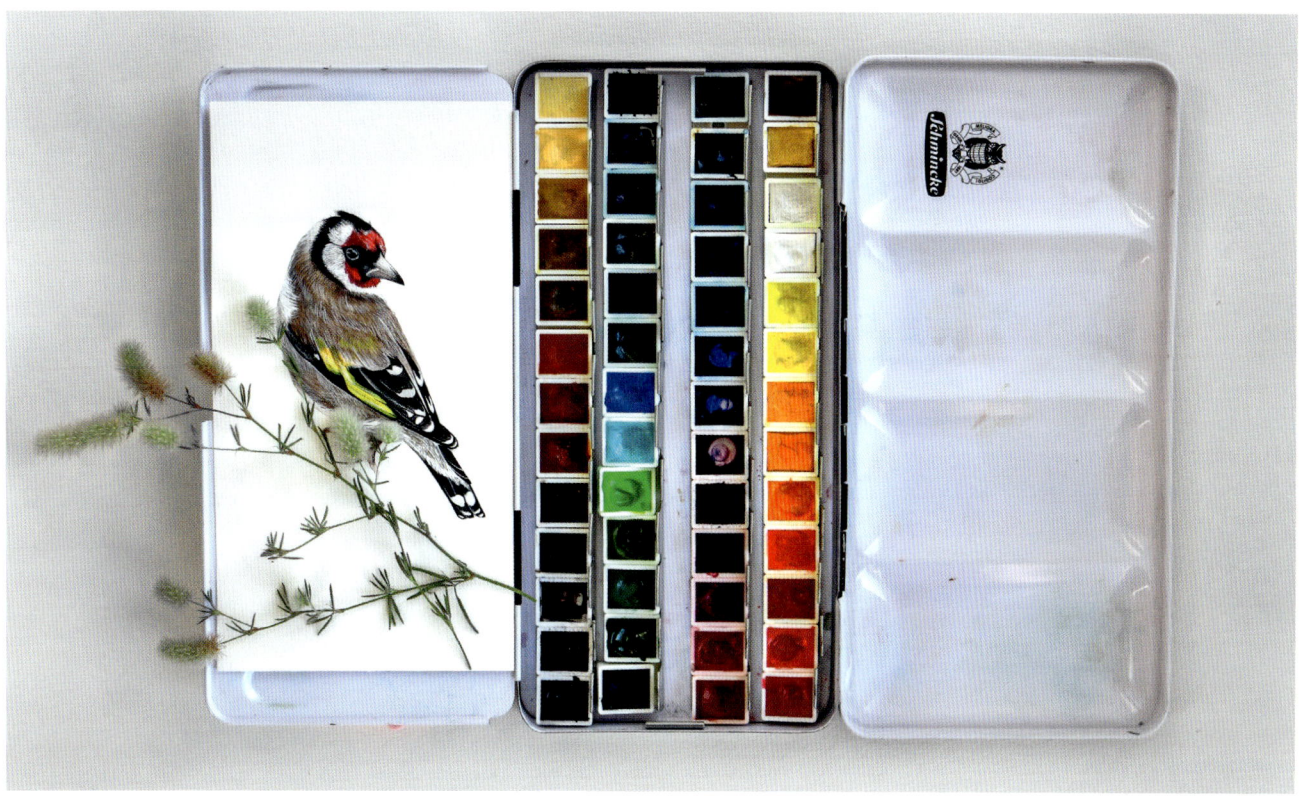

WATERCOLOR BOXES

My first experiences of watercolor painting were with a little watercolor box by Winsor & Newton, which was a gift from my sister. I enjoyed working with these special watercolors so much that I spent more and more of my time watercolor painting. I eventually came across paints by the brand Schmincke and gradually learned more and more about their fantastic reputation. However, the box I had did the trick, and Winsor & Newton paints are really high quality too, so I kept using them a while longer. I put the Schmincke palette on my wish list.

A while later, on my birthday five years ago, it happened: I was holding my new watercolors in my hands. The moment had arrived to try them out for the first time. The Schmincke palette has been my trusty companion ever since. I love the luminosity of the paint, and the colors have completely lived up to my expectations.

Schmincke offers two different versions of its watercolor paints, called Horadam and Akademie. Both options are characterized by their quality and superb lightfastness, so you can be confident that your watercolor paintings will not fade over time. That being said, the Horadam paints are more brilliant than the Akademie range, making them the preferred choice for experienced artists. I have Horadam paints in my paintbox too and I can confirm that the result is great!

"BUY CHEAP, PAY TWICE"

This is a saying that absolutely applies to choosing the right watercolors. When looking for a paint palette of your own, you'll soon see how expensive some brands are. Good watercolors—especially Schmincke's Horadam range—don't come cheap. Even individual pans come with a price tag. However, I believe that quality has its price and cheap paints always give themselves away on the page, which can take away from the fun of watercolor painting.

Of course, perhaps you don't have any experience with watercolor painting and are unsure whether or not you'll actually want to keep going with it. So that you don't end up spending lots of money for nothing, with an expensive box of paint gathering dust in a drawer, I want to give you the following advice.

The Three Base Colors

It sounds simple when I say it, but you really only need three colors to paint an eye-catching watercolor. To show you what I mean, let's take a look at Johannes Itten's color wheel.

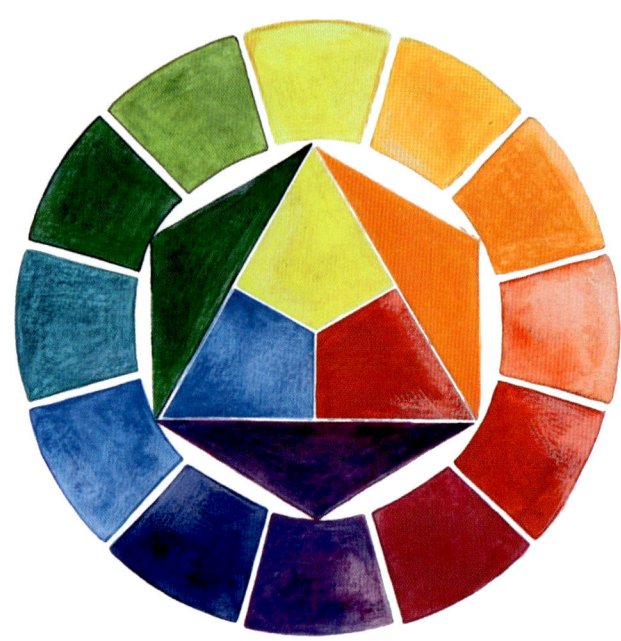

At the center of the color wheel, you can see three base, or primary, colors: red, yellow, and blue. Depending on how you mix the colors, you can create other shades (secondary colors). These can then be mixed with the base colors to create individual accent colors (tertiary colors). If you look at it this way, you actually only need three base colors. You can create all the other shades from your red, yellow, and blue. However, I think a small paint palette containing the base colors, as well as a few individual accent colors, is more fun. These boxes usually contain a black too, which, for my paintings, is essential.

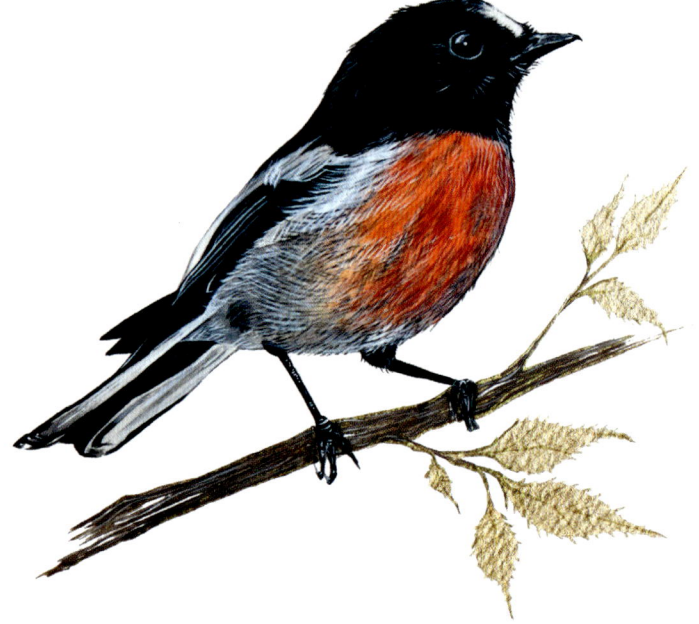

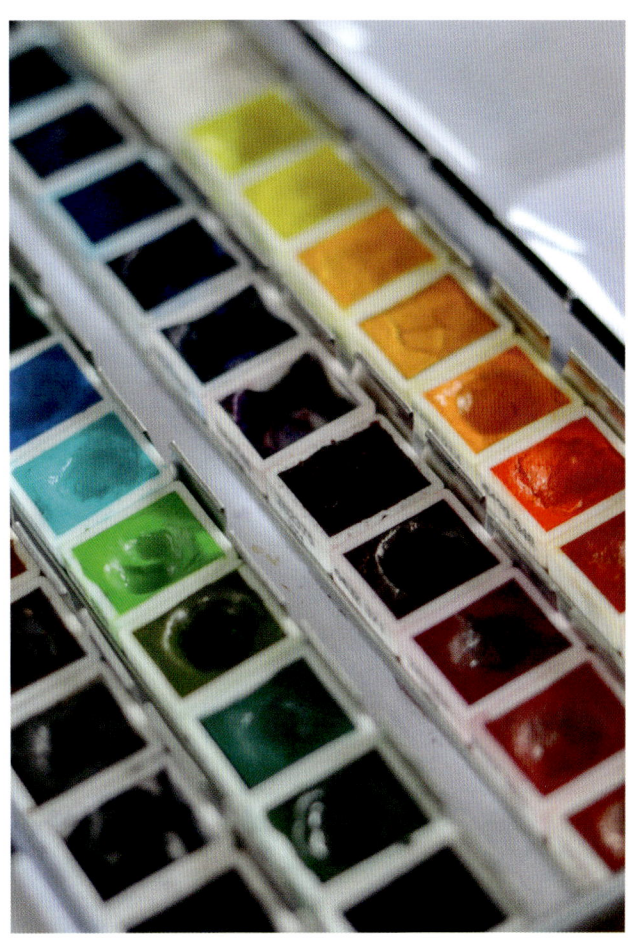

MIXING COLORS

They may be small, but wow! Solid watercolors go a very long way and pack a lot of color. Your pans can be activated by adding a drop of water to the paint with your brush and then waiting a moment. Once the solid surface of the little pan has softened, you're ready to go! Carefully swish your brush over the paint and transfer it to a palette or dish. Make sure to rinse your brush well if you want to take paint from a different pan. With light shades in particular, I make sure my brushes are clean so a yellow doesn't turn into a green, for example.

In general, you should always mix your colors outside of the pans, adding more or less water as required. Take the time to get to know your palette and the colors in it. A piece of scratch paper is helpful for trying out different colors, getting a feel for how much water you need, and the various painting techniques.

Buying Secondhand

Online marketplaces are a reliable source of unwanted watercolor boxes, which are sold at a fraction of their original price. They've hardly been used and need a new home. It's always worth a look!

Tip

You don't need to wash your dish or mixing palette. You can reuse the paints instead. Just add a little water and the dried paint will become liquid again.

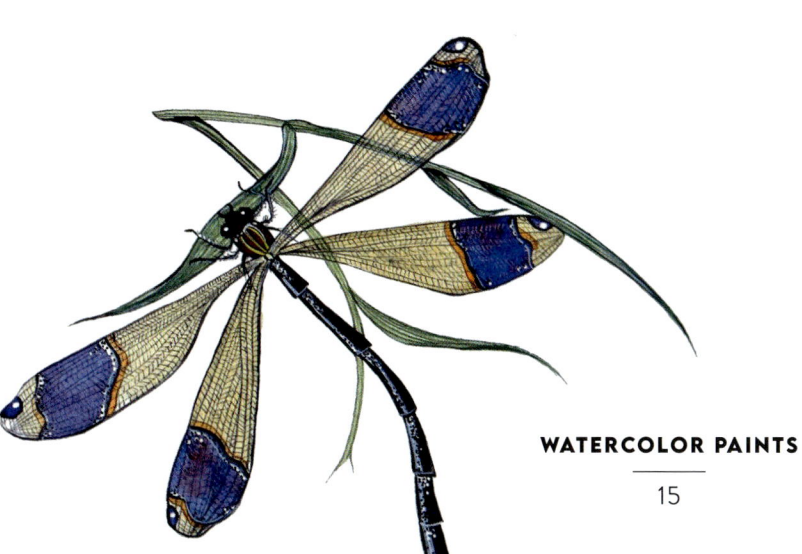

WATERCOLOR PAINTS

METALLIC PAINTS

Over the years, I've come to love the combination of simple watercolors and sparkling metallic effects. It's the blending of these two elements, I think, that has become my trademark as an artist. I've embellished many of my pieces with these unique details to literally make them shine.

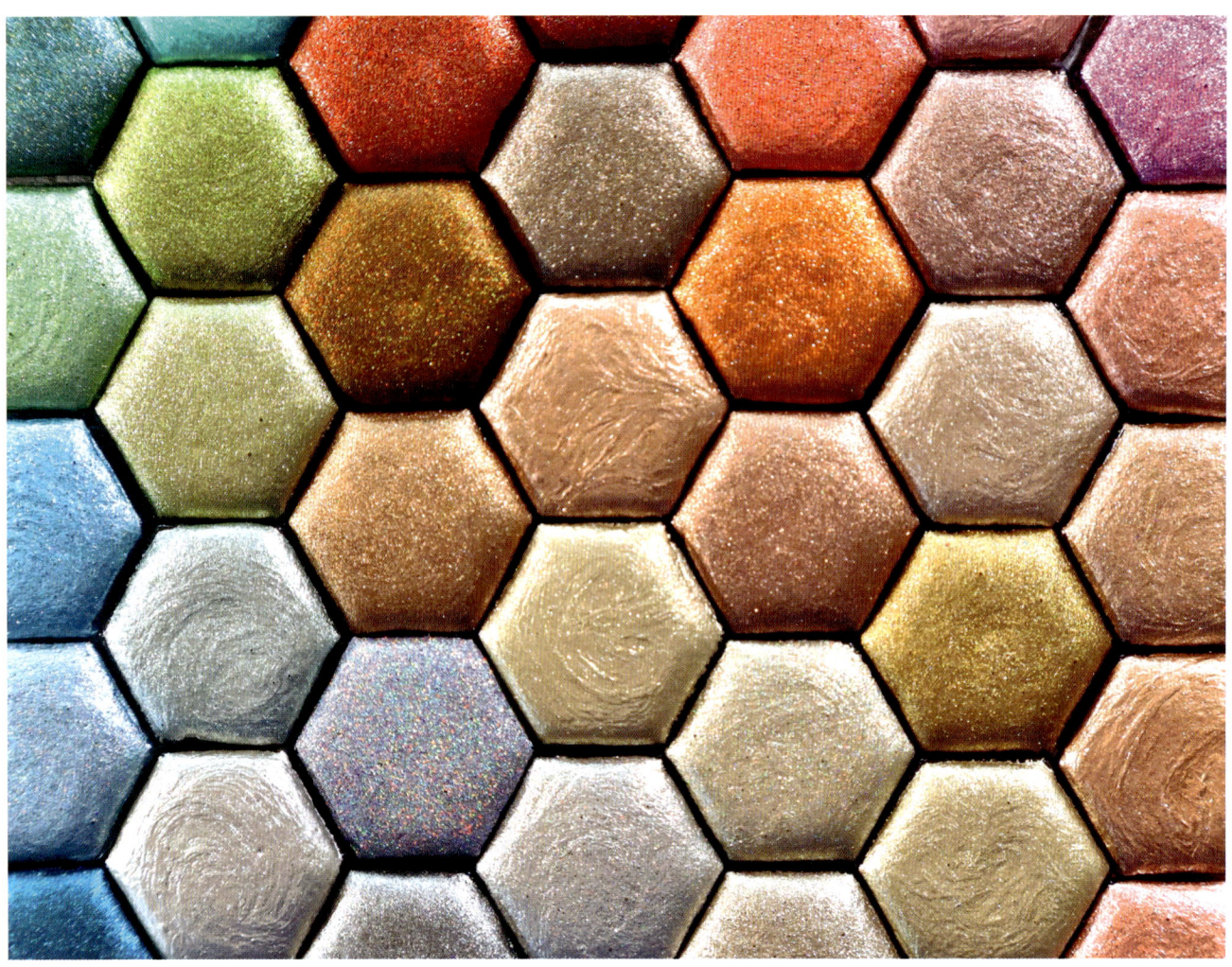

METALLIC WATERCOLOR

16

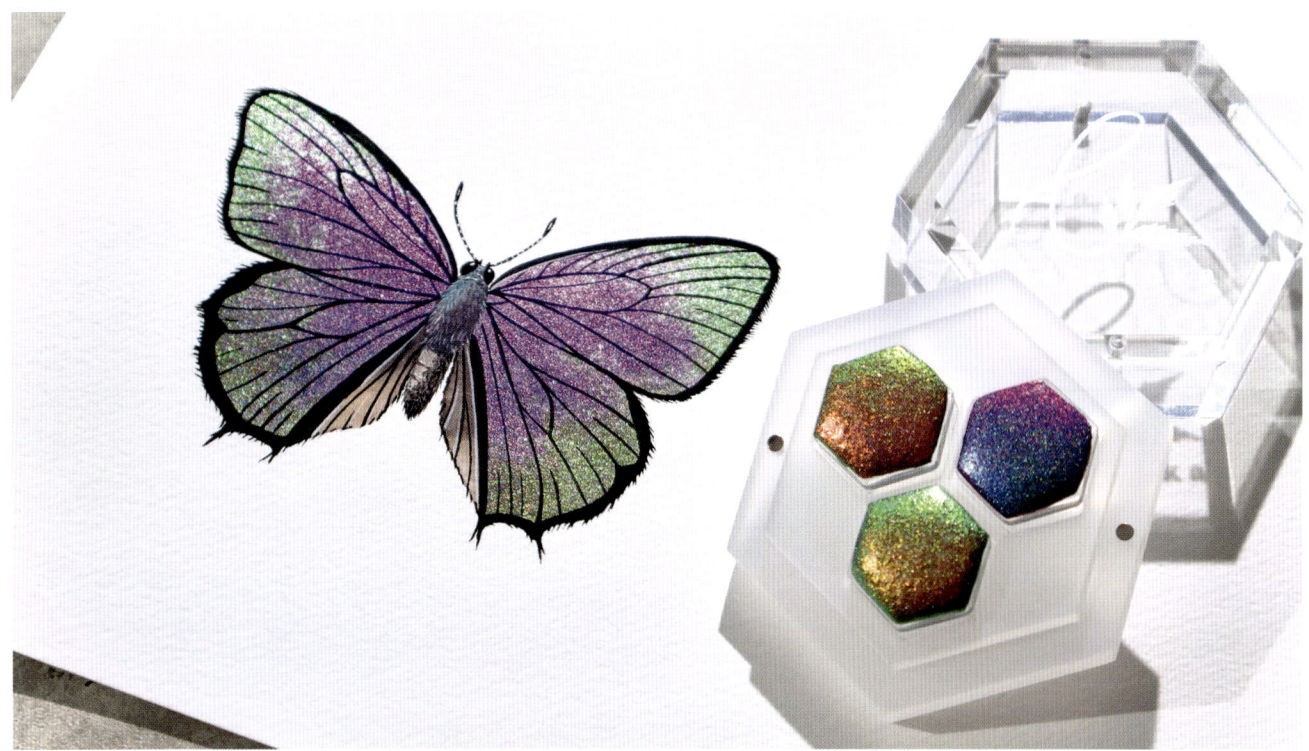

Metallic watercolors are vibrant and shimmering watercolors that create a stunning, eye-catching effect. These colors come in a variety of shades, ranging from soft pastels to very intense hues.

They have a unique metallic appearance that adds an extra shine and shimmer to paintings and drawings.

The two main ingredients in metallic paints are gum arabic (a binder for color pigments) and mica pigments. The latter are minerals whose structure refracts the light to create an intense sparkle. Because of this, the paints always look a little different depending on the light.

As with so many materials in the art world, there are lots of different brands and manufacturers of metallic paint, and I have used many of them successfully in my artwork. Over time, however, I came up with the idea of creating my own metallic colors that glitter particularly strongly after application, making the image come alive even more. In addition to a strongly pronounced sparkle, I also focused my attention on paints that are simple and quick to handle. The selection of the right color pigments were a top priority for me.

After almost a year of research and many unsuccessful attempts, I was able to produce my own metallic watercolor paints that had all of the qualities I was looking for. Today, I use only my own Lisilinka metallic watercolors for my paintings and enjoy their shine every day. I encourage you to try them, but it goes without saying that you can use metallic paints from other brands and have wonderful results.

BRUSHES

We all know that without the right brush, our watercolor won't work. The trick is finding out which brush is the most suitable for our motifs. The right brush is a crucial factor when it comes to painting a picture as it looks in our mind's eye. When it comes to choosing the right brush, the key question is, what do you want to paint?

BRUSH SHAPES

The brushes used for watercolor painting generally come in different shapes and bristle types (natural vs. synthetic material). The most common brush types are the round brush, flat brush, fan brush, rigger brush, and mop brush. Personally, I only use the round brush and rigger brush for my paintings, so I'll tell you a bit more about them. All of my brushes are made by da Vinci and are part of the CosmoTop Spin and Micro-Nova ranges.

The Round Brush

A round brush is so called because the fine bristles are secured in a round ferrule (the metal band connecting the brush head to the handle). The bristles form a tapered point. It is the most common form of watercolor brush and available in a variety of sizes. Round brushes absorb water and paint particularly well, so I like to use my size 3, 4, 6, and 8 round brushes for priming smaller and larger surfaces. The fine tips on smaller round brushes are great for detailing too.

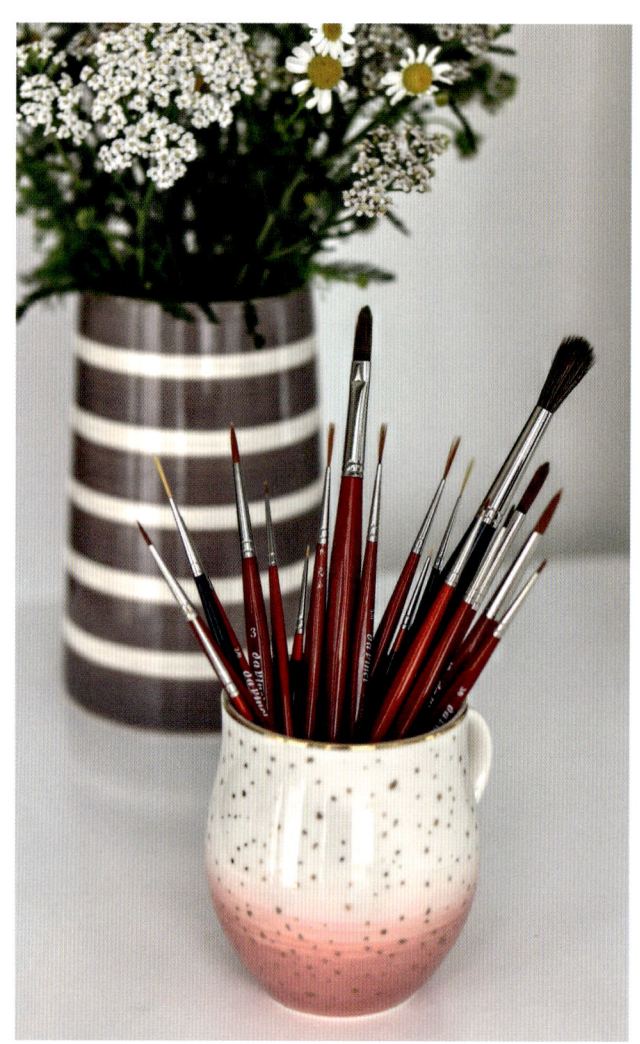

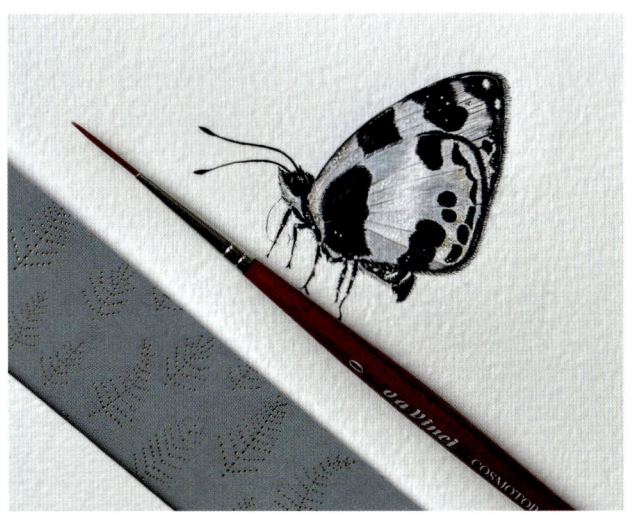

Microbrushes

As I've explained already, a richness of fine details is the trademark of my watercolor paintings. The more hairs I can add to the fur of my animal motifs, the more calming the effect on me. For this delicate work, you naturally need the right tool—and I certainly found it in my microbrushes. The brushes' tiny tips are great for painting the fine hairs on a butterfly's wing or the reflection of light in an animal's eyes.

The Rigger Brush

The rigger brush looks similar to the round brush but has lots of longer bristles. Both types of brush can absorb lots of water and paint. The rigger brush's long tip is particularly good for straight or sweeping lines. It's one of my absolute favorites for sure, as I can use it to color larger areas and paint the finest details. It's a real all-arounder!

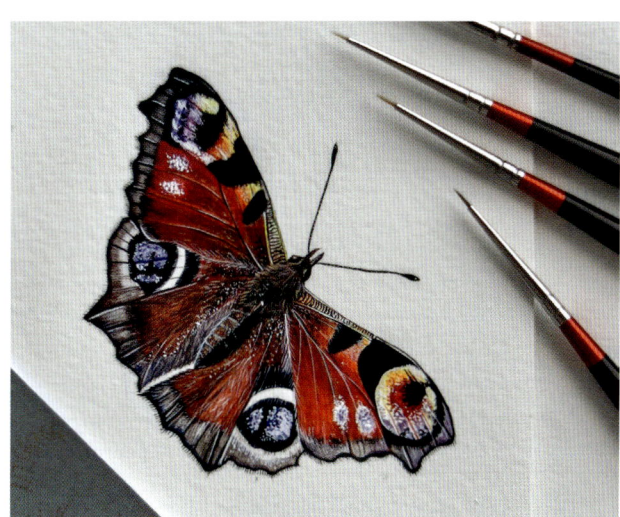

Tip

I recommend buying your brushes from a local shop rather than online. When choosing the right brushes, it's often helpful to hold them in your hand and test the flexibility of the bristles. Not only that, I've twice had the unfortunate experience of brushes I've ordered online getting damaged en route and being delivered with frayed bristles. Especially when it comes to details, the tip of the brush must taper without fraying.

PROPER CARE

You need to make sure you clean and store your brushes correctly. Fine brushes like the rigger brush don't tolerate being stored upside down with their tips pointing downward. I wash my brushes in lukewarm water after use and store them in a cup with the handles pointing downward. This way, your brushes are sure to last a long time.

PAPER

To do watercolor well—and have fun at the same time—you need the right watercolor paper. This is where you enter a whole new world, as finding your preferred paper is a science in itself. It took me quite some time to find a watercolor paper I was completely happy with.

WATERCOLOR PAPER

Essentially, watercolor paper differs from conventional paper in that its texture is much thicker. It needs to be. In watercolor painting, we use a lot of water and ordinary paper would quickly tear or buckle with unattractive waves. Watercolor paper is designed specifically for the conditions of painting with watercolor paints. It's made to withstand a certain amount of moisture, absorb the paint well, and distribute it evenly.

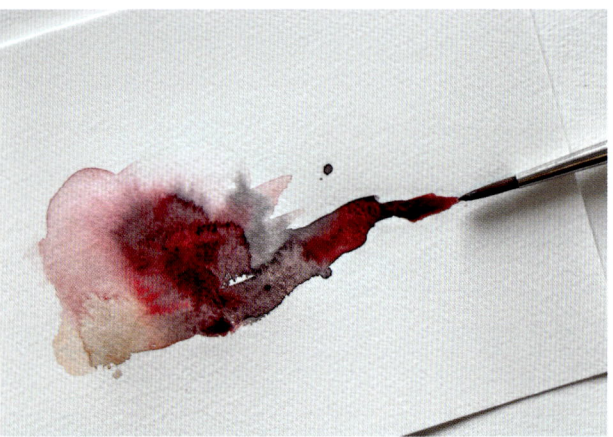

This all sounds very simple and logical, of course, but not all watercolor paper is the same. There are different variations and grades aimed at different painting techniques from the world of watercolor painting.

PROPERTIES

The main differences between watercolor papers are the surface texture and overall strength of the paper in question. Below I'll introduce you to the specialist terms you're most likely to encounter when choosing your paper.

Hot-Pressed vs. Cold-Pressed

Hot-pressed and cold-pressed are two categories referring to the surface texture of the watercolor paper. Hot-pressed paper has a smooth, relatively untextured surface and is great for details and line work, as well as for dry techniques. However, this makes it quite difficult to create gradients and even washes of watercolor. The smooth surface is also more sensitive and less forgiving of mistakes.

Its counterpart is cold-pressed watercolor paper, which is very rough and matte in texture. It absorbs paint and water like a sponge and dries slowly. It's also very robust, so the surface can be worked extensively. Very even glazes can be produced on cold-pressed paper, making it particularly suitable for wet techniques, and therefore for painting landscapes. It does have one disadvantage, however. Its rough texture makes it less suited to fine details.

Weight

Watercolor paper weights are often expressed in both pounds and grams per square meter, or gsm. While the two measurements are related, they are not direct conversions. The figure in pounds refers to the weight of a ream (500 sheets) of that type of paper, but it does not account for the size of the paper. So a 90-lb paper with larger dimensions than 90-lb watercolor paper will actually weigh more. The gsm refers to the weight of each individual sheet of paper, which is exactly 1 square meter. Paper is divided into three different weight categories:

- ✦ **light paper:** 90 lb (120–300 gsm)
- ✦ **medium paper:** 140 lb (300-600 gsm)
- ✦ **heavy paper:** 300 lb (600-840 gsm)

I recommend a happy medium: paper with a weight of 140 lb (or over 300 gsm) you can use with very wet washes, without the paper becoming warped or changing in other ways. Why not try it out by using intense colors to create gradients?

In Conclusion: WHICH PAPER TO USE?

For many years, I've used Canson watercolor paper with a weight of 140 lb (300 gsm). In my opinion, this paper combines the qualities of cold- and hot-pressed paper. It's not too smooth or too rough, meaning I can work with lots of water and also add fine details without too much difficulty. It meets all of my expectations.

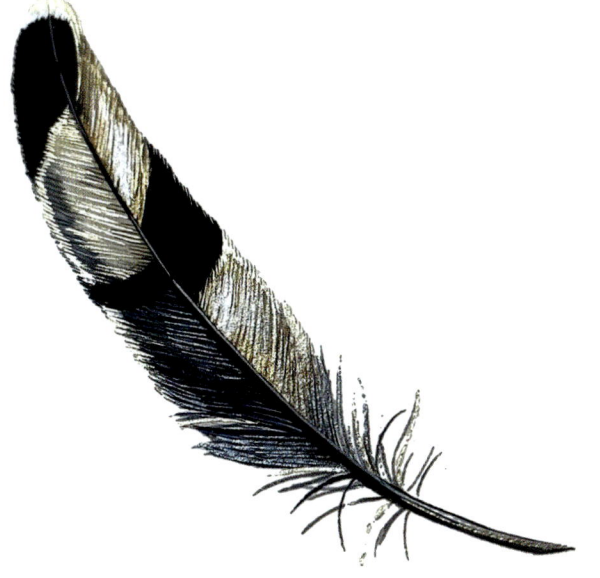

Tip

I'd like to add that paper is a very individual choice. As with choosing your brushes, first you need to think about what style of painting you want to create and what motifs you want to paint. To make the decision easier, I recommend paying a visit to an art supply shop. Here you can explore the texture and feel of the paper for yourself and get a better understanding of the theory.

ADDITIONAL MATERIALS

My pictures are more than just a combination of watercolors
and metallic paints. They're an interaction between lots of
different materials, which I'll show you this in this chapter.
You can then gather your inspiration and decide
which ones you'd like to use for your motifs.

PENCIL

Before picking up my brushes and applying my
watercolor, I like to sketch some fine reference
lines first. For this I use a medium-soft to soft
pencil, keeping the pressure as light as possible.

FINELINER PENS

Whether black or color, fineliners are great for
tracing over the edges of your watercolor, making
certain areas blacker, or contouring.

GEL PENS

You can use a white gel pen to add fine details and
light reflections to your watercolor. This intensifies
the effect of your pictures, giving them a more
three-dimensional look. I recommend Sakura Gel-
ly Roll (white).

ERASER

Once your picture is finished, you'll want to rub
out your pencil lines, so an easy-to-hold eraser is
a must. Just make sure that your paper is sufficiently dry before using it. That way, you'll avoid
any unintended mixing of colors or damage to
your paper.

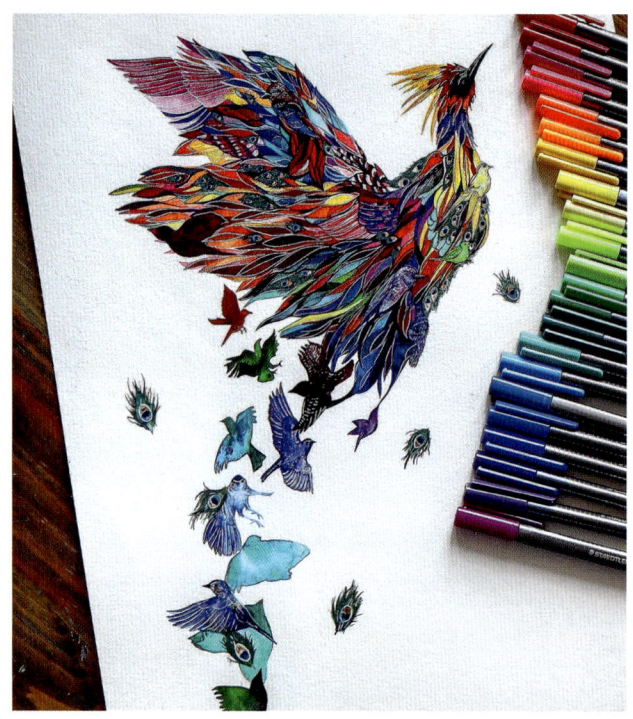

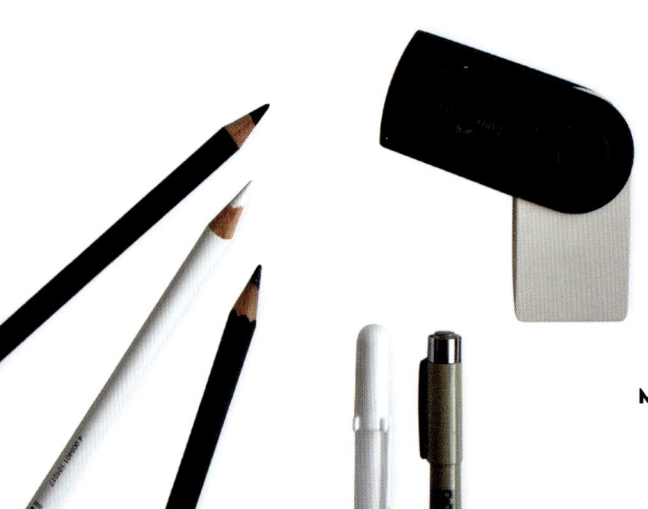

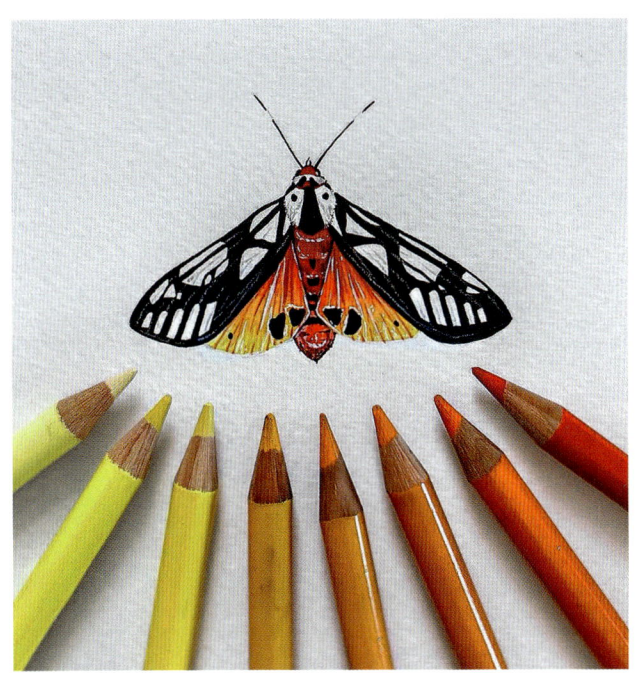

DISH

For mixing my colors, I like to use a little saucer, and I hardly ever clean it. The paints I collect on it can be reactivated again with water at any time. Just make sure that your mixing dish doesn't get dusty; otherwise you'll end up with little bits of lint in your watercolors.

PAPER TOWELS

These are great for wiping excess water and paint from your brushes.

COMPASS, CUP, OR BOWL

If you want to draw a circle for round wreaths of flowers, for example, ideally you'll want to use a compass. I use a cup or a bowl, which I turn upside down and draw around in pencil instead.

COLORED PENCILS

Colored pencils are an important medium in my pictures. I recommend Polychromos by Faber-Castell, which I use for coloring specific parts of my watercolor. A white pencil is great for adding light details to a dark background. When using this technique, just make sure that your watercolor paint is dry first.

TWO GLASSES

When I combine my watercolors with metallic paints, I make sure to use a separate glass of water for each medium. The sparkling mica pigments in the pearlized paints are very intense and disperse in your brush water. If you use just one glass, they'd end up in your watercolor paint and then in parts of your picture that you want to keep matte. Make sure to use a clean brush when switching between the two paints too.

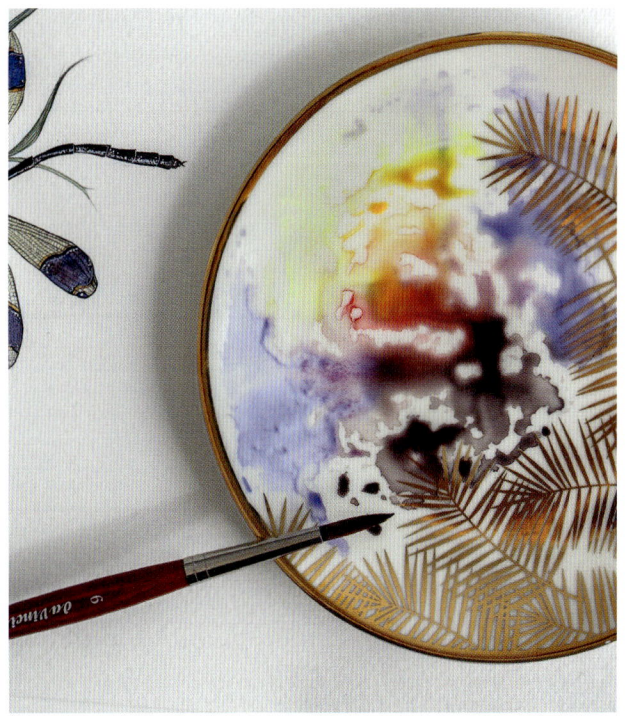

Technique

Watercolor mixing and brushwork are things that come very intuitively to me. While drawing I try not to think too much about what I'm doing. Then watercolor painting becomes a great way of finding inner peace. That's why, before writing this chapter, I needed to read a little bit more about the theory. That way, I can explain clearly how my intuition works and how it ties in with the theoretical aspects of drawing.

THE DO'S & DON'TS OF WATERCOLOR PAINTING

In the course of my research, I stumbled upon some "rules" of watercolor painting. These included "Paint light to dark," "Never use opaque white paint," and "Black is forbidden." While, in my opinion, applying paint from lightest to darkest is indeed the foundational technique of watercolor painting, I've broken the other two rules many times.

White is an important component of my pictures, as it helps me develop really intricate details. The much-scorned "opaque white" is perfect for achieving this finish. However, I must also add that something else is implied by this rule, the so-called negative painting technique. In this commonly used element of watercolor painting, white areas are created by leaving some areas unpainted. When it comes to avoiding the color black, I can say this: I'm all too happy to use it, and often, for accents and outlines. For darker areas such as these, strong, dark colors, such as indigo or perylene green, also work.

The Bottom Line Is THERE ARE NO RULES

The bottom line for me is that I can't identify with rules in a world where creativity is meant to flow. In my opinion, experimentation and trying out new things are the lifeblood of art. Combining different materials and techniques together is an exciting journey culminating in a picture in the artist's very own handwriting. Rules would stunt these individual journeys rather than encourage them.

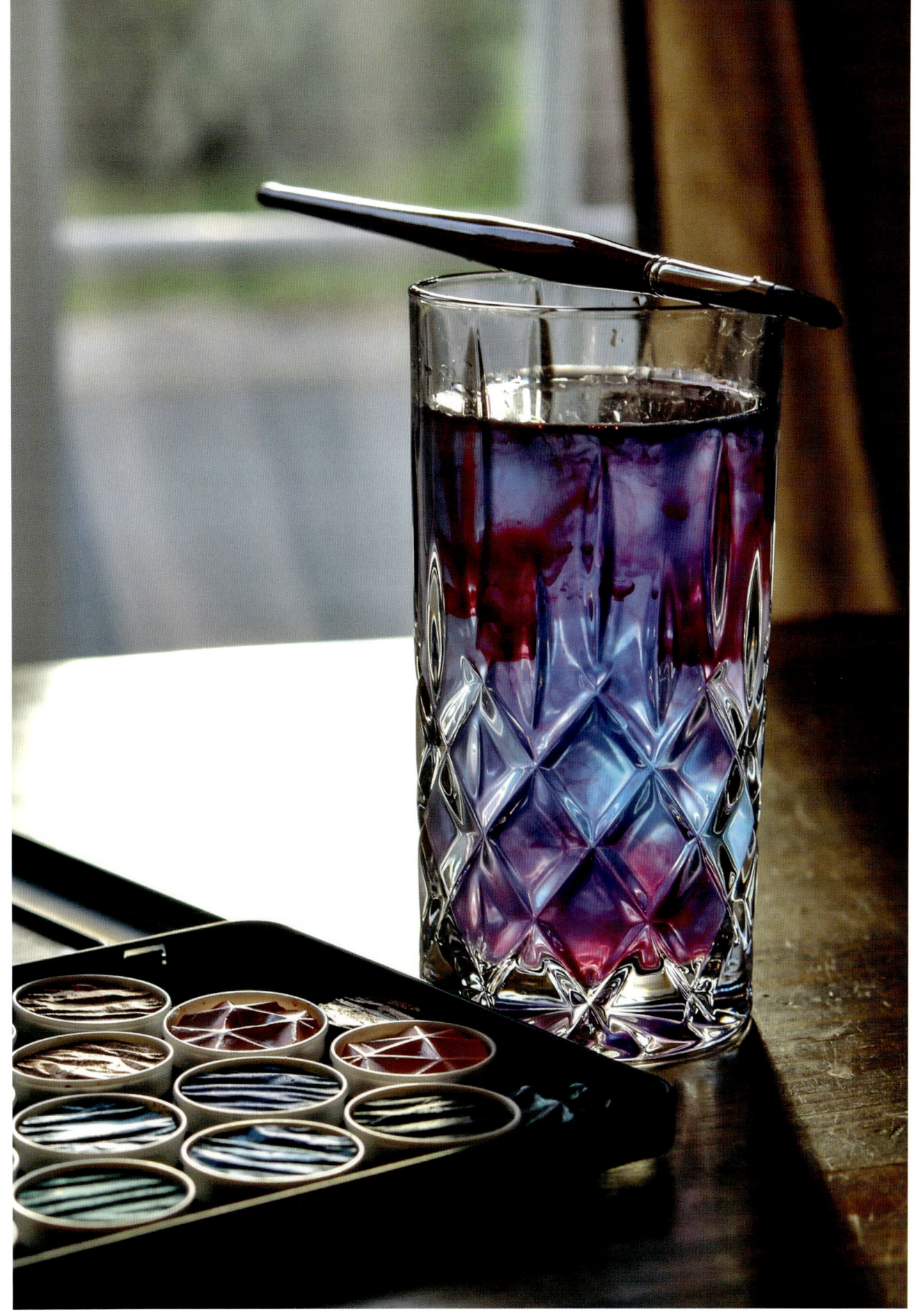

WATERCOLOR TECHNIQUES

Watercolor painting is a multifaceted craft that uses specific techniques. Over the next few pages, I'll introduce these techniques in more detail so you can use them in the motifs shown from page 34 onward. The exercises will also help you get to know your paints and brushes better.

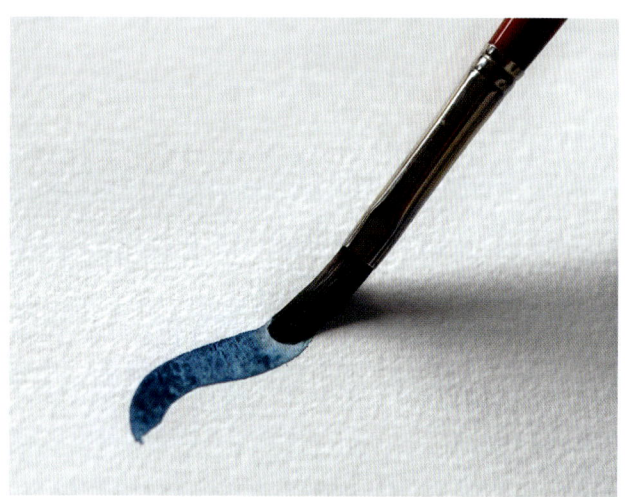

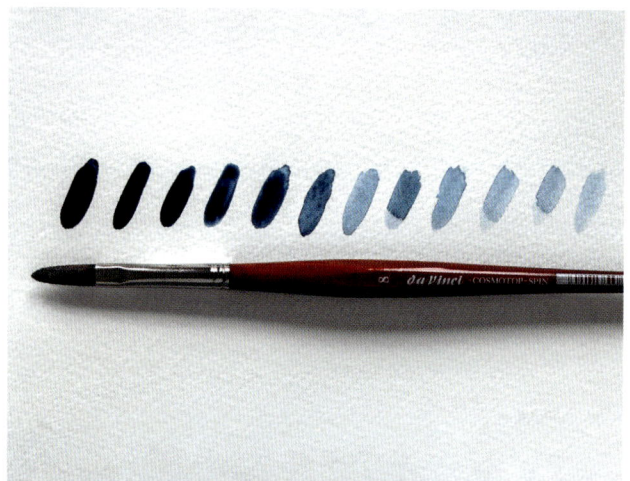

WET-ON-DRY TECHNIQUE

In the wet-on-dry technique, paint is applied to a dry surface. You thin the watercolor paint with lots of water on a dish or mixing palette and paint it onto dry paper with your brush. We work with different paint layers in watercolor painting, so you need to let every layer dry sufficiently before adding the next one.

The wet-on-dry technique is great for your first watercolor, as it gives you a lot of control over the flow of the paint.

Exercise: Wet-on-Dry Technique

If you don't have any experience with watercolors yet, I highly recommend this exercise. It'll help you get to know the properties of your paint and see how it behaves when combined with water.

For this exercise, you need a round brush, watercolor paper, your paints, and a glass of water. First, dip your brush into the water and then into a watercolor paint of your choice. Once you've activated the paint and it's become liquefied, apply it to your dry paper (a small stroke is enough).

Now dip your brush back into the water and paint another stroke next to the first one (without loading your brush with any more paint). Repeat so you can see how your color changes under the influence of the water. The stroke of paint becomes lighter and lighter and your shades steadily change.

Tip

The quantity of water can be used to control or influence the intensity of your colors, so it's always helpful to mix your colors on a dedicated palette or dish. You can add as much water as needed for designing your motif.

WET-ON-WET TECHNIQUE

The wet-on-wet technique can be used to create an intense gradient and flowing transitions. Although this method gives us less control over our paints, it produces striking effects, which makes it very popular. In this context, wet-on-wet means moderately damp rather than saturated. Your paper should be well moistened, not dripping with water or creating puddles.

Using your brush, apply the well-thinned paint to your wet surface and watch how the pigments spread across the paper. The dry parts of your paper form an invisible barrier that the watercolor paint won't cross. More layers of paint are now added to the first layer while it's still wet. That way, the colors are able to run into one another.

Exercise: Wet-on-Wet Technique
This exercise will help you get a feel for how different colors interact and harmonize.

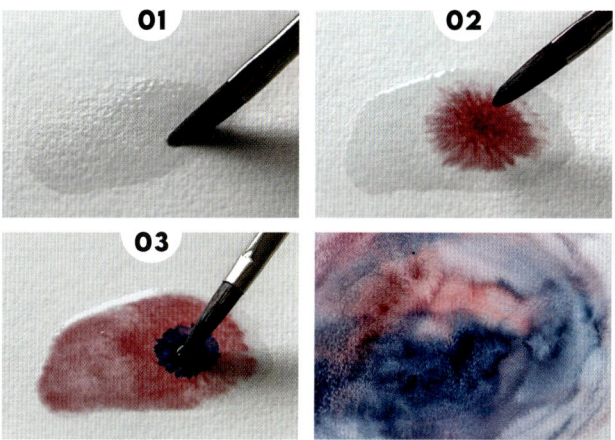

Take your brush and apply clean water to a section of your paper (01). Thin the paint and apply it to the dampened area. You'll see how the paint spreads across the damp surface (02). Add another color and the different shades will blend and run into each other (03). Make sure that the area you're painting is dampened through. This simple exercise is helpful for testing out different color combinations for creating gradients. The more paint you apply, the darker your watercolor will appear.

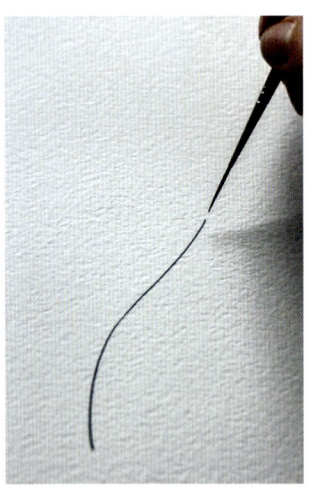
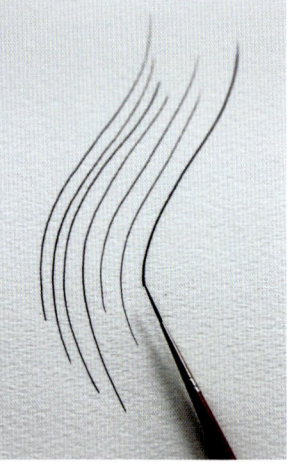

Hold your brush between your thumb and index finger and try to paint a sweeping line from the wrist in one go without stopping. With a bit of experience, you'll get a sense for how much pressure you need to put on the tip of your brush to get the result you want.

Please don't feel discouraged if the first lines aren't as fine as you'd like. No one is born a master and you'll see that your skills will improve consistently with a little practice. So it pays to stay on the ball!

PAINTING LINES

On social media, I'm always asked how I get my details so fine and my lines so thin and even. For delicate elements like this, the right tool and a little practice are important starting points.

For a long, fine line like a flower stem, I only ever use my rigger brush (see page 19). In my experience, this gives the most even results.

It's important to make sure that you load the right amount of water and watercolor paint onto your brush. If the tip of your brush is too damp, it'll cause damp splotches on your paper. If the tip of your brush is too dry, your lines will be patchy, as the paint won't be distributed evenly.

Exercise: Painting Lines

The same applies to painting lines as applies to many things in life: The proof of the pudding is in the eating! Grab a sheet of scratch paper and get painting. You'll soon find out how much paint and water you need to get an even stroke.

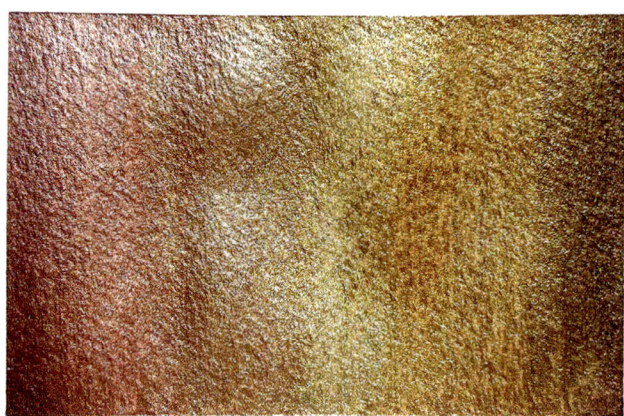

GRADIENTS WITH METALLIC PAINTS

Creating gradients is a great way of finding out which color combinations look best together.

I especially like this method for painting with my metallic paints. A flowing transition makes me feel happy, and the sheen of the pigments makes the picture look more expressive too.

In the following exercise, I'll show you how you can paint gradients with your pearlized paints.

Exercise: Gradients with Metallic Paints

Activate your metallic paint with a round brush and sufficient water. Add a drop of water to the surface of the paint and leave for a while until the pigments have become liquid (01). Once you have a creamy consistency, you can start working with your metallic paint. Test it out to get a sense of how much water you need. Now transfer the paint onto the watercolor paper with your brush and distribute your paint over an even area (02). Due to its creamy consistency, metallic paint has great coverage. It's highly pigmented too, which produces an intense sheen. Clean your brush and activate another metallic paint, adding it to the area you've just painted. Make sure, however, that your paints stay wet so the different pigments can blend smoothly into each other. At the point where the two colors meet, I use a dabbing motion to make the overall appearance more even (03). Once the paint is completely dry, you'll be able to see the flowing transition between the two colors in full. The shimmer of the mica pigments will look different depending on the angle you hold your picture at, enhancing your painting's unique shine (04).

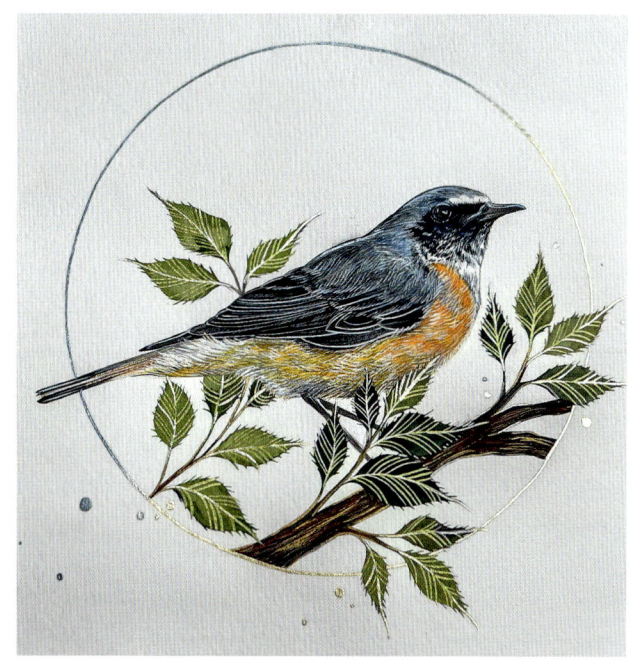

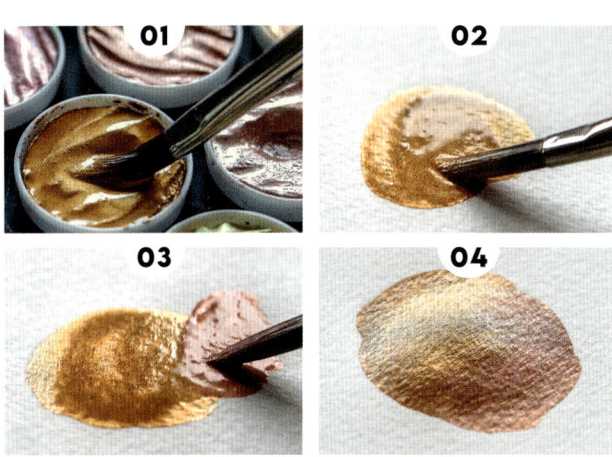

GEOMETRIC SHAPES WITH METALLIC PAINTS

I like to integrate geometric shapes into my realistic motifs, especially circles outlined in metallic paint.

Elements like these offer an abstract counterbalance. The shimmering metallic paint also transforms a very naturalistic painting into an eye-catching masterpiece. The finer you paint a shimmering circle, the more delicate your watercolor will look, so it's worth practicing a little.

However, practice isn't the only thing you need to create elements like this. When outlining your geometric shape, you need the right tool. A thinner brush is undoubtedly one of these tools. As I've already mentioned, I always use my rigger brush for fine lines, whether straight or sweeping. Its long, flexible tip makes it easier to get a consistent result.

Exercise 1: Painting Geometric Shapes with Metallic Paints

Draw a geometric shape of your choice on the watercolor paper in pencil (01). Now activate your metallic paint with water until it has a creamy consistency. Load the paint onto a rigger brush (02). Make sure that your brush is loaded with enough paint and its bristles aren't frayed. That way, you'll get a fine, even line. Now start tracing carefully over the pencil line of your shape (03). When tracing over a circle, I like to turn the paper around in the direction of the curved line. Give yourself plenty of time and try not to rush. Fine lines like these need lots of concentration and a steady hand. You'll see how your outlines gradually become more delicate with a little practice and experience (04). Rather than drawing my circle all in one go, I put my brush down from time to time.

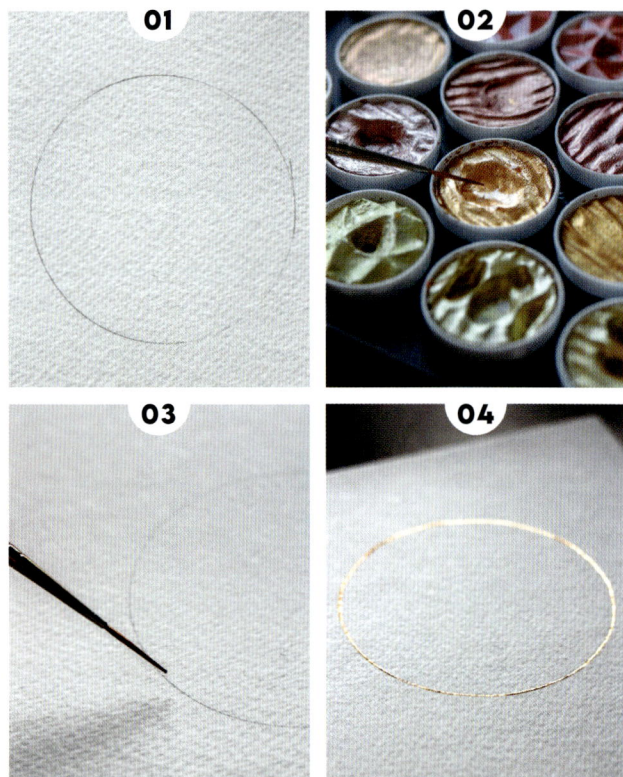

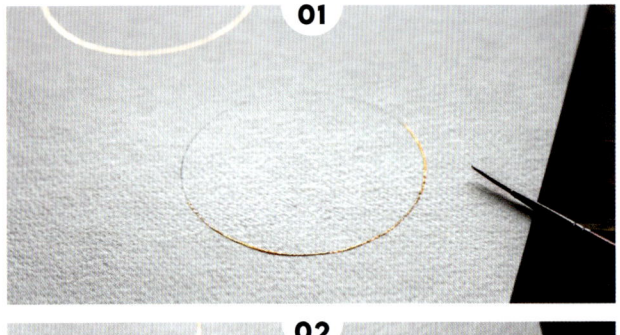

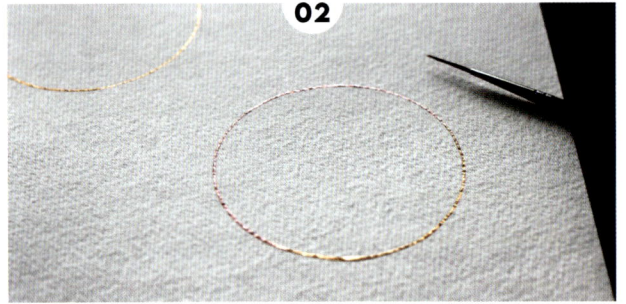

Exercise 2: Geometric Gradient

After we've practiced the outline of our geometric shape, we can increase the difficulty and add a gradient. To do this, draw a shape of your choice on your watercolor paper in pencil, then trace over half of the outline with the metallic paint you used before (01). Now choose another color, activate it with water, and switch to your rigger brush. Trace over the other half of your shape with this new shade. Try to make the transitions between colors as seamless as possible by painting one color lightly over the other (02).

ABOUT
THE PROJECTS

Before you attempt the first project, I'd like to share a few
thoughts on choosing and working through my motifs.

IDEAS AND INSPIRATION

The projects I've chosen are taken from the world
of plants and animals. It's the subject that I enjoy
painting the most and that fills me with the most
joy. Nature's diversity is breathtaking and complex
at the same time. It creates bright colors and min-
ute details that are important points of reference
in my watercolors.

DIFFICULTY LEVEL

The motifs I've selected are an exciting challenge
for beginners and experienced artists alike. I've
divided them into four categories of gradually
increasing complexity and time commitment.
I've color-coded each category so you can see
which level of difficulty you're trying. In each of
the four categories, you'll find the instructions
for five motifs.

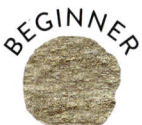
BEGINNER

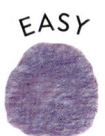
EASY

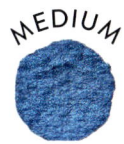
MEDIUM

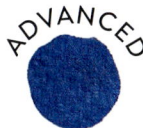
ADVANCED

DOWNLOADABLE SKETCHES

Most of the projects begin with a pencil sketch.
You can draw them freehand or download and
trace them.

Scan this code to access the
downloadable sketches.

CREATE YOUR OWN ARTISTIC
SIGNATURE

Although I'll be giving a step-by-step explanation of
how to copy my watercolors, I want to encourage
you to let your own creativity flow into your paintings. In my opinion, it's obvious when a picture has
"just" been copied and when it carries the artist's
own signature. This personal touch, your stamp as an
artist, will emerge on its own with every picture you
paint. Take your time and give it a go. Eventually
you'll discover that you've developed your very own
style. So please feel free to swap the colors I've used
for your own—they're just suggestions.

SHARE YOUR WORK WITH ME

I'd love it if you shared the pictures you've painted
using my book! Get in touch with me on Instagram
with the hashtag #inspiredbyLisilinka or by tagging
me (@lisilinka) in your post.

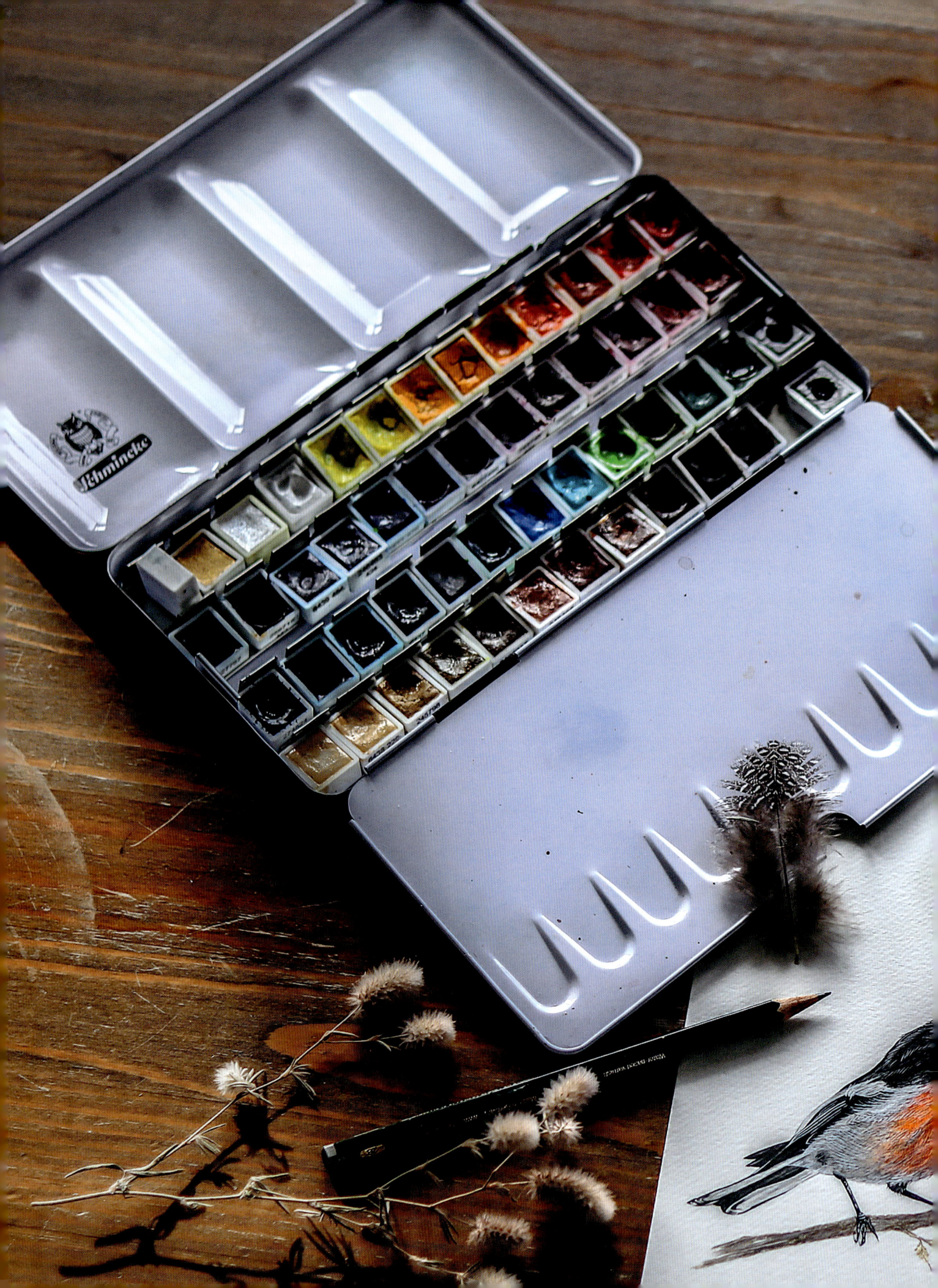

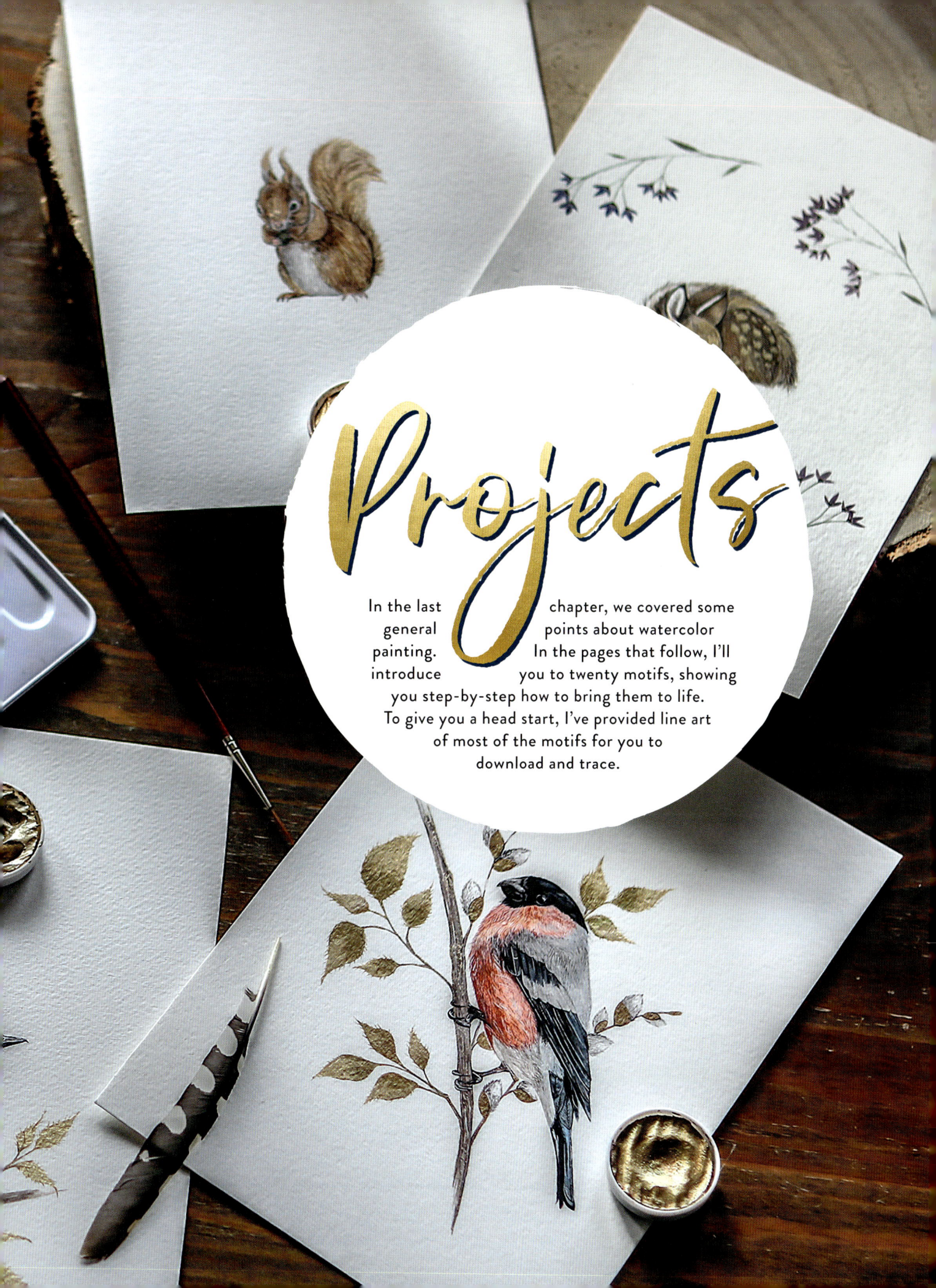

Projects

In the last chapter, we covered some general points about watercolor painting. In the pages that follow, I'll introduce you to twenty motifs, showing you step-by-step how to bring them to life. To give you a head start, I've provided line art of most of the motifs for you to download and trace.

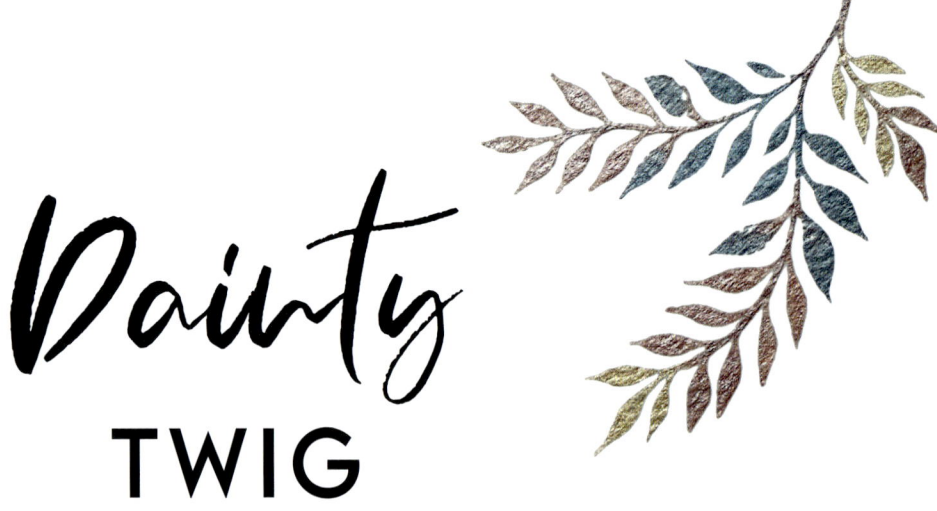

Dainty
TWIG

This twig of young leaves will teach you how to incorporate delicate details into your paintings. What makes this motif stand out is the variety of metallic accents and the flowing transition from a light to dark shade.

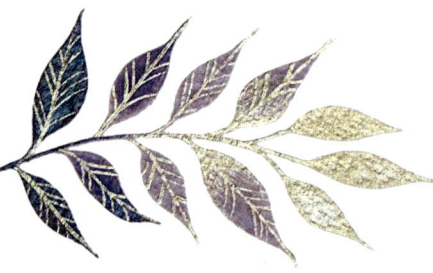

MATERIALS
RIGGER BRUSH | WATERCOLOR PAPER

MY COLOR PALETTE

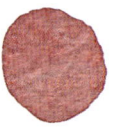   

METALLIC PAINTS

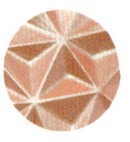 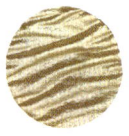 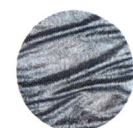

ROSE   LIGHT GOLD   PALE BLUE

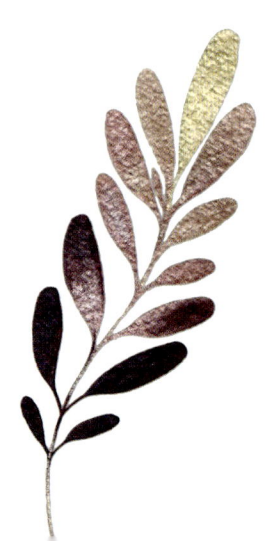

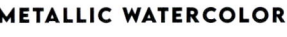

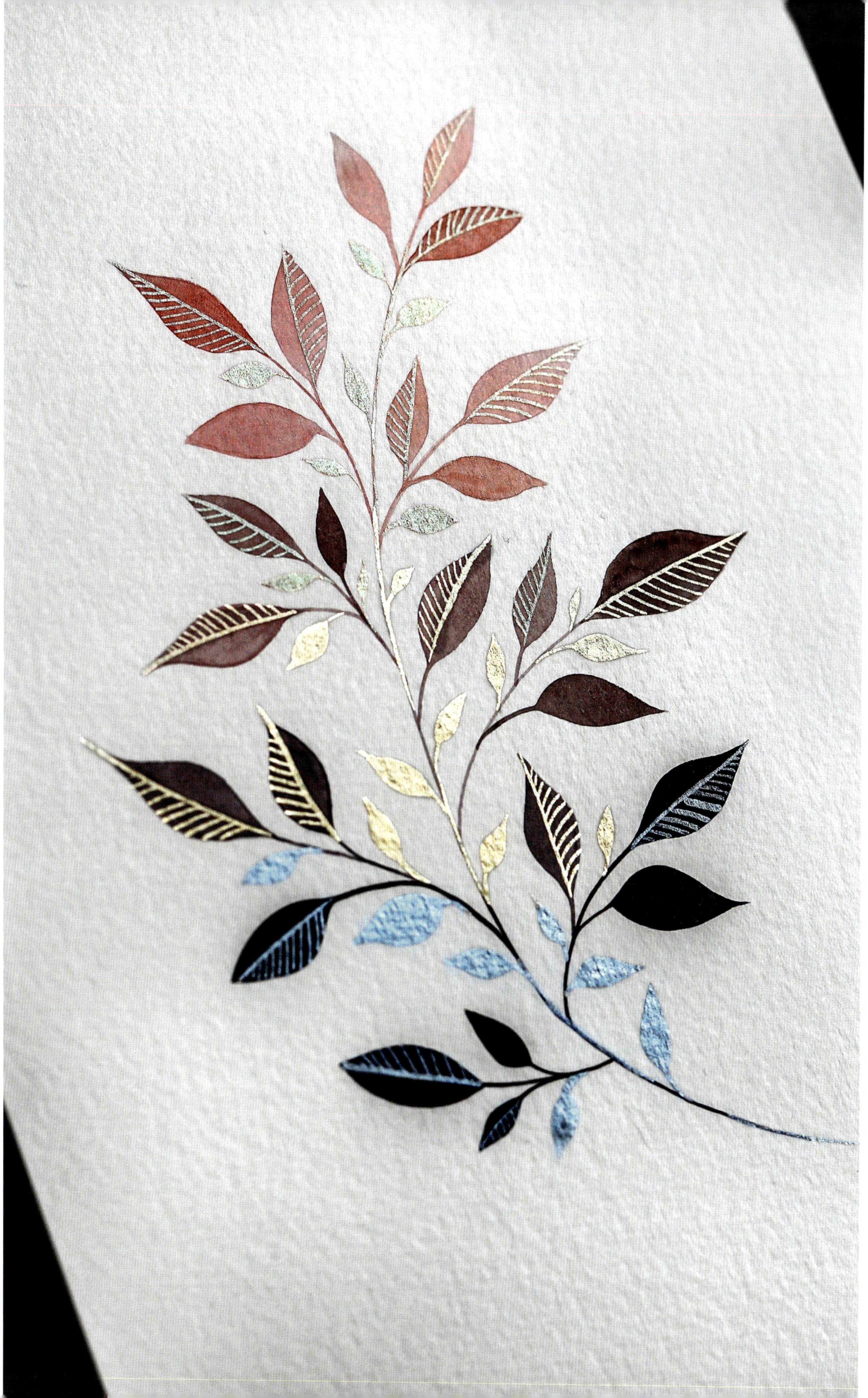

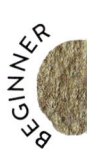

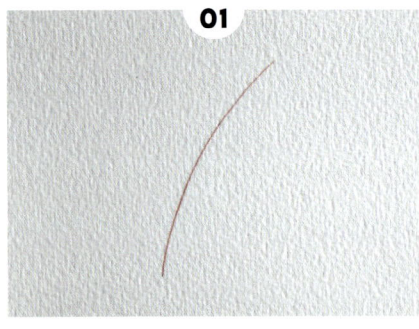

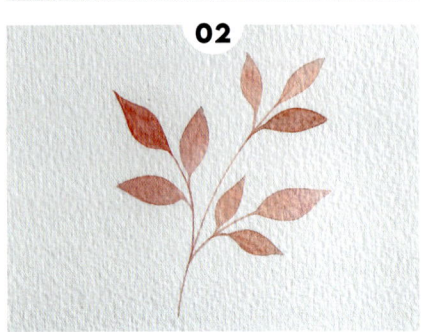

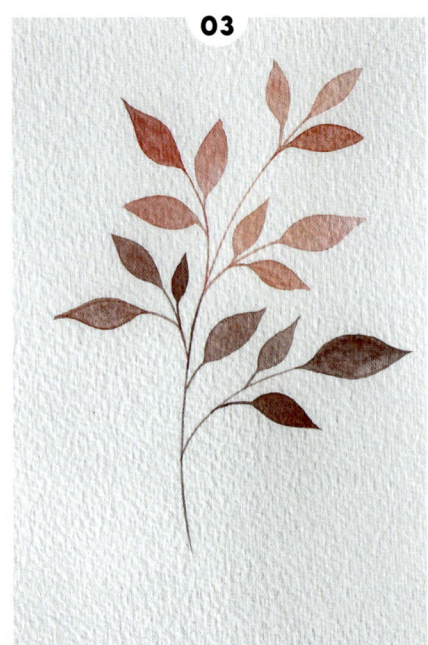

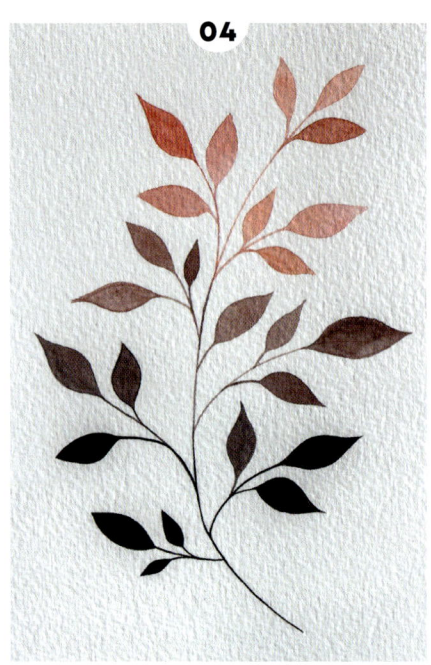

01 I deliberately chose not to make a sketch for my twig. Instead, start at the top of the twig and, using a thin rigger brush, paint a fine line from the wrist. Use the lightest shade of paint and concentrate on the top part of the twig first.

02 Add small branches with leaves at each end coming out of the first thin twig. This is the top part of our painting. It's also the lightest part, as the rest will become increasingly dark.

03 On a dish or paint palette, mix your paint to make it darker and apply it with your brush. Try to make the transitions as smooth as possible by changing the concentration of paint with your brush. Now extend the twig with the darker shade of paint and add even smaller branches, as well as leaves of varying sizes. Try to keep the lines as even as possible.

04 Repeat this process with the final—and darkest—shade. In my example, I've used a very darkly pigmented taupe, which is one of my favorite colors in my watercolor box. Add a few more leaves and the colorful base of your twig is finished.

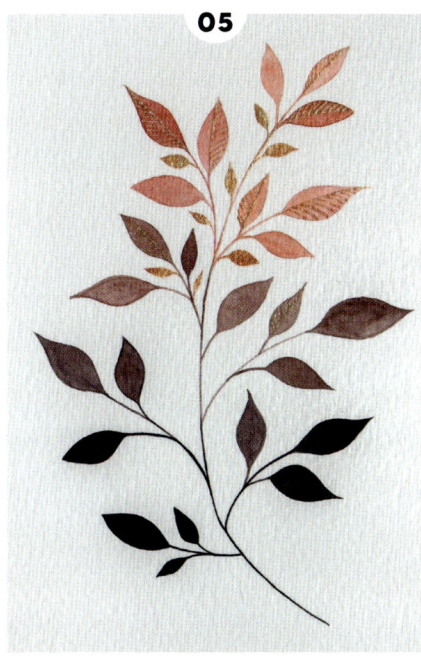

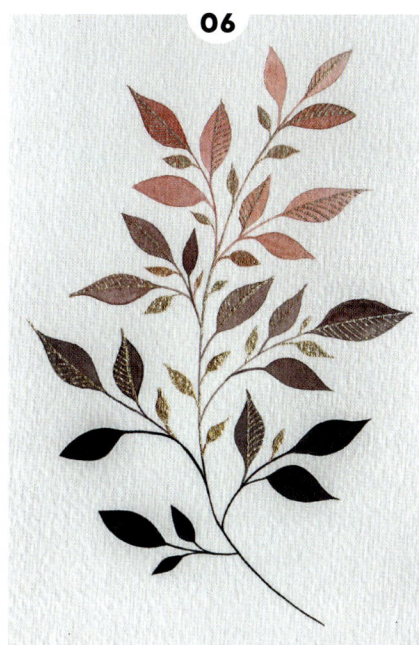

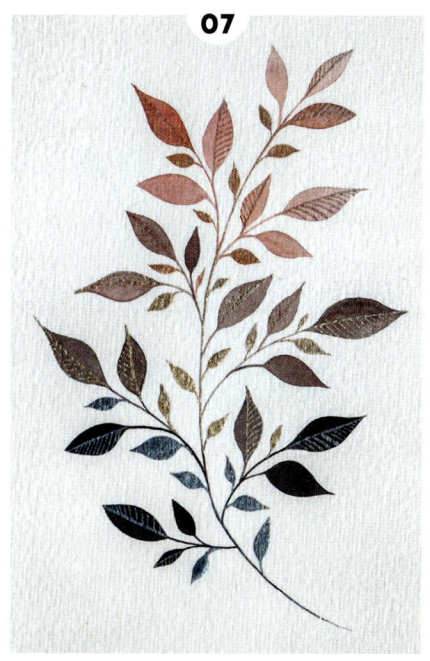

05 Our twig is made up of just three different shades of paint. To these, we'll add details in three different metallic paints. These details include little veins, which I've painted onto just one side of several leaves, as well as a few more small leaves on the smaller twigs. I chose rose metallic paint for the lightest area of paint.

06 You can paint the same details and little metallic leaves in the middle part of the twig too. I've chosen the light-gold shade, making sure that the gaps between each delicate leaf vein are as regular and even as possible.

07 Finally, I chose pale-blue metallic paint. Repeat the process from the last two steps in the darkest part of the twig. The motif now has an enchanting gradient with fine metallic accents that enhance the effect because of the contrast between the two colors.

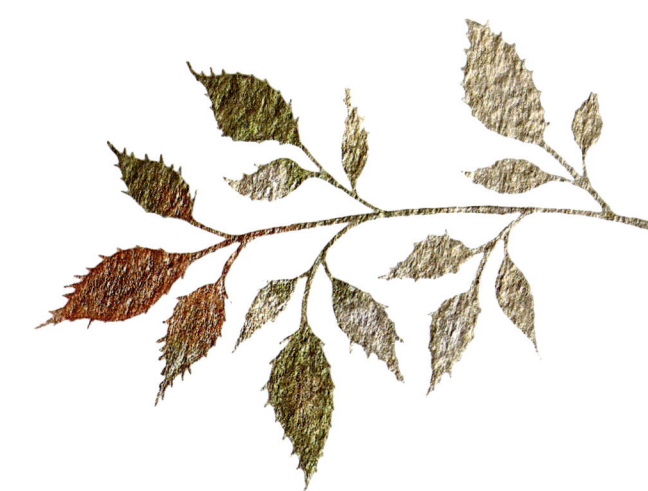

A Shimmering
UNDERWATER WORLD

The colorful underwater world of the ocean is perfect for developing creative ideas and making them a reality with intense colors and shimmering metallic accents. I have thousands of ideas for watercolors inspired by this theme. Here I'll show you how to magically paint this abstract seahorse onto the page.

MATERIALS

RIGGER BRUSH | ROUND BRUSH | PENCIL | WATERCOLOR PAPER

MY COLOR PALETTE

    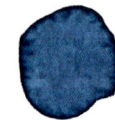 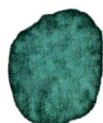

=== METALLIC PAINTS ===

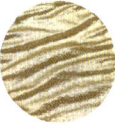

LIGHT
GOLD

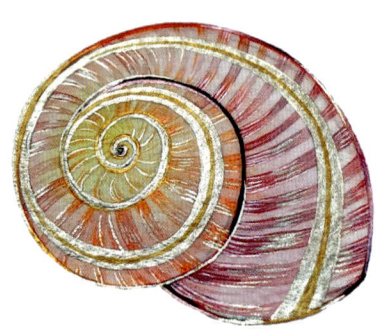

METALLIC WATERCOLOR

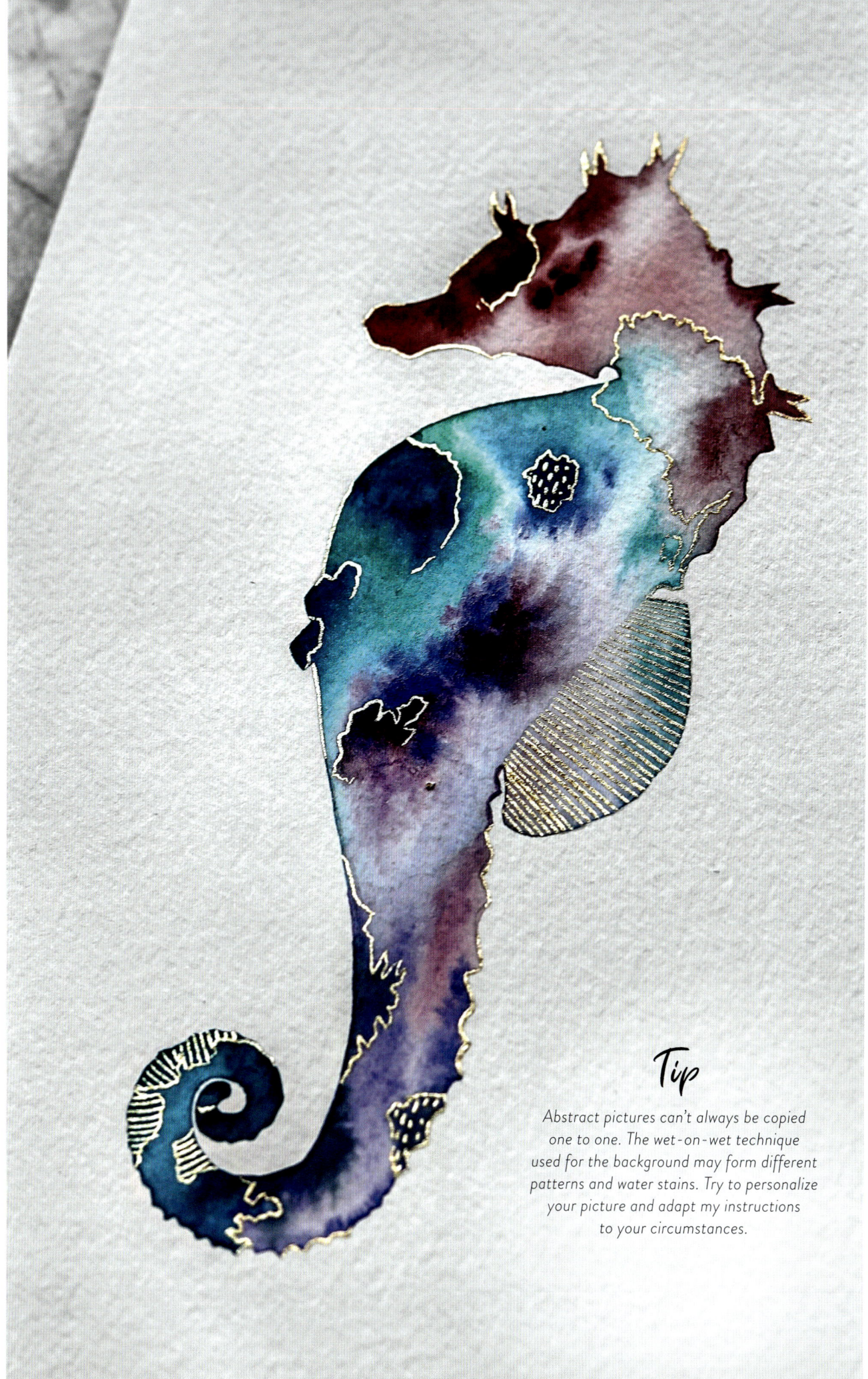

Tip

Abstract pictures can't always be copied one to one. The wet-on-wet technique used for the background may form different patterns and water stains. Try to personalize your picture and adapt my instructions to your circumstances.

01

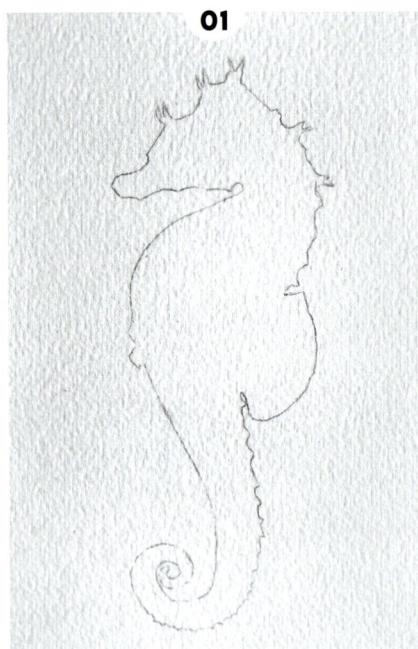

02

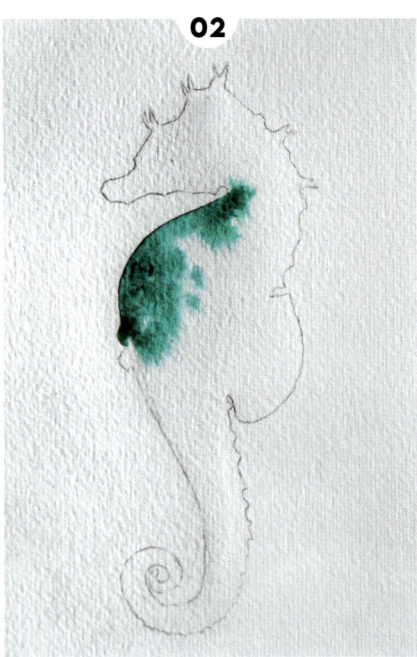

03

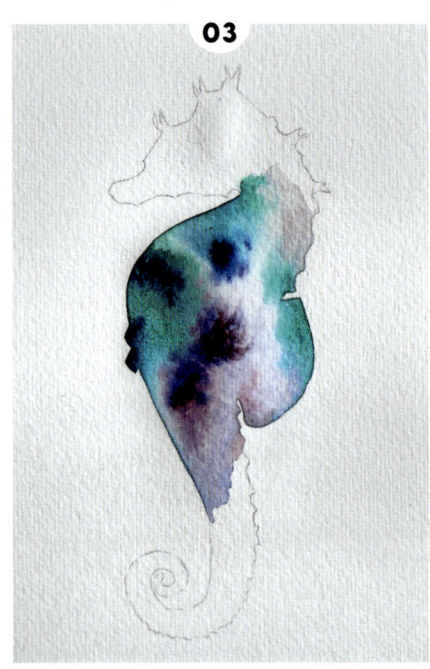

01   Using a soft pencil, sketch the silhouette of a seahorse. (You can also scan the QR code on page 31 to download a traceable sketch.) Try to keep the pencil lines as light as possible so they can be easily erased at the end. Then take a clean round brush (size 3) and clean water and paint the whole area of the seahorse.

02   Load your brush with a color of your choice (I've opted for turquoise) and apply it to the wet surface of your seahorse. With the wet-on-wet technique, your colors are distributed evenly and blend into one another easily.

03   Repeat this process with new colors. Choose shades that harmonize with one another and create attractive contrasts. Using light dabbing motions, you can apply the pigments so that in certain areas, the colors become more intense. The more water you add to your mixture, the lighter the resulting color will be. Work at a steady pace so that the surface of the paper doesn't dry out before you've applied all your colors. If this happens, you can take a clean, wet brush and carefully go back over the areas that are still without color. Make sure that your brush isn't too wet. There should be no puddles on the paper.

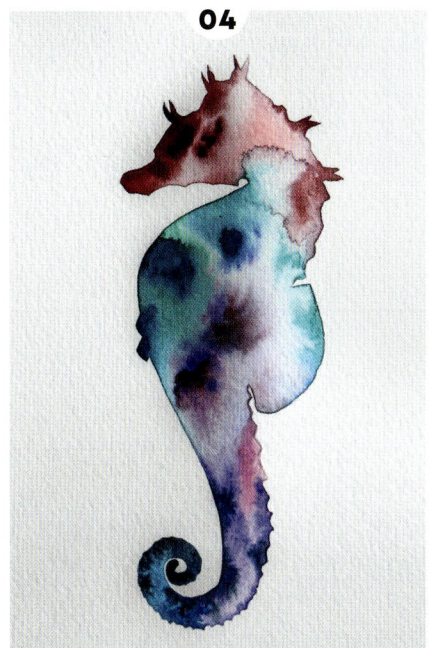

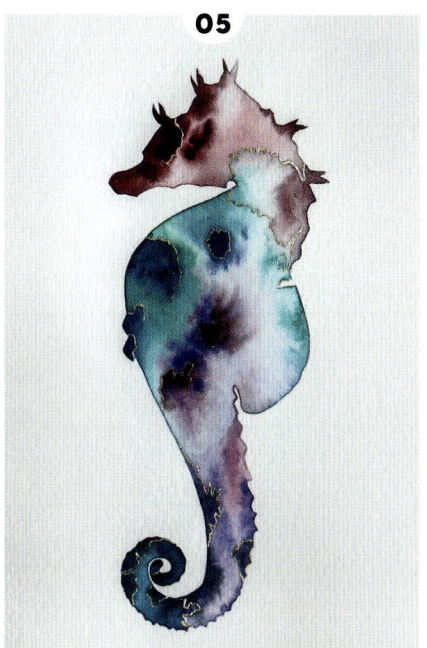

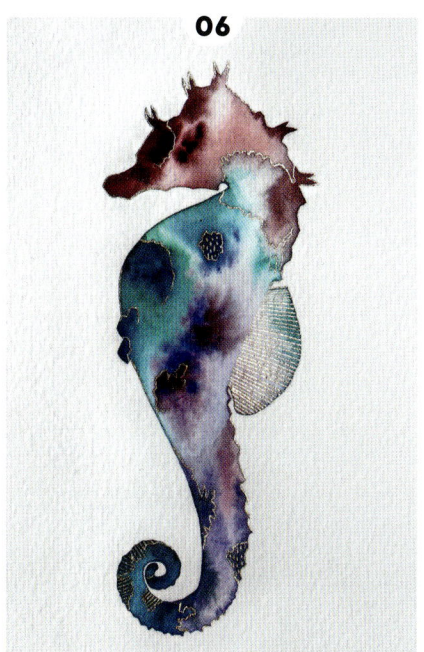

04　I chose a vibrant magenta for the seahorse's head. It varies in brightness and goes well with the other shades.

05　Leave your seahorse to dry completely. (You can speed up this process with a hairdryer.) When the paints are dry, patterns and water stains become more visible. I've traced over the outlines of these water stains in light gold to make them stand out.

06　In the last step, I've used a fine brush to draw little patterns and shapes in the outlines and give the seahorse a dorsal fin. Make sure that you draw fine details like these as accurately as possible and that the spaces between the lines are roughly even. This precision will make your motif look more elegant.

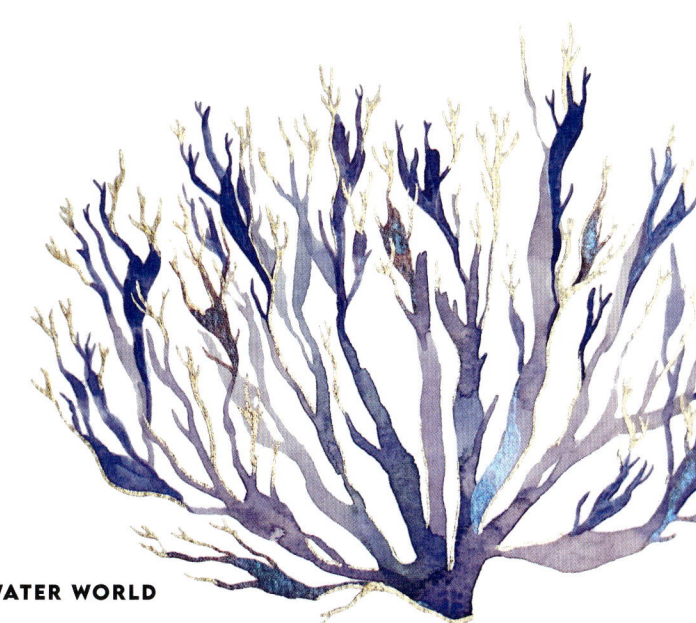

A SHIMMERING UNDERWATER WORLD

Romantic
ROSES

If you want a motif for a homemade greeting card or birthday card, I highly recommend these delicate roses. They're pretty straightforward, as they don't take long to paint. They're suitable for new artists too. Their gentle appearance is really eye-catching and sure to bring a smile to your loved one's face!

MATERIALS

RIGGER BRUSH | ROUND BRUSH | PENCIL | WATERCOLOR PAPER

MY COLOR PALETTE

 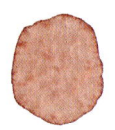 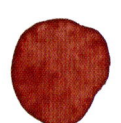 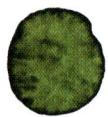 

=== METALLIC PAINTS ===

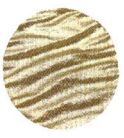 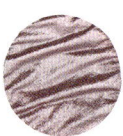

LIGHT
GOLD

LIGHT
VIOLET

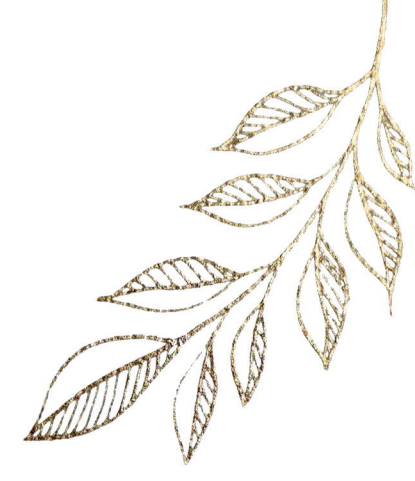

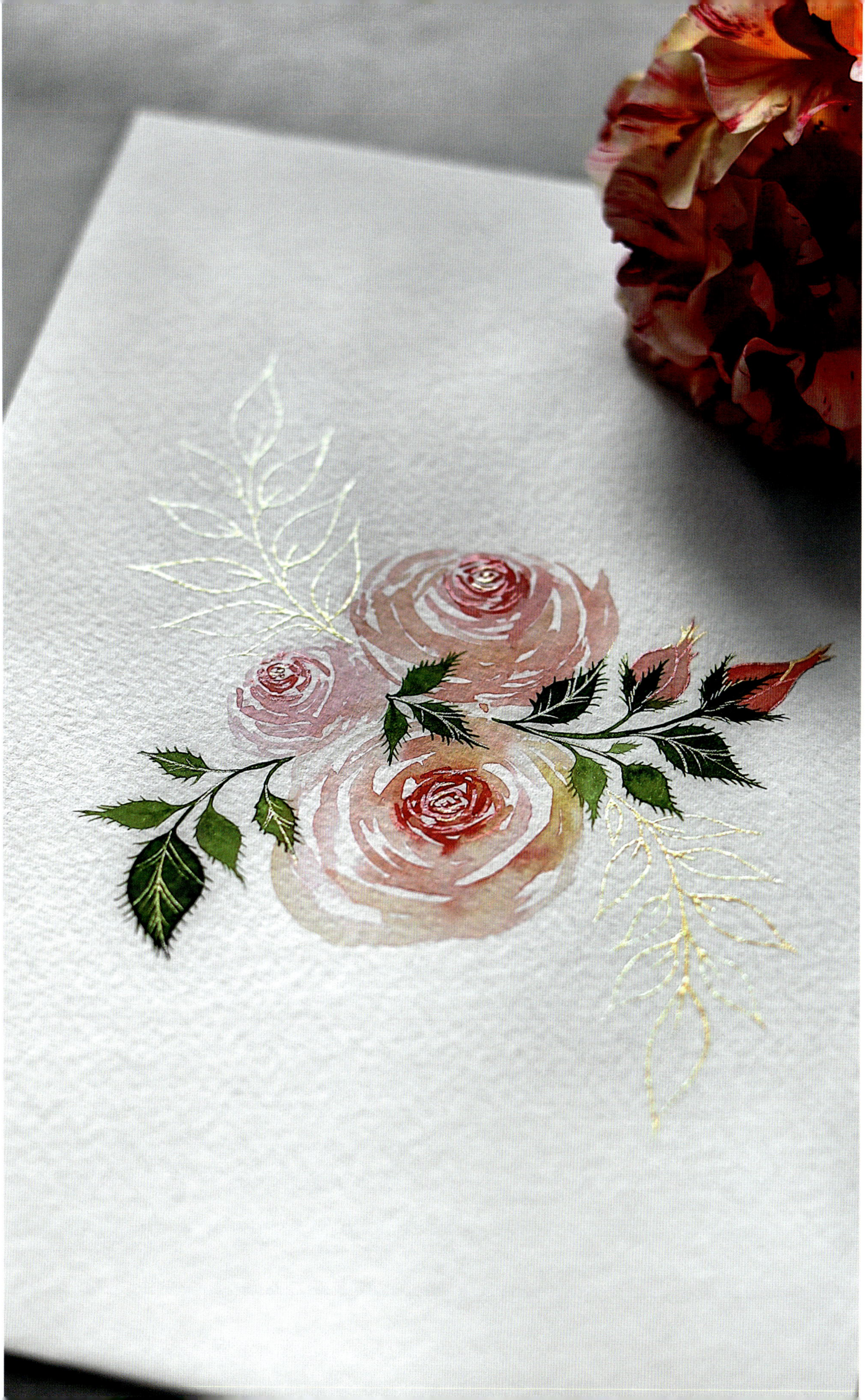

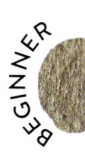

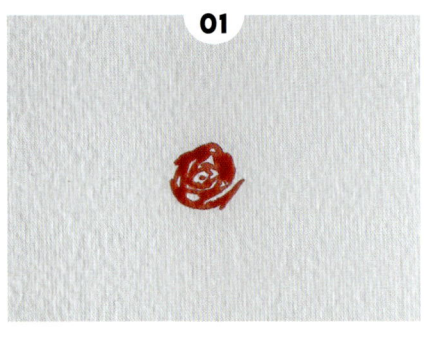

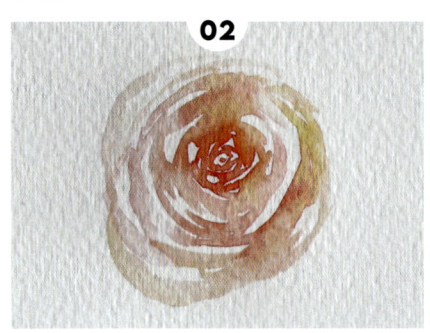

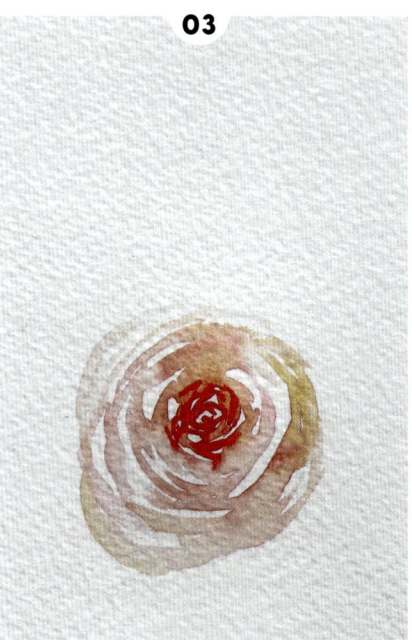

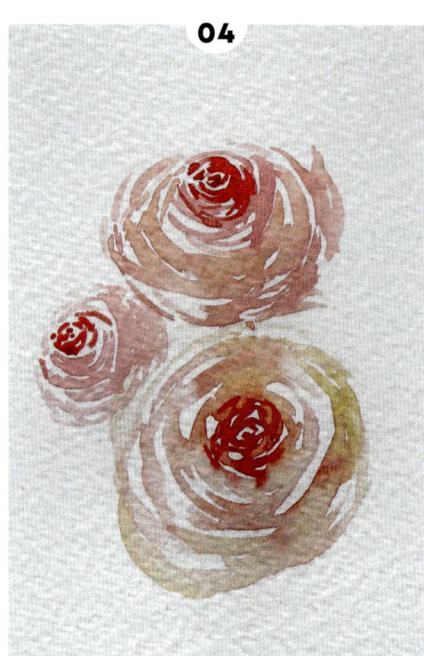

01 For the roses, start in the middle of the flowers, dipping your round brush (size 3) into paint and working from the inside outward in small semicircles. I used a light pink for my roses, mixed with a little yellow.

02 The petals in the middle of the rose are still very close together and open out as your flower's circumference gets bigger. Try not to use too much paint, so the inside of your rose looks darker and the outside gets increasingly lighter.

03 To increase the contrast between the inner and outer petals, you can add more paint to the middle of the rose. As long as the surface is wet, the transitions will flow smoothly into one another.

04 You can add more flowers to your finished rose using the same technique. Make sure that the size, color, and position of each rose is a little different so your arrangement looks consistent.

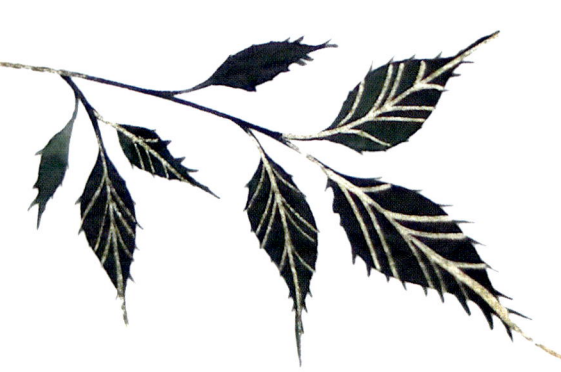

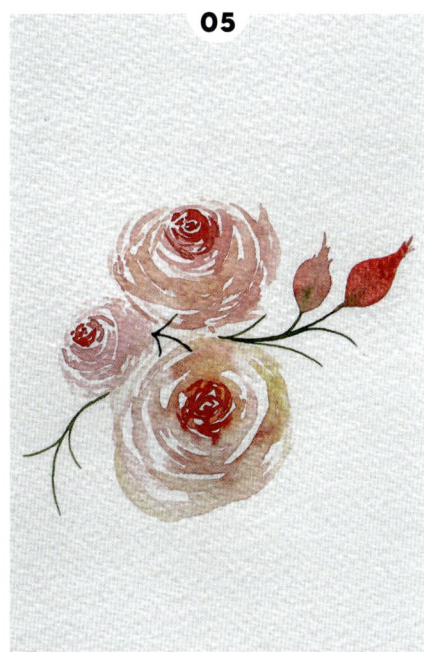

05

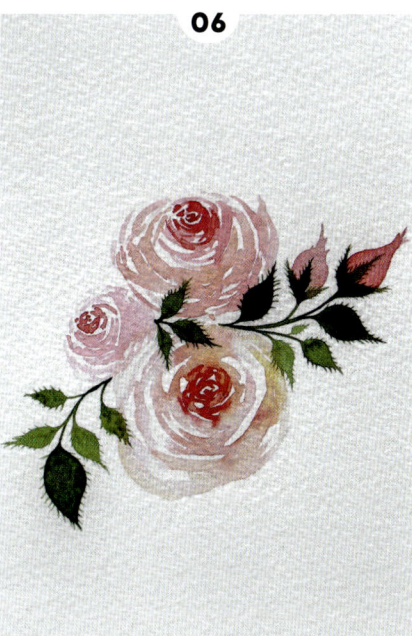

06

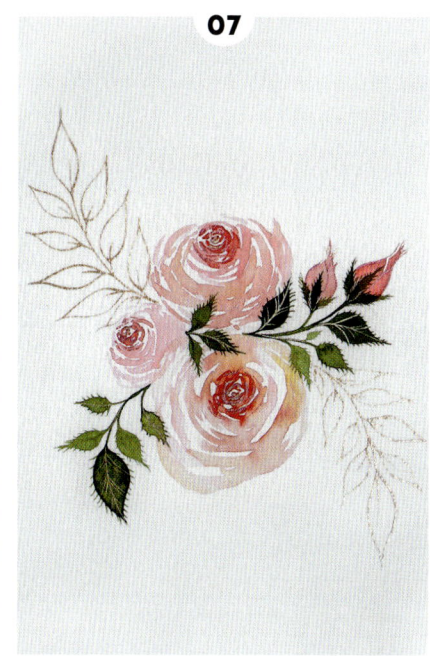

07

05   To perfect your rose flowers, you can add some buds and leaves. Look carefully at your painting and decide where these would look best. In my painting, I've drawn the roses facing left, so I decided to draw the little twig of buds in the opposite direction. For this, I chose a warm olive green that I applied with a rigger brush. Additional leaves have been added between the roses and around their edges. I then painted the buds using the same pink I used for the open flowers.

06   Finish your twigs and buds with delicate leaves that are toothed at the ends. This is what gives the rose leaves their characteristic appearance. I used the same olive green as before.

07   Now it's time to add some metallic accents to your flowers and leaves. Using the light gold color, I added fine veins to a few of the leaves and then traced over the outlines of the buds to make them stand out from the background. I also added a delicate leafy twig above and below the roses. Last but not least, I highlighted the inside of the flowers with a little light-violet paint. Make sure you don't add too many metallic elements to your painting. That way, your watercolor won't become overloaded.

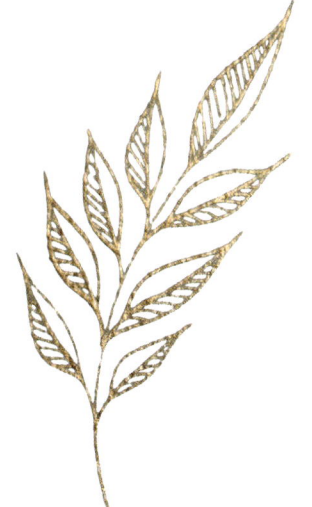

ROMANTIC ROSES

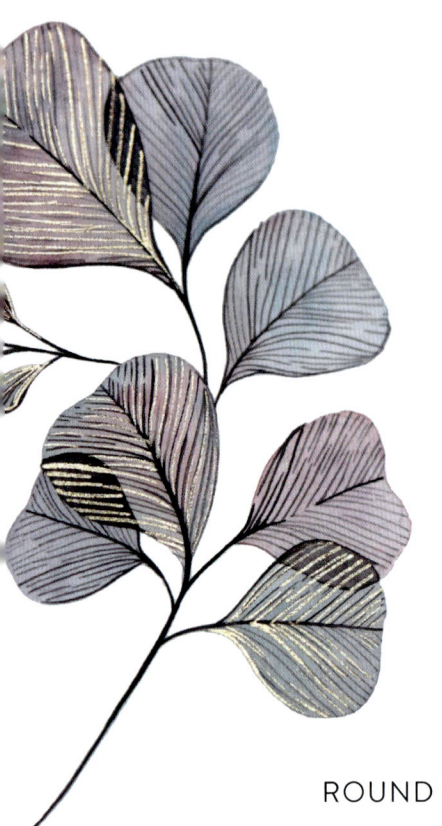

Delicate
EUCALYPTUS

Not only does eucalyptus look great in a vase, it also makes a great motif for a delicate watercolor.

MATERIALS

ROUND BRUSH | RIGGER BRUSH | WATERCOLOR PAPER | PENCIL

MY COLOR PALETTE

 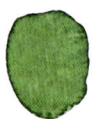 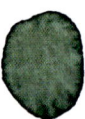

═══ METALLIC PAINTS ═══

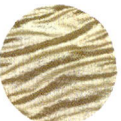

LIGHT
GOLD

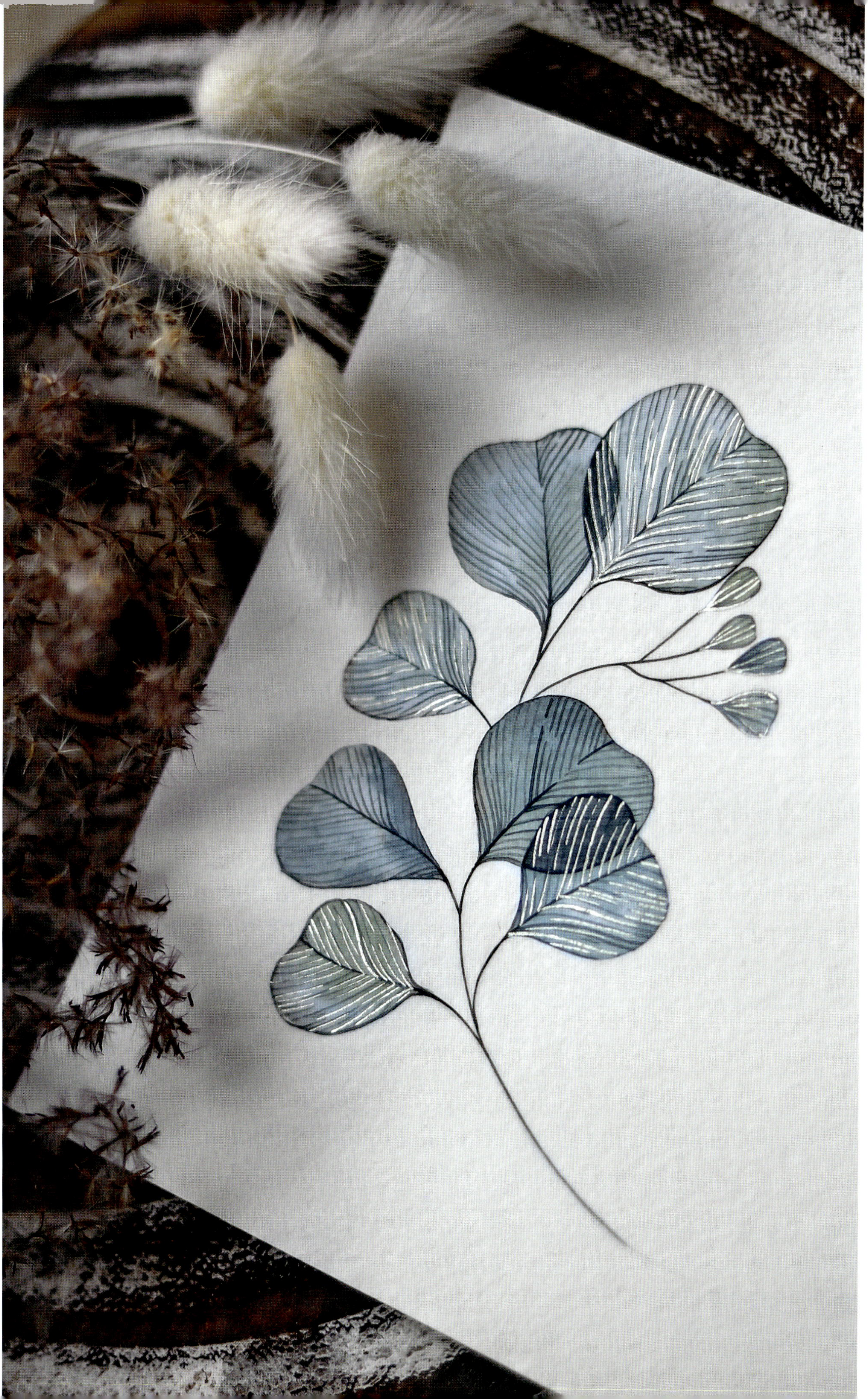

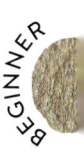

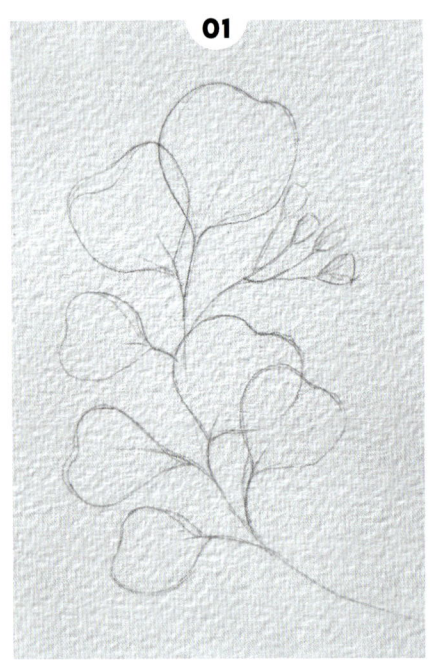

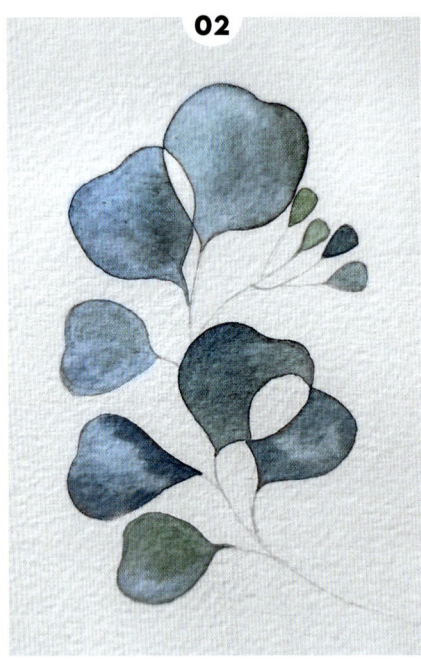

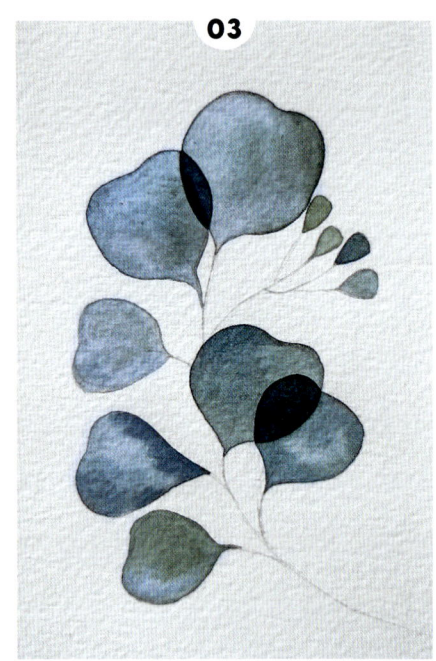

01   Take a soft pencil and draw the outline of a eucalyptus twig. (You can also scan the QR code on page 31 to download a traceable sketch.) Try to position the leaves so that some of them are overlapping.

02   Using a clean round brush (size 3) and clean water, paint over the whole surface of the leaves so they're ready for paint to be added. At this stage, leave out the part where two leaves overlap. Mix shades of blue and green with a little yellow and you'll get the typical eucalyptus mint. The shade can vary a bit. Apply your paint using the wet-on-wet technique.

03   After your leaves are sufficiently dry, intensify your mint shade, then apply this darker shade to the unpainted areas with the overlapping leaves. This increases the impression of two objects overlapping.

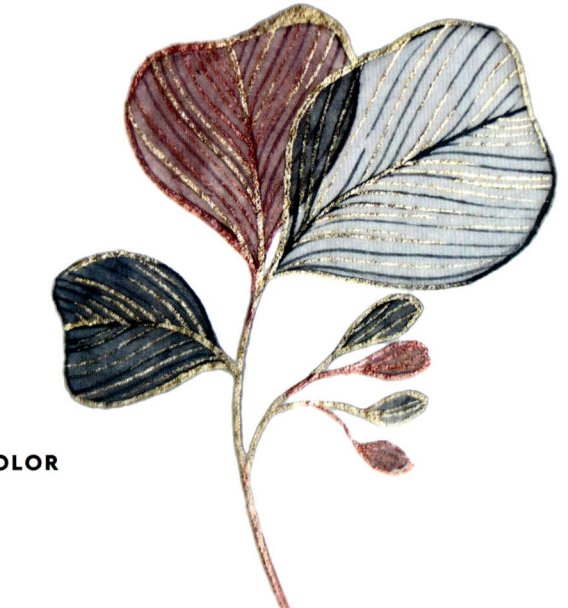

METALLIC WATERCOLOR

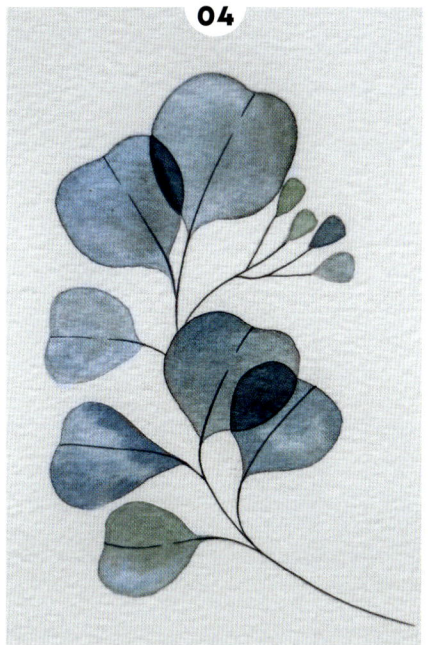
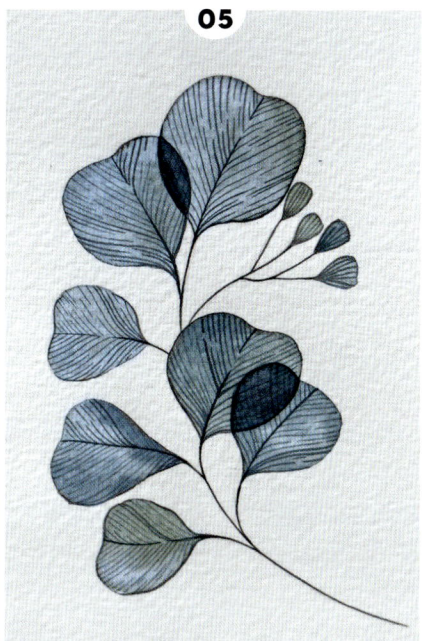
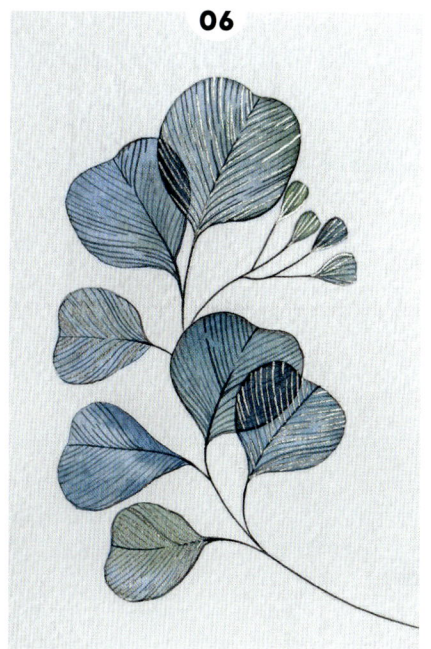

04   Using a thin brush, such as the rigger brush, paint the middle part of the eucalyptus twig and the fine outlines of the leaves. I've used the darker shade of mint to make them stand out from the leaf surfaces.

05   To give the leaves their delicate appearance, add some thin veins in the dark-mint shade. The veins don't need to reach all the way from the center of the leaf to the edge. There can be breaks in them. Make sure that the spaces between the veins in the leaves are even.

06   In the final step, it's time to add some metallic accents and give your painting that little something extra. I've traced over some of the veins in the leaves with light-gold metallic paint.

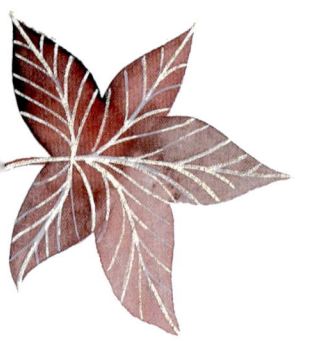
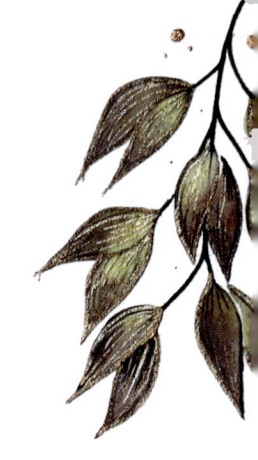

Fall
TREASURES

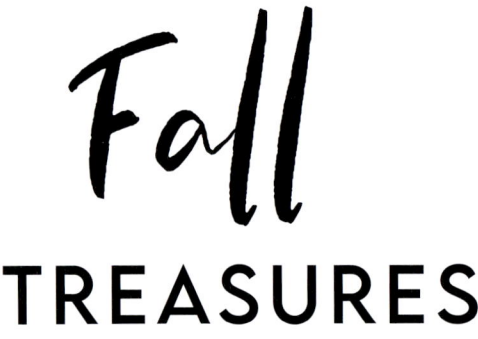

No season is as intensely colorful as fall. Green foliage transforms into radiant yellow, orange, and red and beckons you outdoors for a beautiful walk. The blazing colors of fall are a source of inspiration for me every year, so let's paint a fall-themed watercolor together.

MATERIALS

ROUND BRUSH | RIGGER BRUSH | PENCIL | WATERCOLOR PAPER

MY COLOR PALETTE

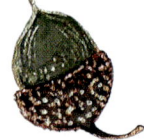

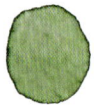  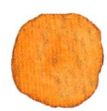 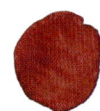

=== METALLIC PAINTS ===

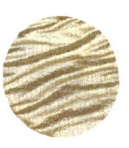 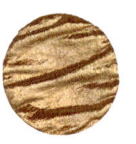 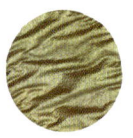 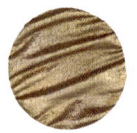 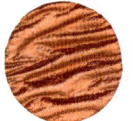

LIGHT GOLD   BRONZE   PALE OLIVE   LIGHT BROWN   RED BROWN

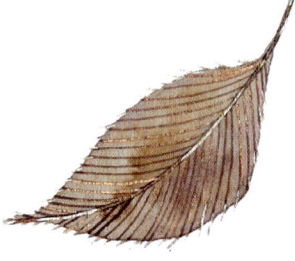

METALLIC WATERCOLOR

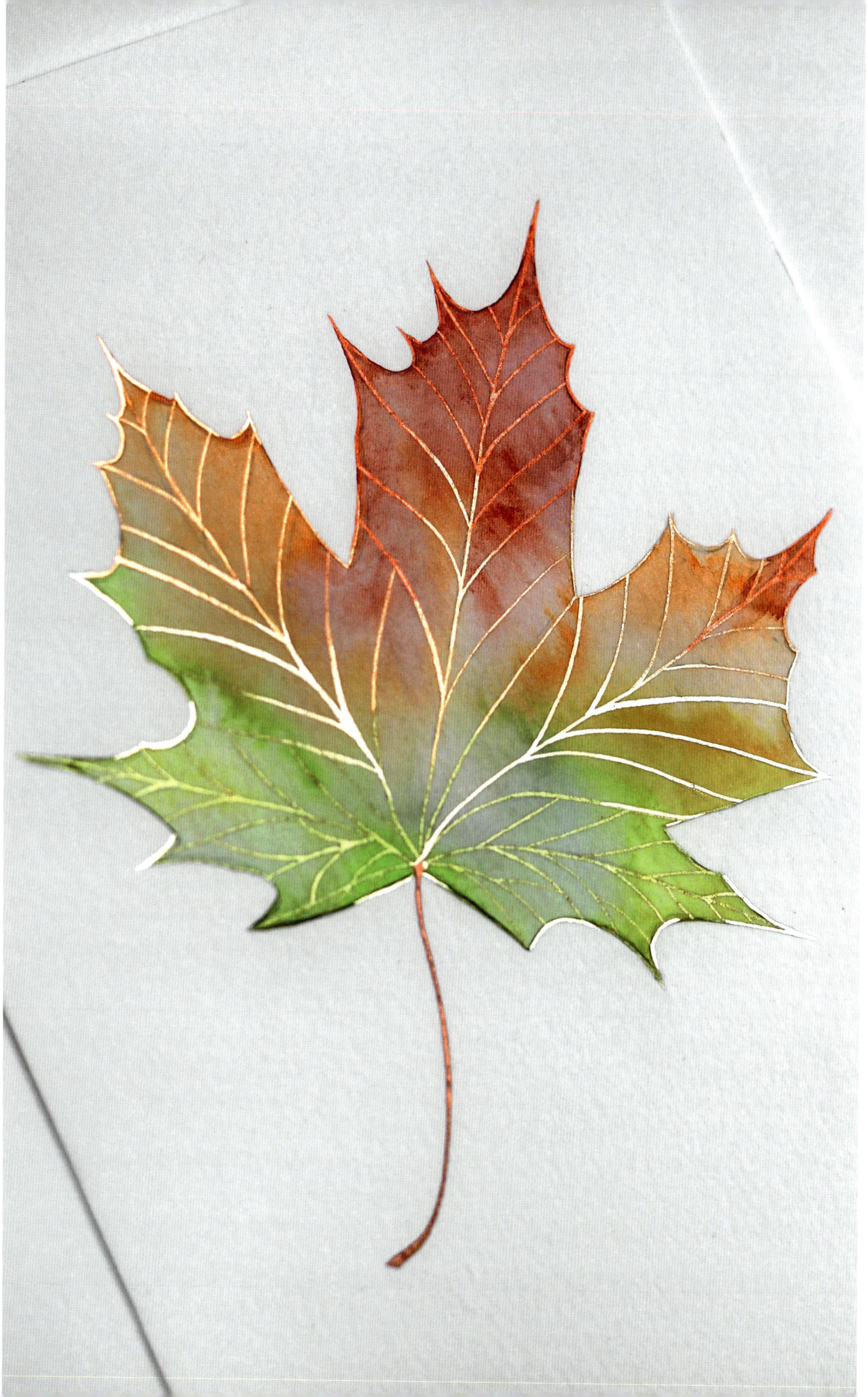

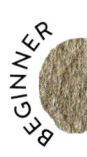

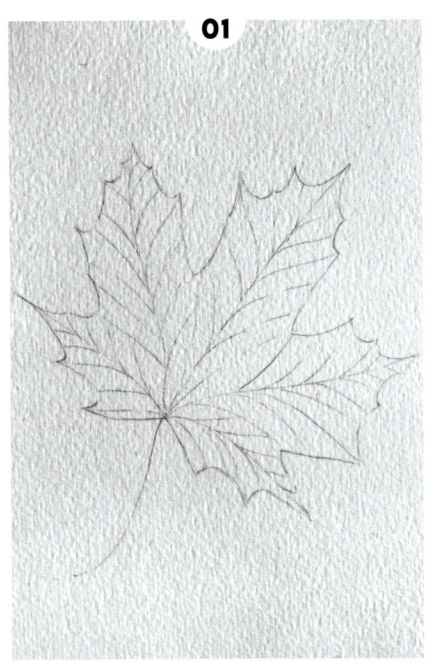

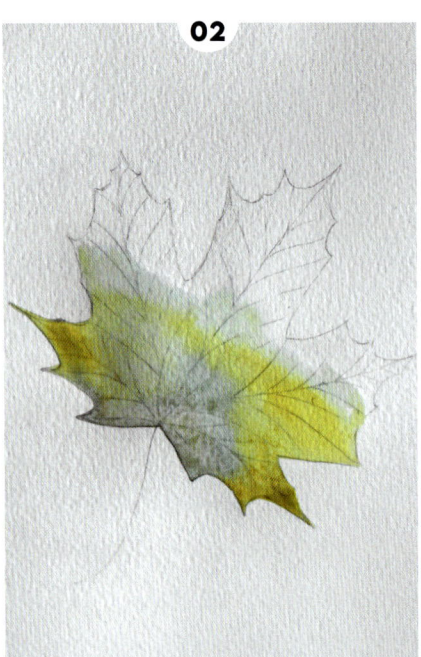

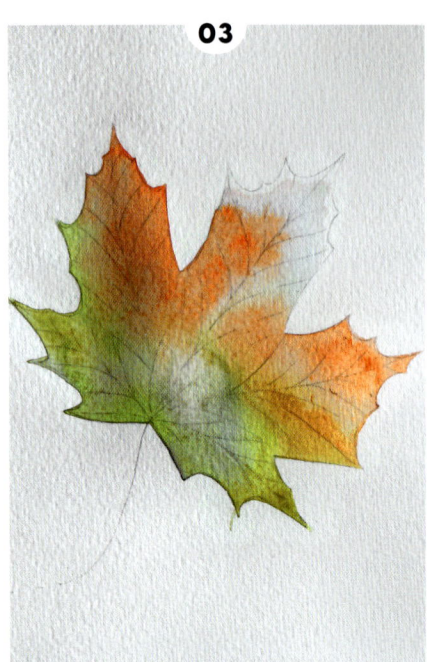

01 Using a soft pencil, sketch the outlines and thin veins of a fall leaf of your choice. I've chosen a maple leaf for my example. (You can also scan the QR code on page 31 to download a traceable sketch.)

02 Dip your clean brush into clean water and moisten the whole area of the leaf. Then apply your paint to the damp surface using the wet-on-wet technique. I've chosen a gradient that starts at the bottom of the leaf and progresses to the tip. I began with a light forest green, making it warmer by gradually adding more yellow. The wet-on-wet technique allows the colors to flow evenly into one another.

03 I then continued with a deep orange, making sure that all surfaces were sufficiently damp.

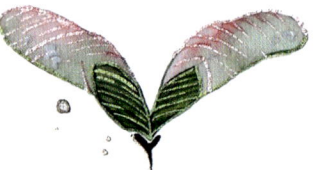

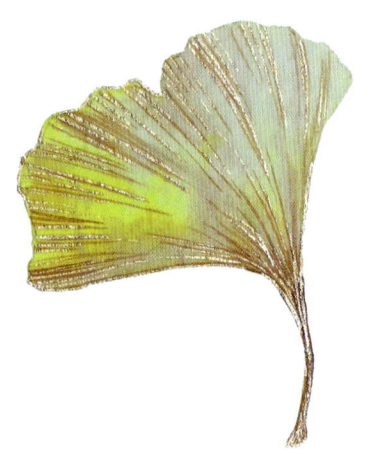

METALLIC WATERCOLOR

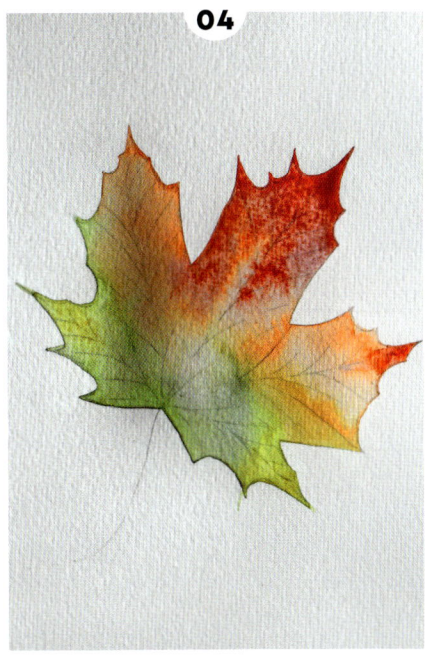 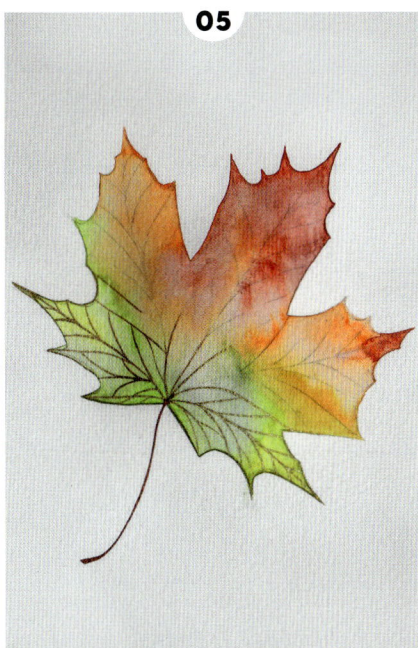 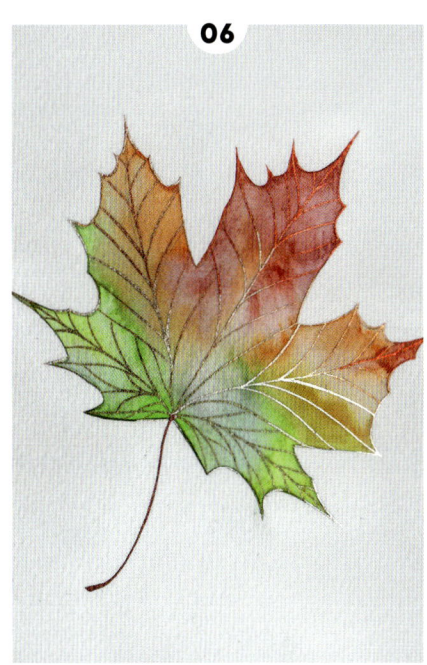

04 To make our leaf shine in typical fall colors, I chose a vibrant red for the tip.

05 Before adding the metallic accents, make sure that your watercolor is sufficiently dry. That way, the metallic paints won't blend with the watercolors. You can choose five different metallic shades for the fall leaf. Then work from the bottom of the leaf to the tip. For the stem, I chose the light-brown metallic paint. I then traced over the veins in the green parts of the leaf with the pale-olive shade.

06 I've painted the veins in the yellow-green area using light-gold metallic paint. For the orange part of the leaf, I've chosen bronze, and for the red area, red brown. You can then trace over some of the leaf tips to make the edges look clean and neat.

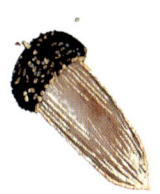

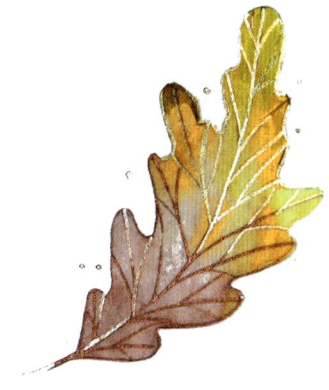

Fall Treasures

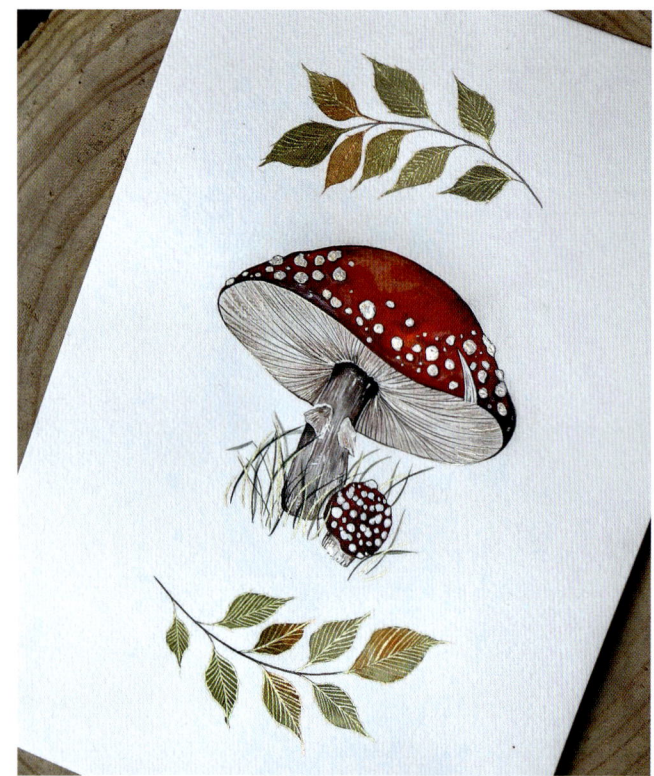

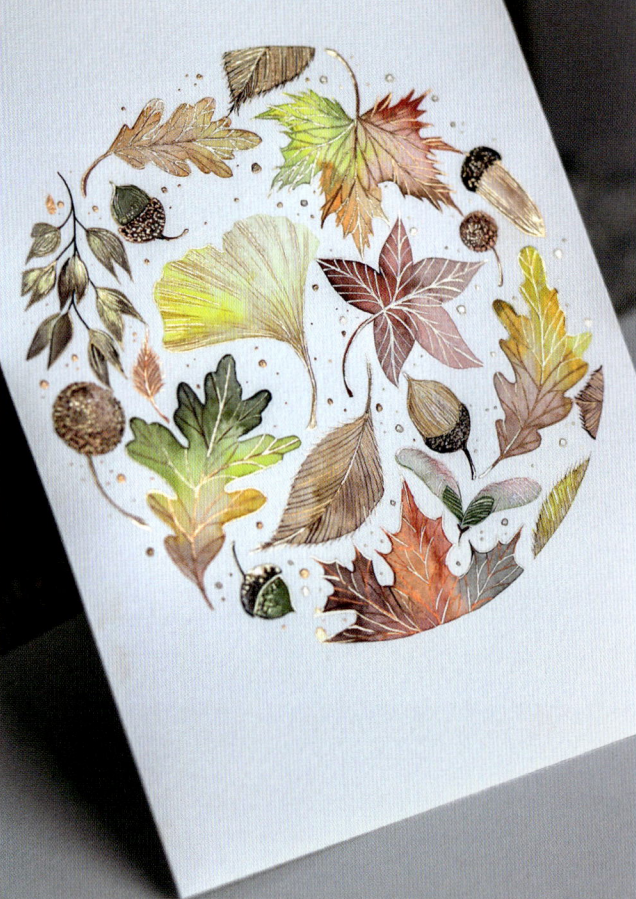

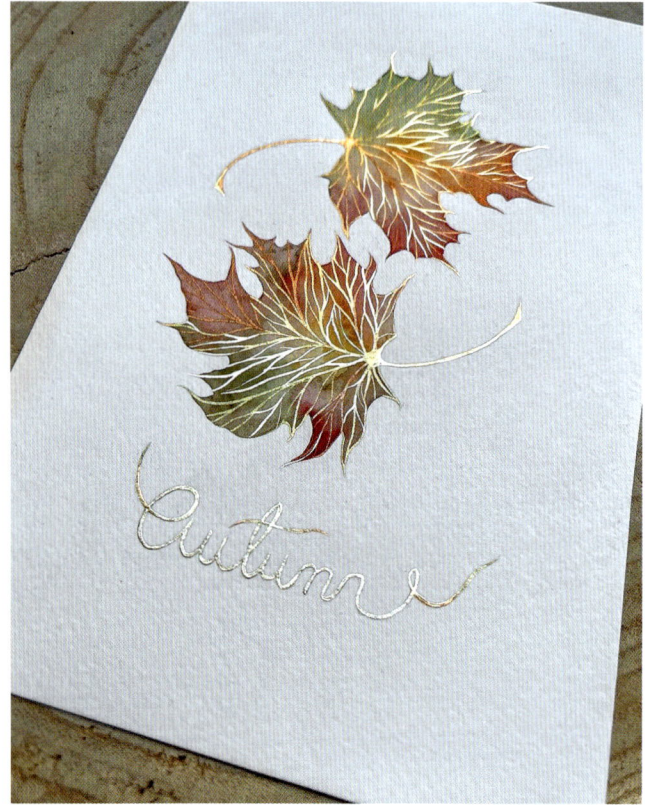

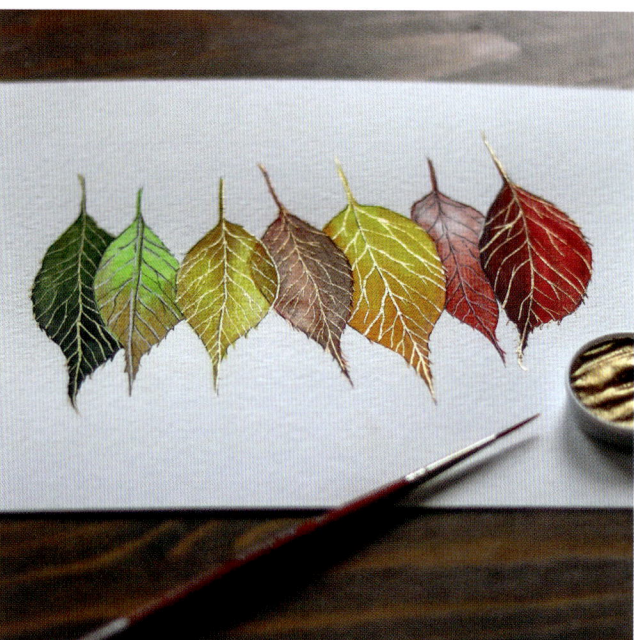

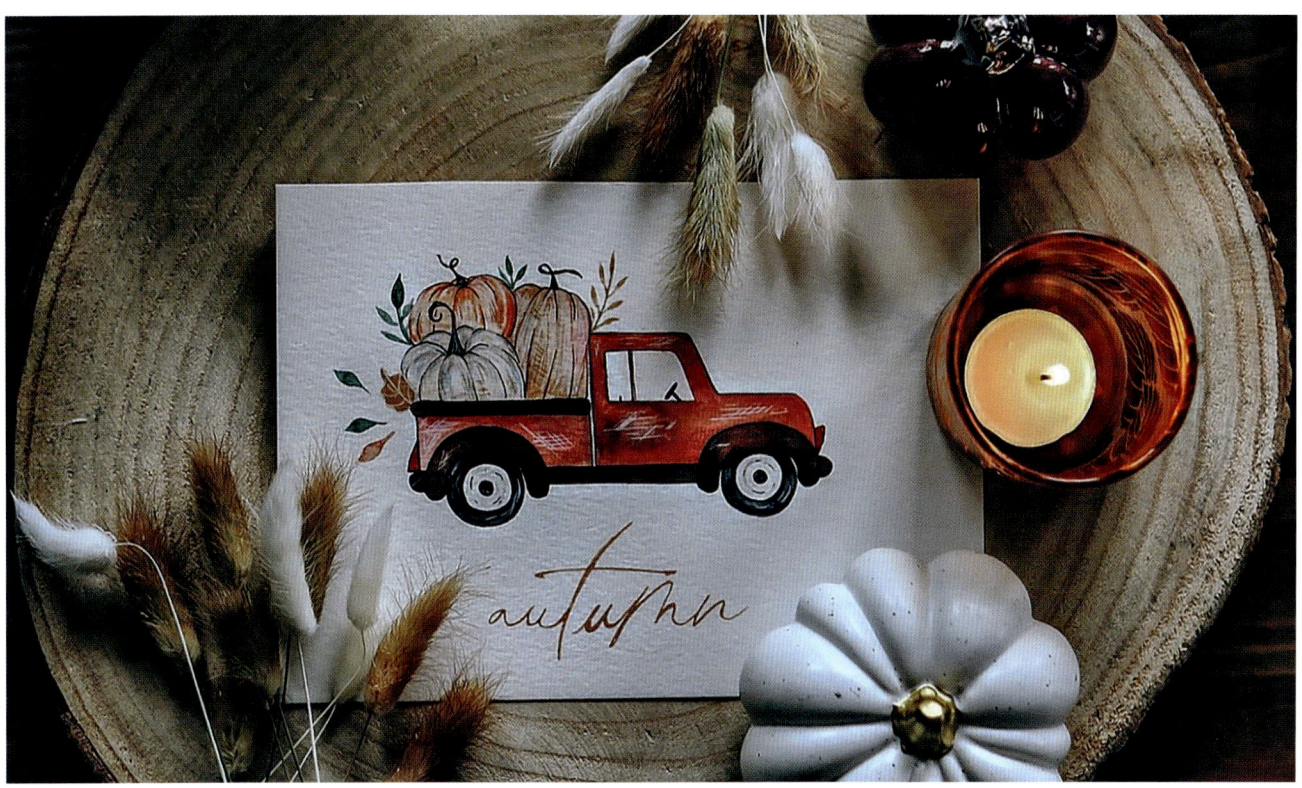

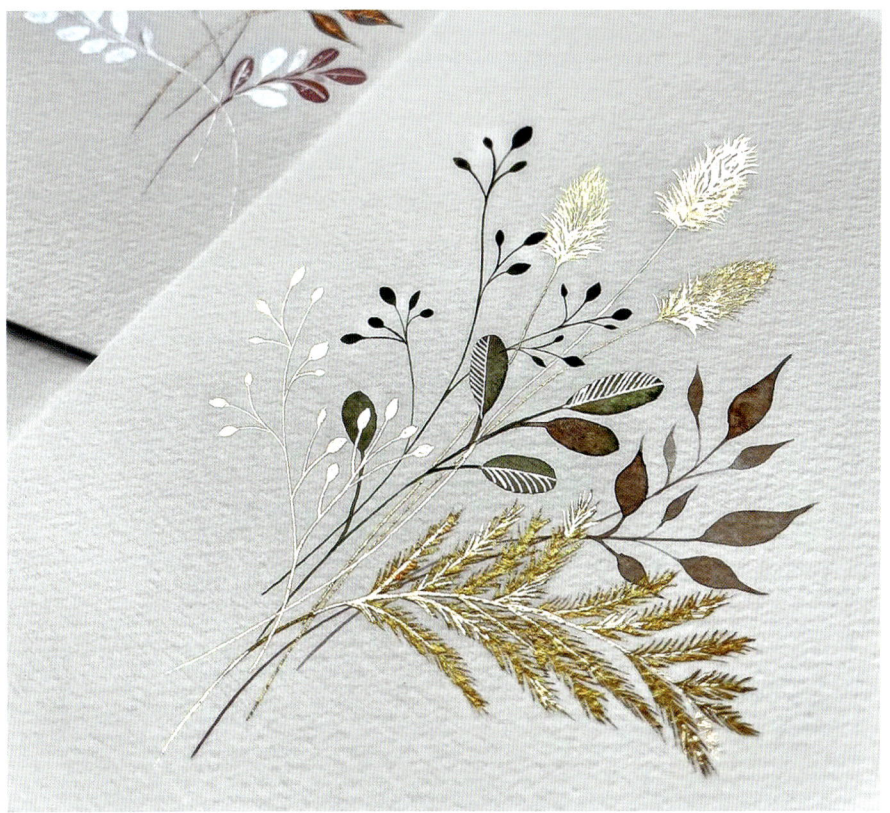

Tip

It's not just fall leaves that make great motifs for your paintings. This colorful season brings with it all sorts of treasures that are worth a closer look. Why not go for a walk in nature to observe these little signs of fall, then gather a few to integrate into your paintings? It's a great way to find inspiration for color schemes, as well as motifs of a variety of fall treasures.

Fuzzy
BUMBLEBEE

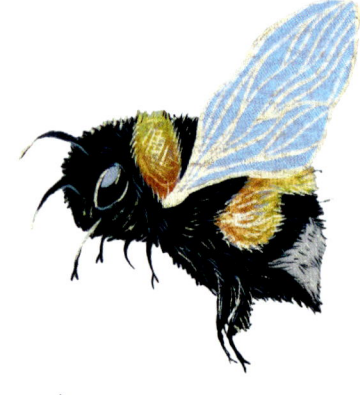

This furry bumblebee marks the beginning of the second of our four categories. As you'll see, the paintings will now become a bit more detailed.

MATERIALS

ROUND BRUSH | RIGGER BRUSH | MICROBRUSH | PENCIL |
WATERCOLOR PAPER | OPTIONAL: WHITE GEL PEN

MY COLOR PALETTE

 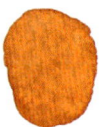  

=== METALLIC PAINTS ===

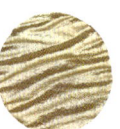 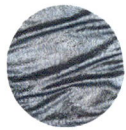

LIGHT
GOLD

PALE
BLUE

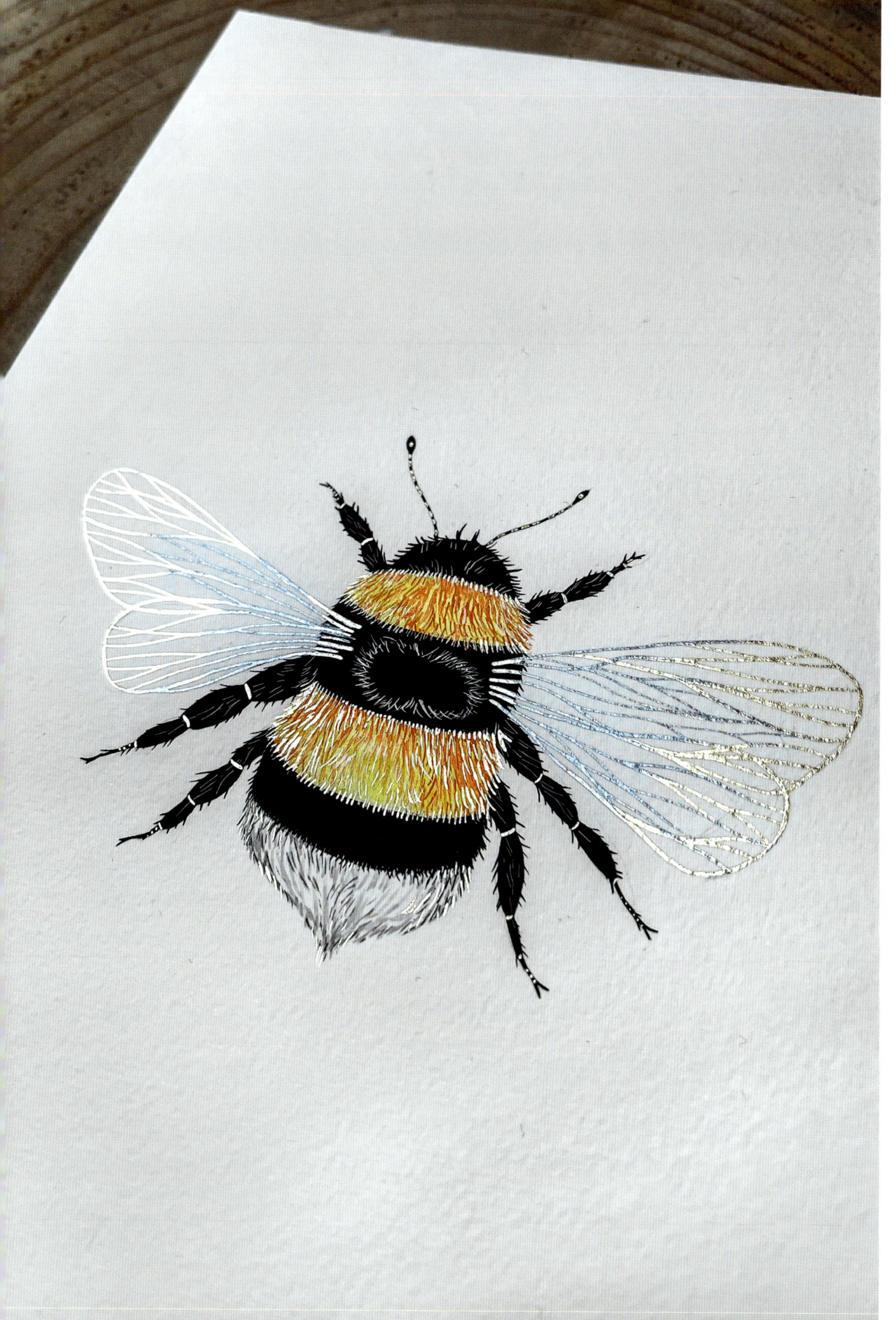

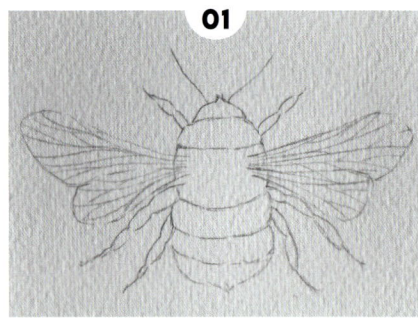

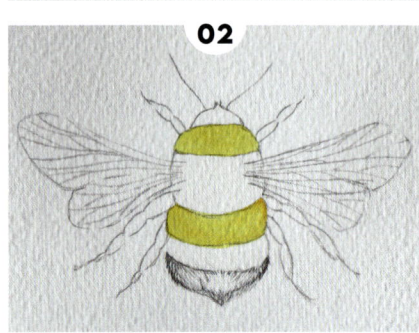

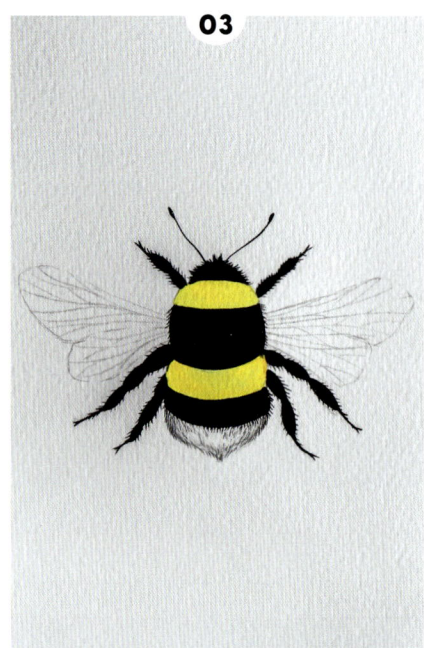

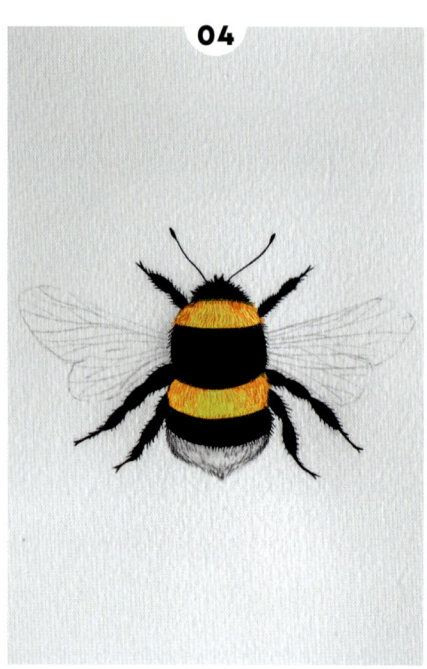

01   Use a soft pencil to draw the outlines of the little bumblebee. (You can also scan the QR code on page 31 to download a traceable sketch.) It's fine to just indicate the outlines. For this motif, we'll be using the wet-on-dry technique. This means that you don't need to prime the surfaces with clean water.

02   Start with the yellow parts of the bumblebee's body. Apply the paint with a brush. I've used a size 1 round brush. While the yellow areas are drying, take a microbrush and paint some little light-gray hairs on the bumblebee's bottom. Make sure that you make the middle lighter or leave a small area unpainted.

03   We can now fill in the rest of the bumblebee's body with black and add little hairs to the body and legs—this will make your bumblebee look as fluffy as possible. Give yourself plenty of time and brush the hairs outward from the body.

04   The bumblebee's yellow stripes look quite striking now. To integrate them into the rest of the body, I've added some little orange hairs with a fine brush. Try to make them as even as possible and show the direction the hairs are growing. Allow them to extend slightly into the bumblebee's black stripes.

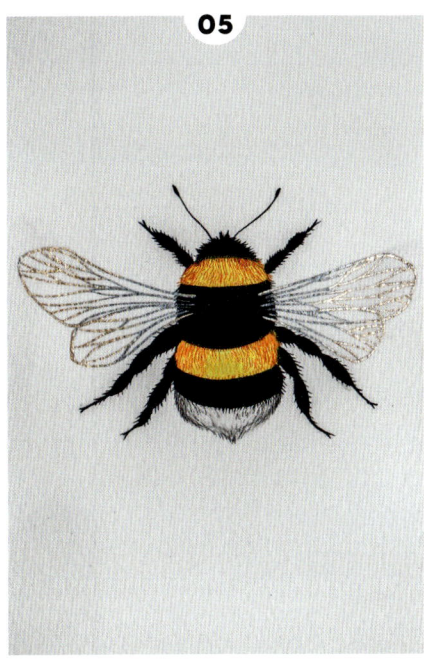

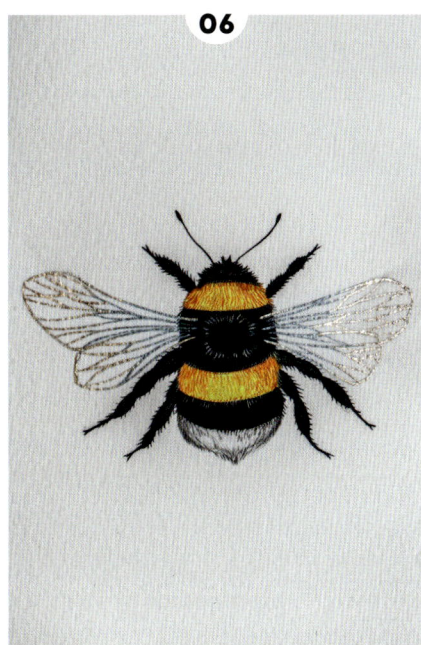

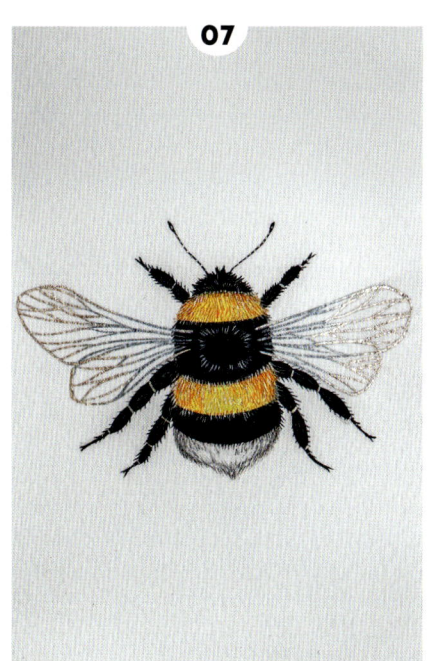

05 We've still got to add the finishing touches to the body. However, first we're going to make a start on the bee's wings. When painted with metallic paints, they look really eye-catching. Use two different shades that gently blend into each other. For the inside of the wings, I chose pale blue. For the outside, I chose light gold. Once you've drawn the metallic accents with your rigger brush, the bee's wings are done.

06 Now that the wings are finished, we can turn our attention to the other details on the body. Using your rigger brush or microbrush, add a few individual white hairs. I've used the white from my watercolor palette. You can use a white gel pen instead if you want.

07 Finally, you can add some more fine hairs to the yellow stripes of the bumblebee in light gold. I've also added some lightly shimmering accents to the bee's fluffy rear end and joints. Now your bumblebee is finished!

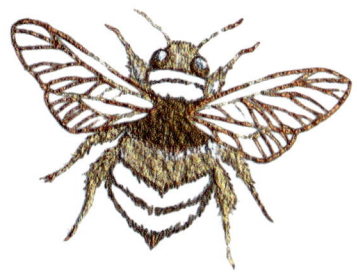

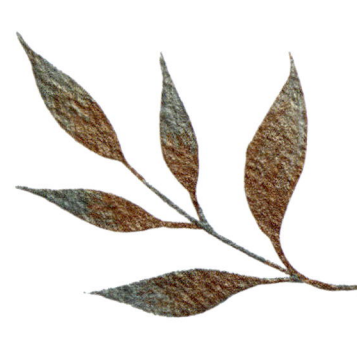

Shiny
LEAVES & TWIGS

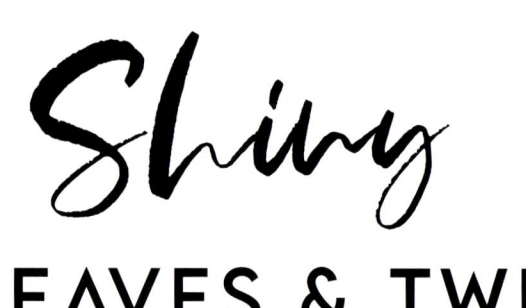

Compositions with a variety of twigs, leaves, and flowers are some of my favorite motifs. I usually don't spend too much time thinking about these creations—I just let my intuition guide me. More often than not, I don't really know how the picture is going to turn out.

MATERIALS
RIGGER BRUSH | PENCIL | WATERCOLOR PAPER

MY COLOR PALETTE

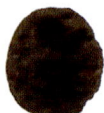  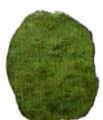   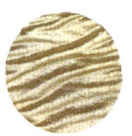

METALLIC PAINTS

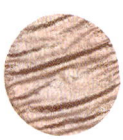 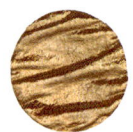 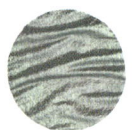 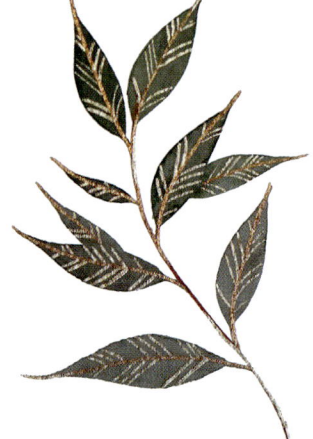

LIGHT GOLD   PALE PINK   BRONZE   MINT

METALLIC WATERCOLOR

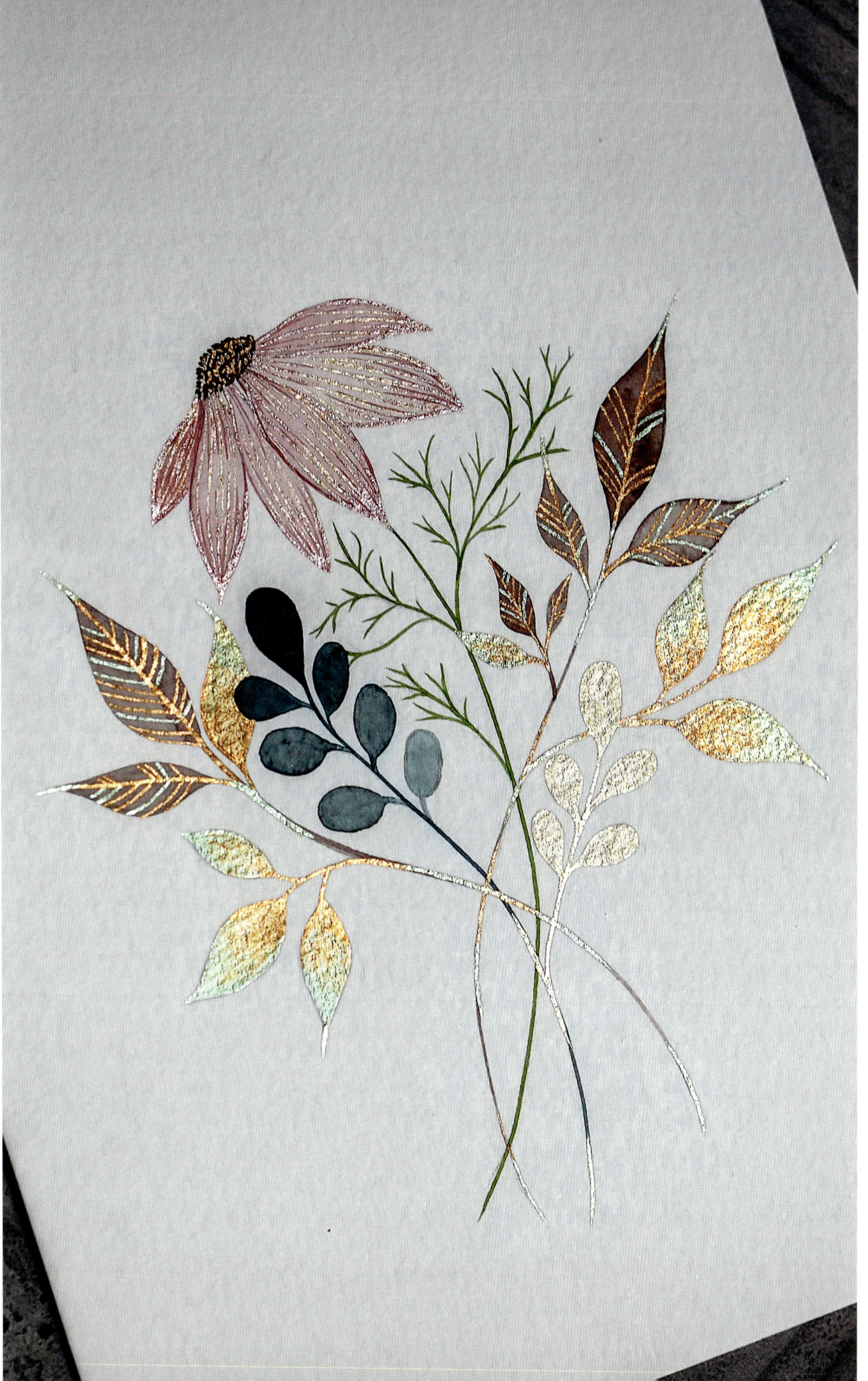

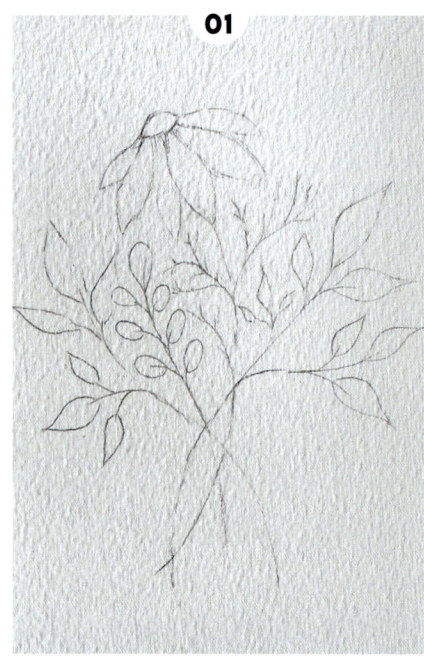

01

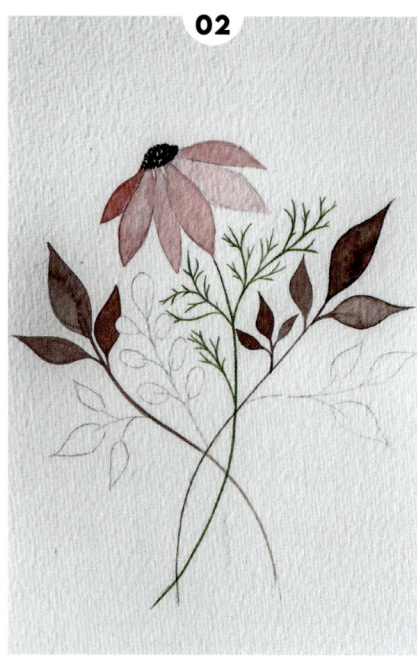

02

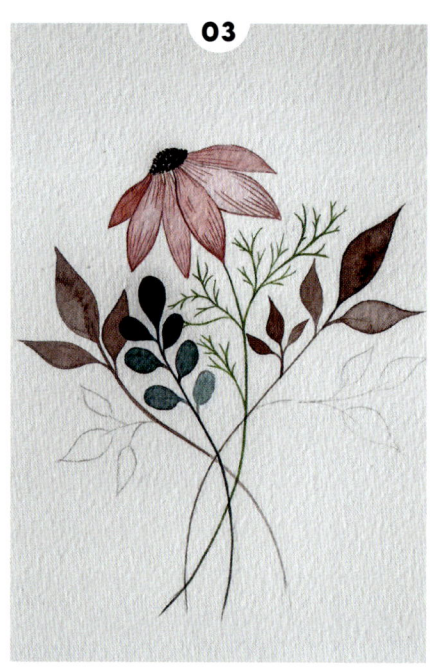

03

01 In this style of watercolor, I don't usually sketch any outlines in advance. I just paint. However, you can sketch the outlines of the leaves and each individual flower in pencil if you wish. (You can also scan the QR code on page 31 to download a traceable sketch.)

02 In an arrangement of multicolored leaves and twigs, we work from the lightest to the darkest color. I chose a soft pink for the flower in the middle. Apply it to the dry paper with a rigger brush. I've painted the flower's center in a dark brown using individual dots. For the stem and the delicate petals, I mixed a warm green. The two twigs on the outside are painted in a dark taupe. I've also left one twig unpainted on each side. I'll paint these in metallic paint at the end.

03 Once all of the painted areas are entirely dry, add fine veins to the flowers with a rigger brush in a darker shade of pink. Then mix a cool green by adding blue and coloring the little twig with its round leaves. It's a nice idea to create gradients, with the shades becoming lighter or darker.

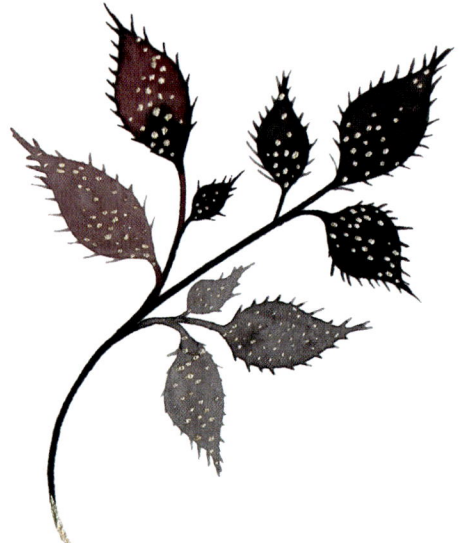

METALLIC WATERCOLOR

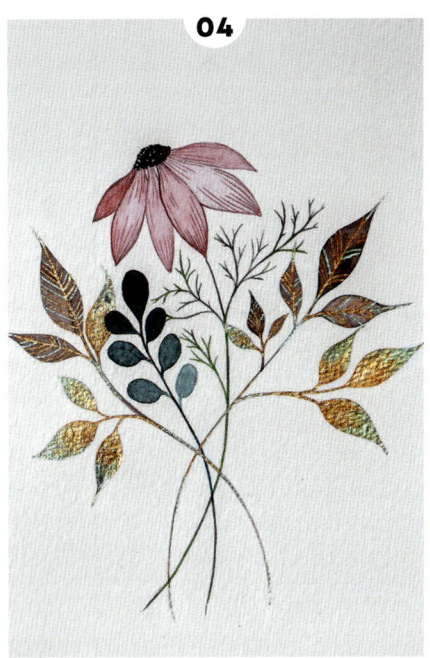

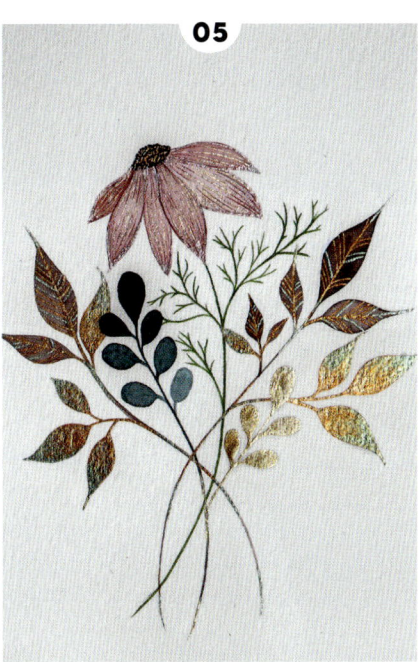

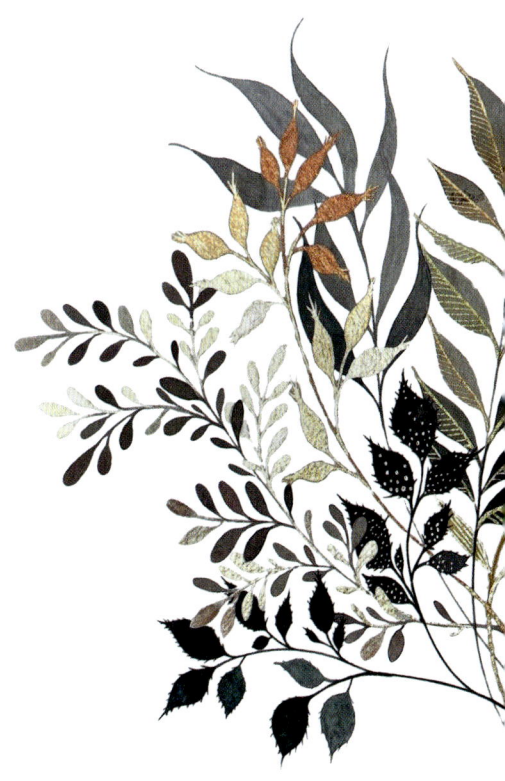

04 There are still a few leaves left unpainted. For these, I chose the bronze and mint metallic paints to create a strong contrast with the other floral elements. Try to vary the shape and color of each leaf in your composition a little. I've used both colors to paint delicate leaf veins and whole metallic leaves, creating a wonderful gradient.

05 In the final step of our watercolor painting, I added a few last details to the flower with pale-pink metallic paint and the rigger brush. Little metallic dots can also be added to the center in bronze. As a final detail, I drew another twig with round leaves in light-gold metallic paint.

Peacock Butterfly
AMONG THE ROSES

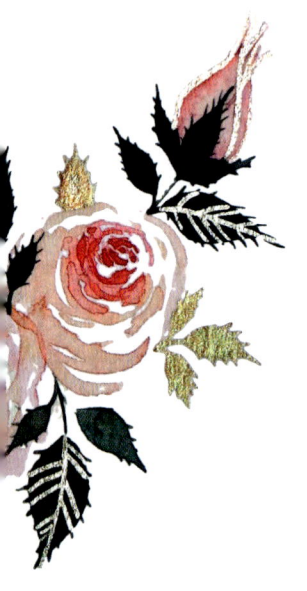

In this motif, we're going to be working the rose tendrils in more detail. The peacock butterfly, meanwhile, will appear in outline only. The effect looks all the more striking since we're using metallic paint.

MATERIALS

RIGGER BRUSH | ROUND BRUSH | PENCIL | COMPASS OR BOWL | ERASER | WATERCOLOR PAPER

MY COLOR PALETTE

 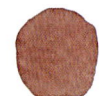  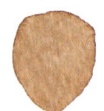 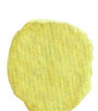 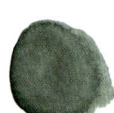

— METALLIC PAINTS —

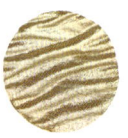 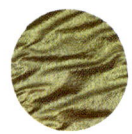 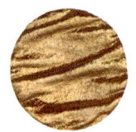

LIGHT   PALE   BRONZE
GOLD   OLIVE

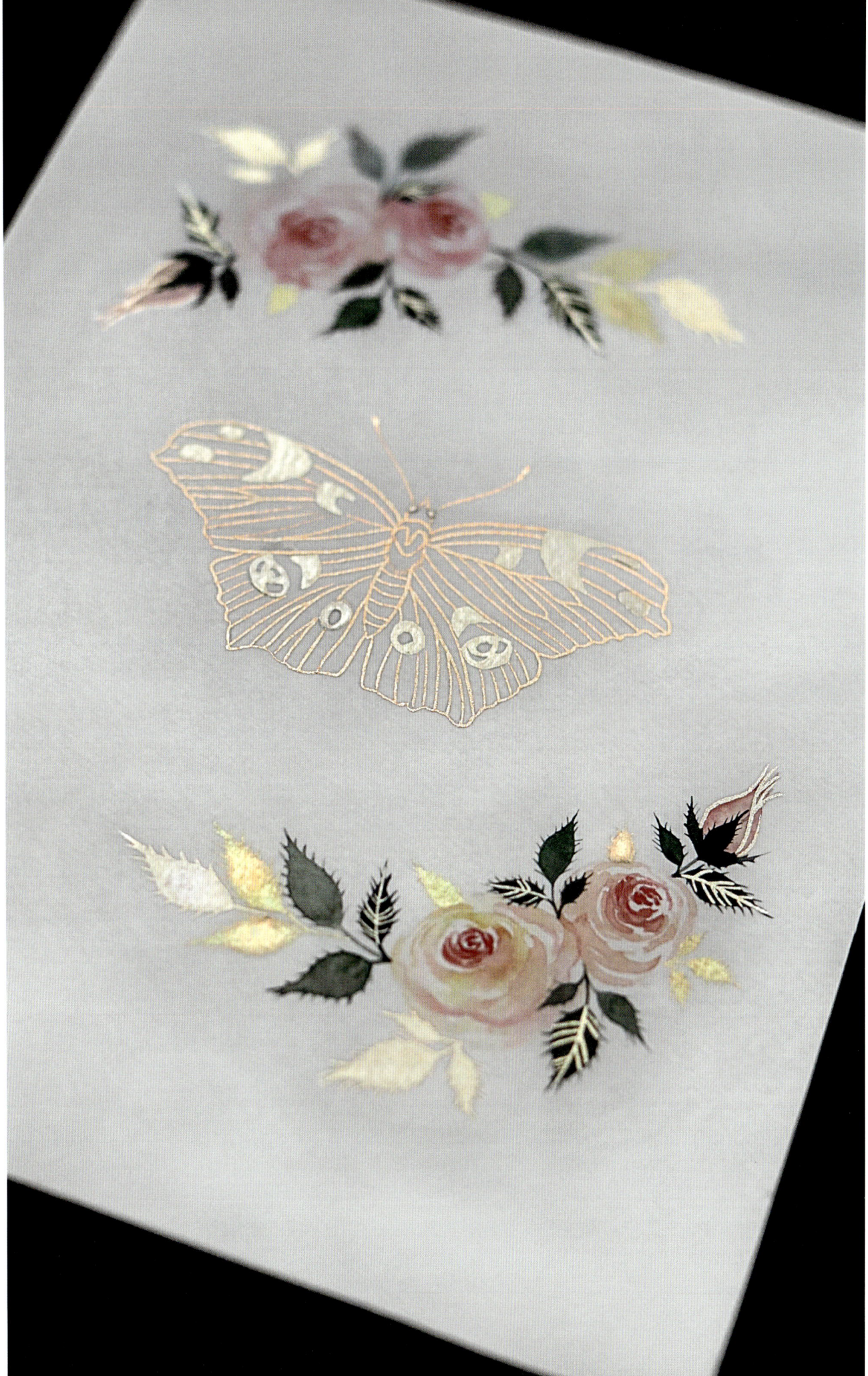

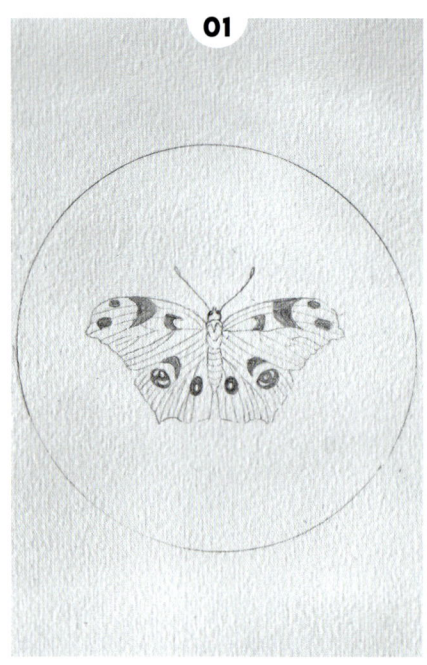

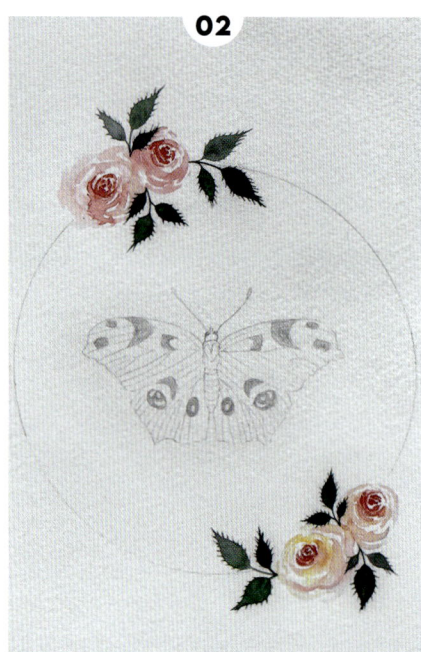

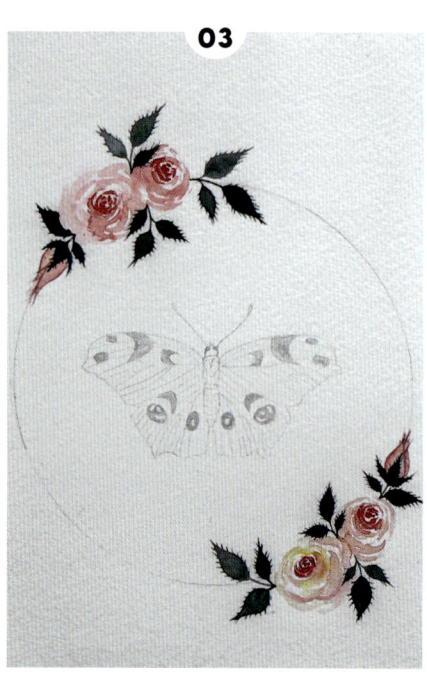

01   With a compass or an upside-down bowl, draw a circle. Try to keep the lines as light as possible so you can erase them later. In the middle of the circle, draw the silhouette of a butterfly, including the pattern on its wings. (You can also scan the QR code on page 31 to download a traceable sketch.)

02   Referring to the motif for the roses on page 42, paint small roses at the top and bottom of your circle in the color of your choice. For my roses, I mixed a light pink with a little yellow. I made sure that the flowers were placed in the center of the pencil line. Add delicate leaves in a dark-green shade and keep the arrangement looking more or less symmetrical.

03   Using the same method, I added some little rosebuds next to the flowers, also placing them on the outline of the circle. This keeps your border looking round.

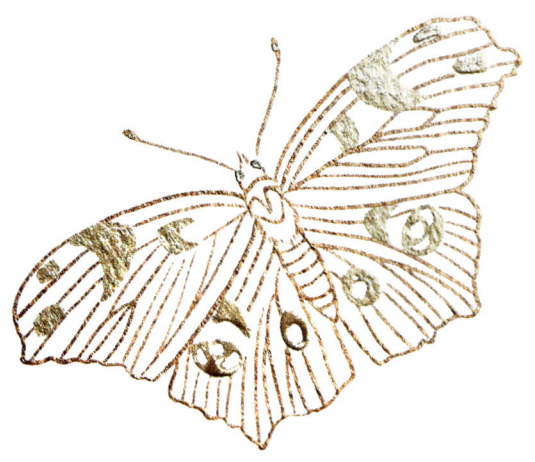

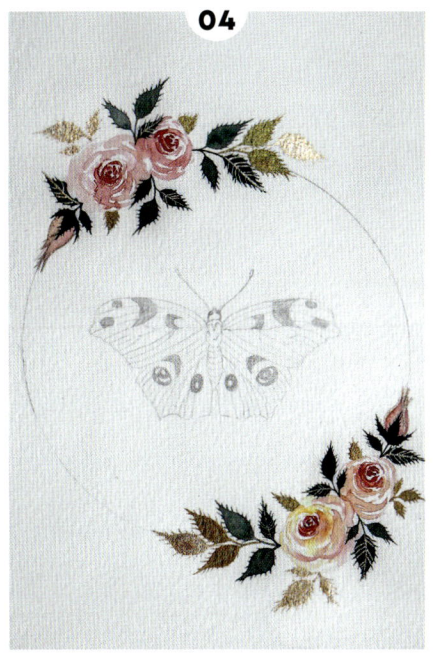
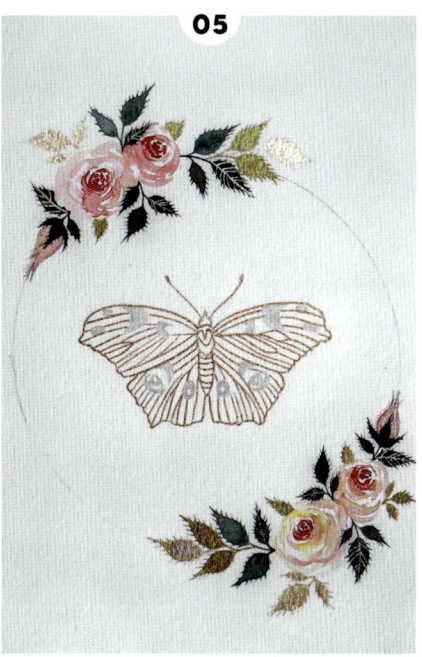
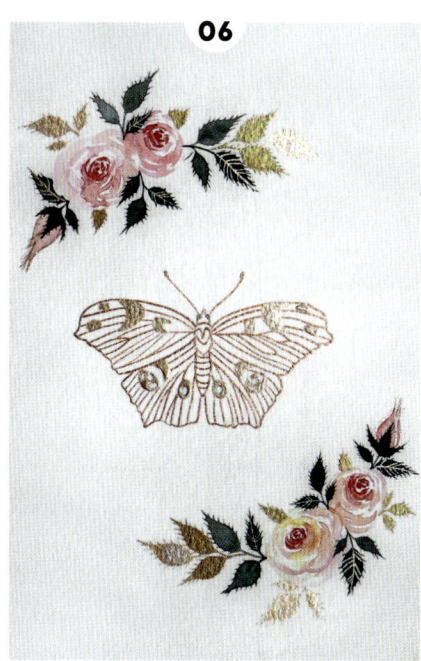

04   Finish off the motif with metallic paint. Add a few more delicate leaves in pale olive and light gold. Again, I've tried to keep everything looking more or less symmetrical. With light gold, you can add some texture to a few of the dark leaves. Details like this make your pictures look subtle and refined.

05   For the outline of the butterfly (and the fine veins in its wings), I've chosen the bronze metallic paint. Apply the metallic paint with the rigger brush. That way, your lines will look even.

06   I then used light gold to highlight the individual elements of the pattern on the butterfly's wings. Once your drawing is completely dry, you can erase the reference line for the circle.

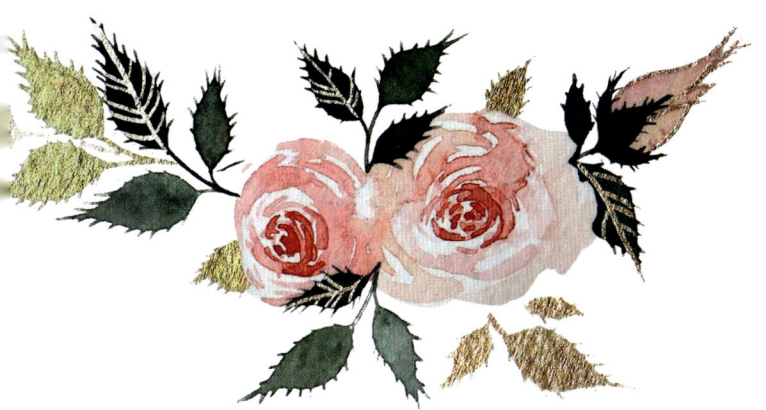

PEACOCK BUTTERFLY AMONG THE ROSES

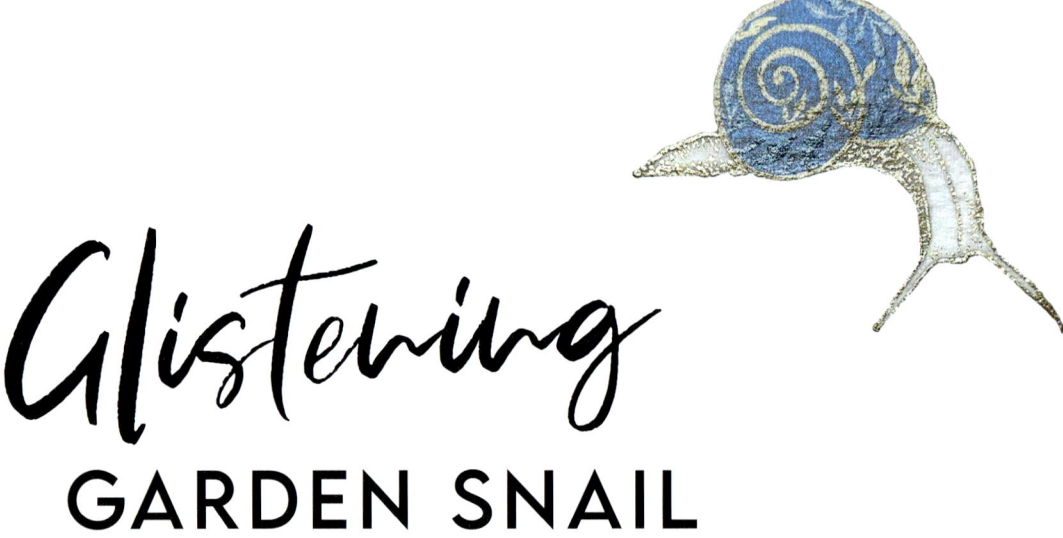

Glistening
GARDEN SNAIL

Imagine all snails glistened as beautifully as this one. Gardeners would fall in love with the little creatures in an instant! As a child, I loved snails and gazed in wonder at their different shells. Our most well-known snail is of course the yellow garden snail, and this is what I'd like to paint with you over the next few pages.

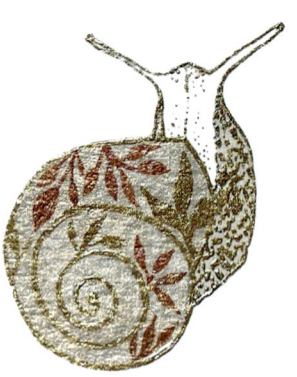

MATERIALS

ROUND BRUSH | RIGGER BRUSH | PENCIL |
WHITE GEL PEN | WATERCOLOR PAPER

MY COLOR PALETTE

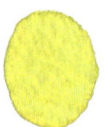 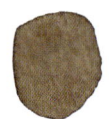  

=== METALLIC PAINTS ===

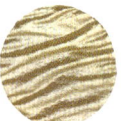

LIGHT
GOLD

METALLIC WATERCOLOR

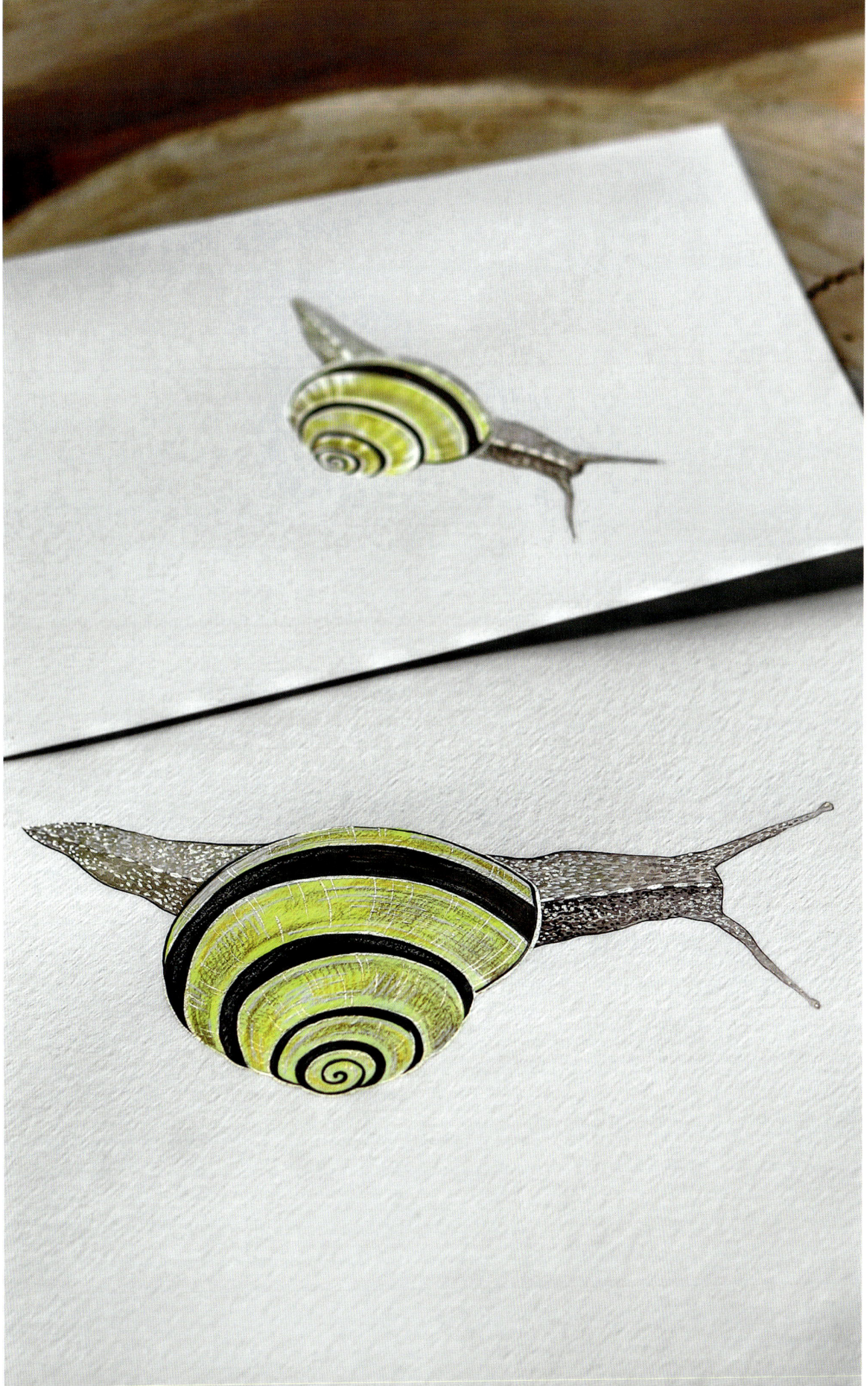

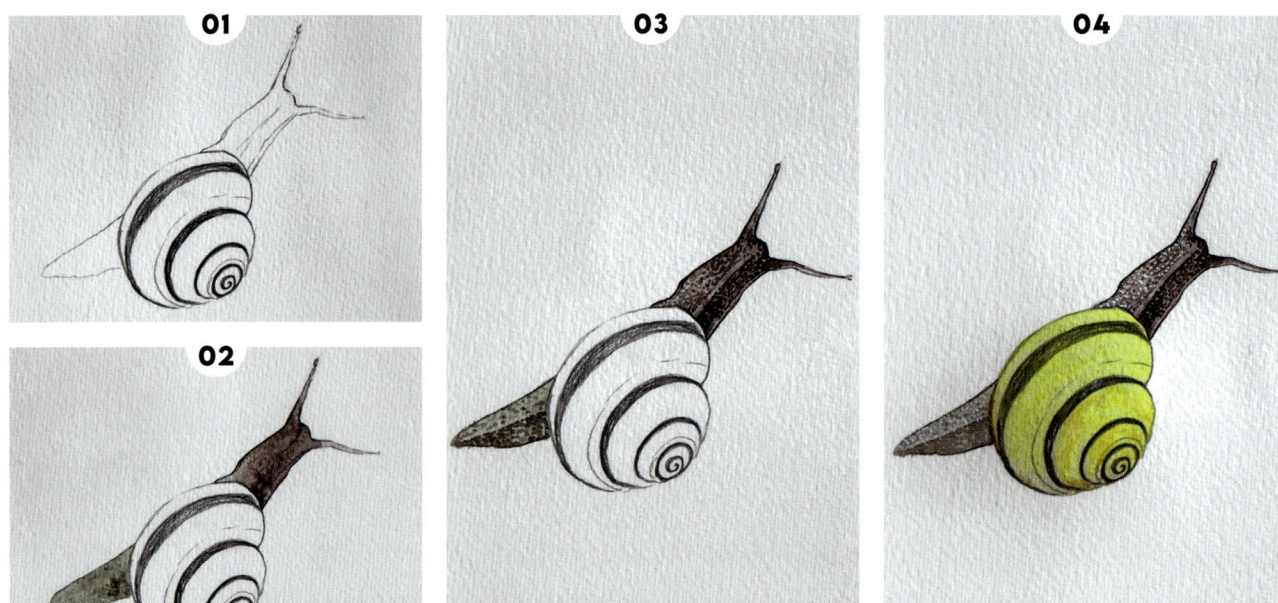

01   As always, we'll start with the pencil outline for our motif. (You can also scan the QR code on page 31 to download a traceable sketch.) I generally try to make the outline as light as possible, but in this instance, I've made the outline of the pattern on the snail's shell slightly darker so I can see how the pattern runs.

02   For the snail's body, mix an olive green with brown and green shades until you get the right color. Apply it to the dry paper with a round brush (size 1). Make sure that you only color the body and not the shell.

03   I added more pigments (brown and gray) to the color I've already mixed for the body. I'll then use this darker shade to paint the fine texture of the snail (in the form of little pads). As you can see in the picture, I've left a thin line unpainted in the center of the body. I've also made the top half of the body slightly lighter. This gives the illusion of light shining down on the snail from above.

04   I've heightened this optical effect with little white details on the top half of the body. Wash your brush (and change your water if it's been tinted by your previous paints) and apply a bright yellow to the snail's shell. Don't worry if you paint over the pencil lines on the inside.

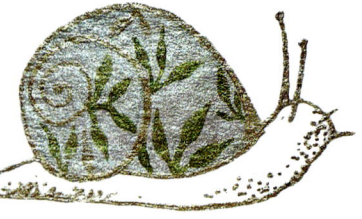

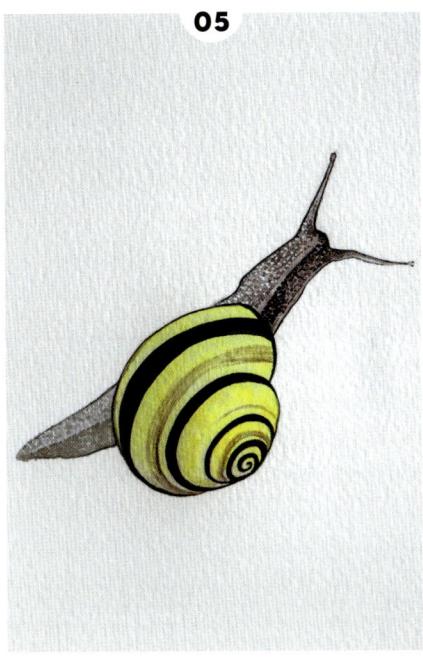

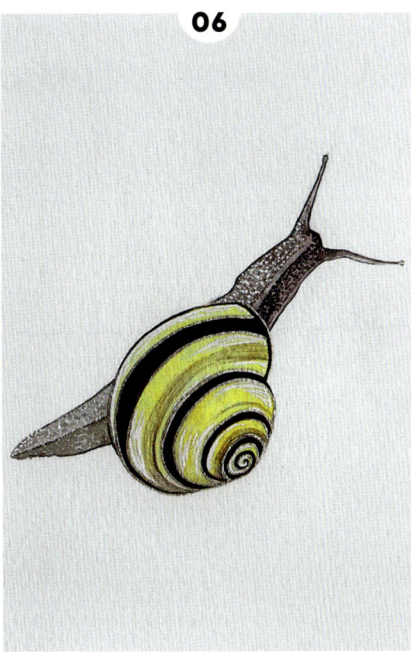

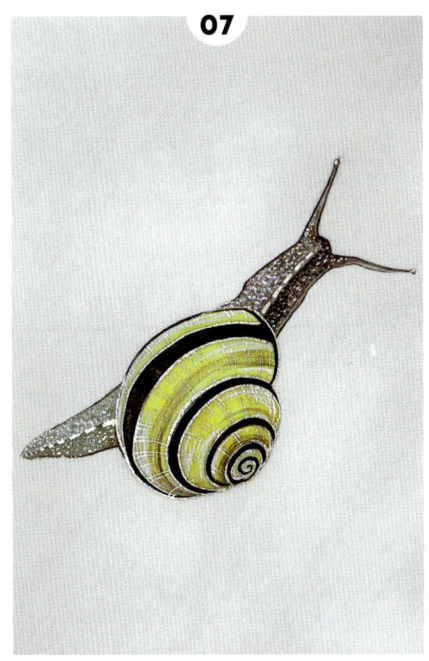

05 After the yellow paint has completely dried, highlight the texture of the shell with a very thin brown to make everything look more three-dimensional. I then traced over the shell's outline lightly with a very dark black-brown and painted the spiral pattern on the inside of the shell. Try to keep the lines as clean as possible.

06 Once your watercolor has dried, you can add more textures to the shell with a white gel pen. Next comes the metallic paint. Trace over the spiral pattern and part of the outline with light-gold paint.

07 Using the same metallic shade, I then painted more textures and patterns on the shell, the snail's body, and its eyes.

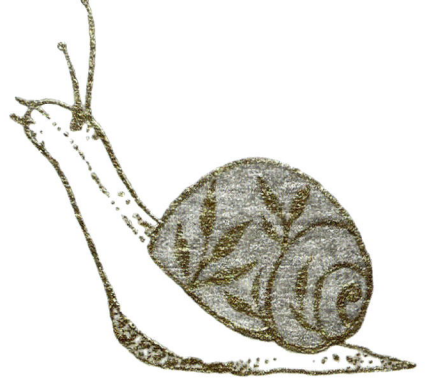

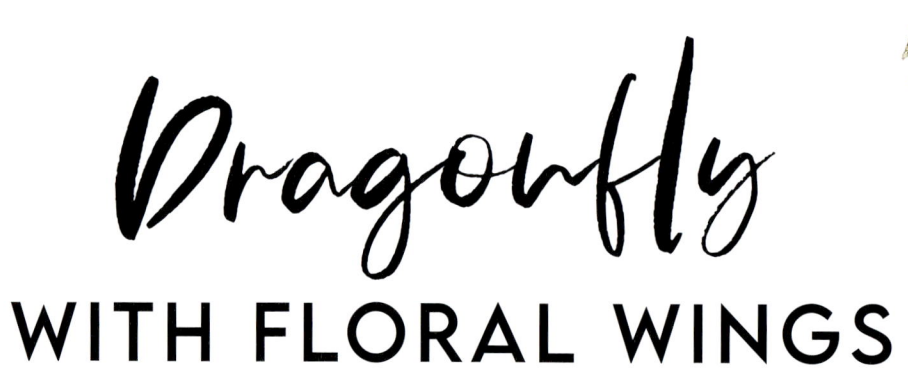

Dragonfly
WITH FLORAL WINGS

I always enjoy painting animals with floral details on certain parts of their bodies. In this chapter, I'd like to introduce you to this style of painting with a dragonfly. It's the final motif in the medium difficulty level and, in my opinion, a glittering finale.

MATERIALS
PENCIL | RIGGER BRUSH | WATERCOLOR PAPER

MY COLOR PALETTE

 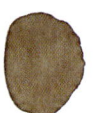 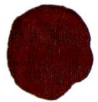  

METALLIC PAINTS

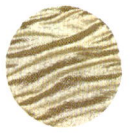 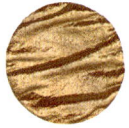

LIGHT GOLD   BRONZE

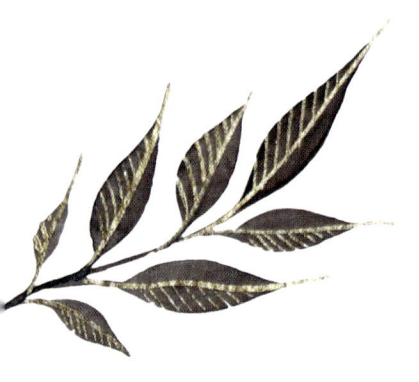

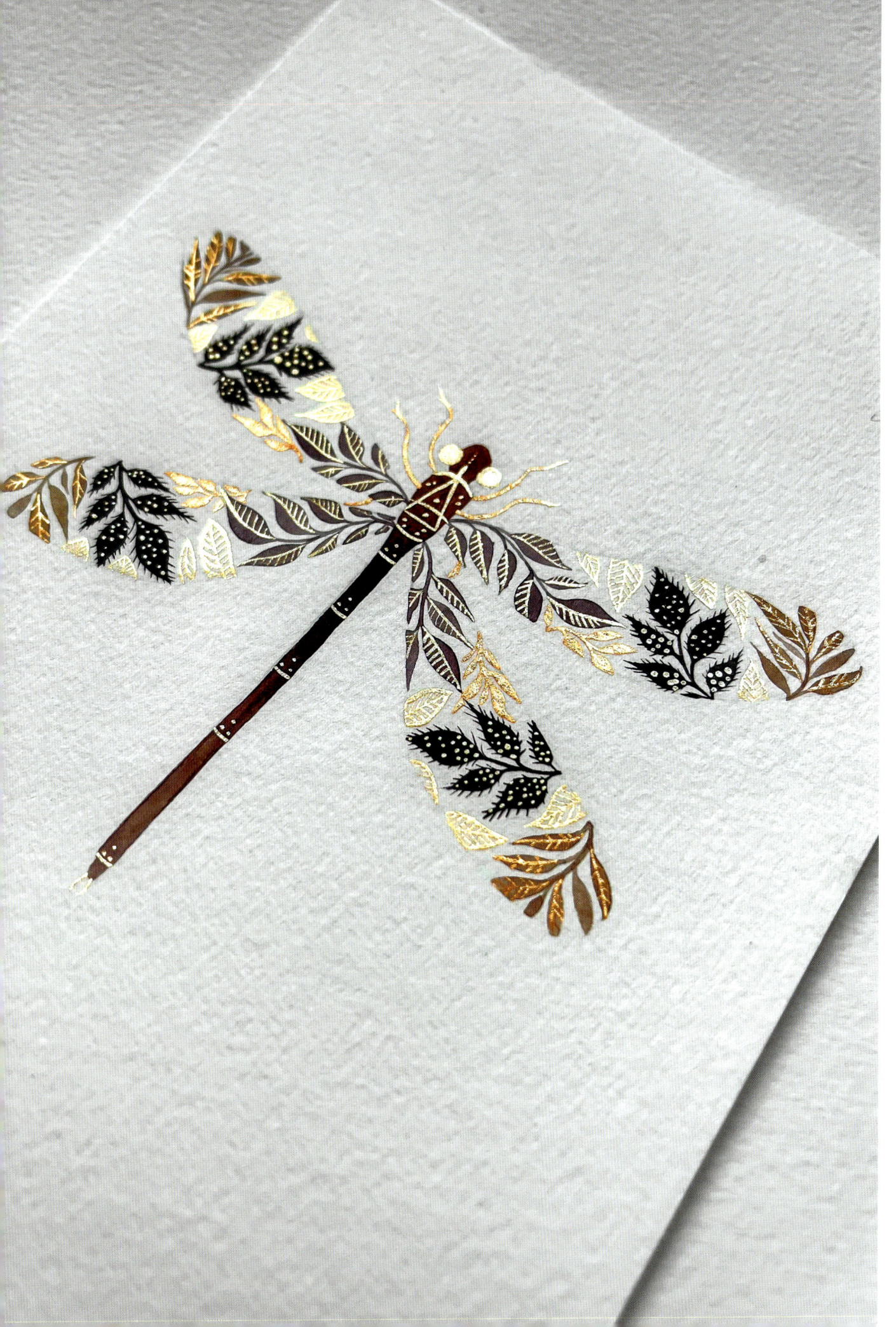

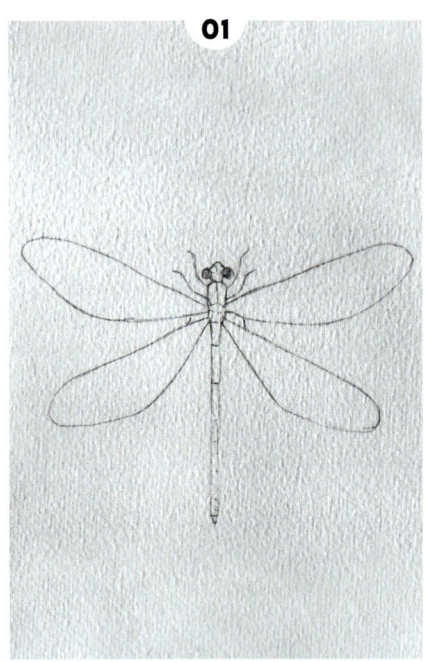

01

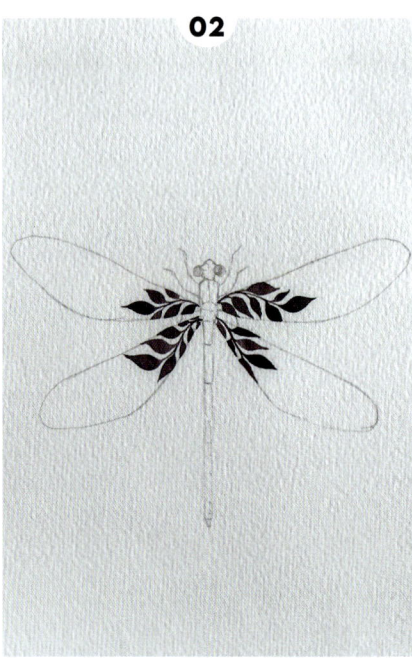

02

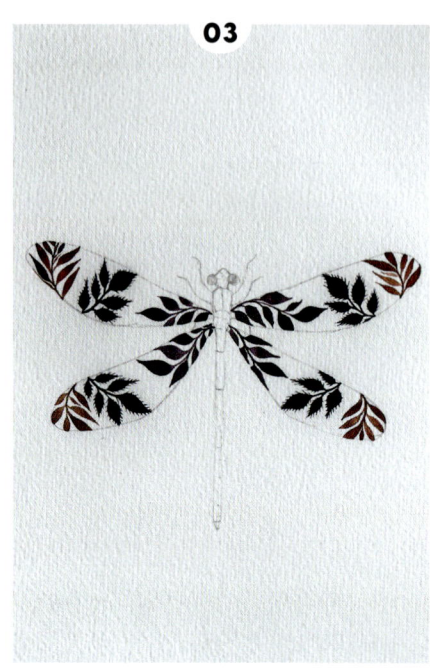

03

01 Sketch the outline of the dragonfly with a soft pencil. (You can also scan the QR code on page 31 to download a traceable sketch.)

02 I painted the entire dragonfly with the rigger brush, which I used to draw the fine details and thin, even lines as well. First, we're going to finish the floral pattern on the wings. You can try out your own color scheme too. I prefer more subtle colors. For the inside of the wings, I chose a dark taupe (a "neutral" shade in makeup). In each of the four wings, you can paint a twig with leaves starting from the dragonfly's body.

03 Now it's time to fill each of the dragonfly's wings with different leaves and twigs. Make sure you keep to the shape of the wings and the pattern inside their edges. In motifs like this, I always try to keep things more or less symmetrical so the wings don't jar with the rest of the motif. For this reason, it's a good idea to repeat the pattern.

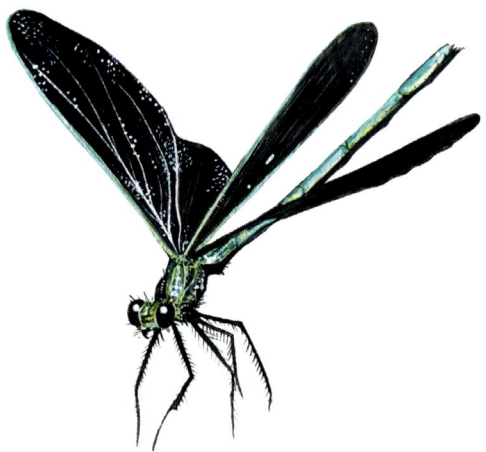

METALLIC WATERCOLOR

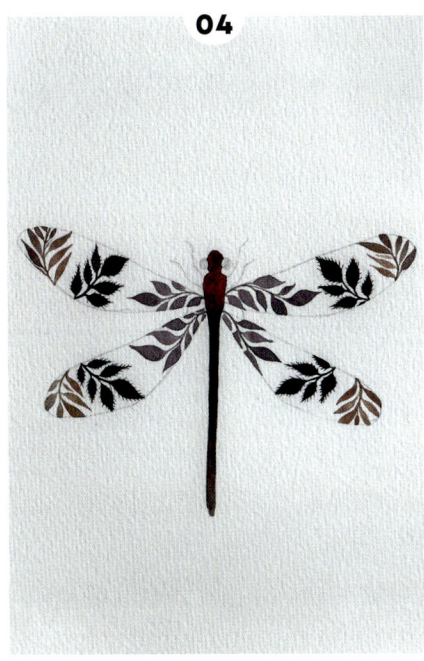
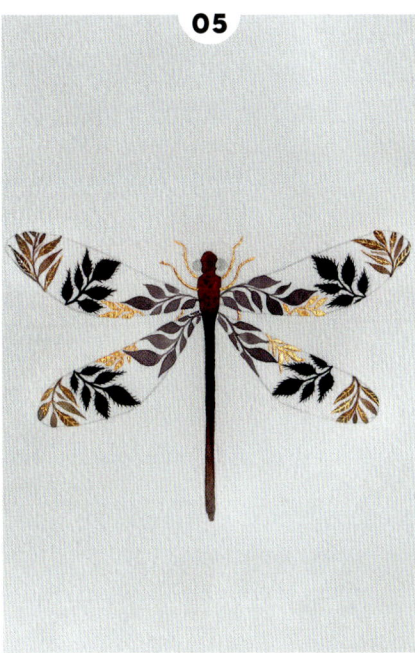
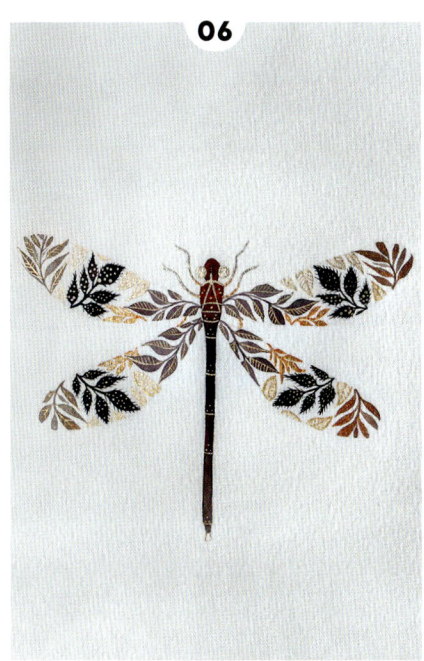

04 Before filling the unpainted areas inside the wings with metallic paints, I turned my attention to the dragonfly's body. For this, I chose a warm chestnut brown that blends into the dark taupe at the rear of the dragonfly and fades at the end.

05 Now choose two metallic paints. I've chosen bronze and light gold. I used the bronze to paint the dragonfly's thin legs, the fine veins of the leaves, and the leafy twig in each of the four wings.

06 Light gold is always a great choice for iridescent accents, which is why I use it so much. I've used this shade to paint other patterns on the leaves and the dragonfly's body. I've also filled in any remaining gaps in the wings and painted the eyes in metallic paint.

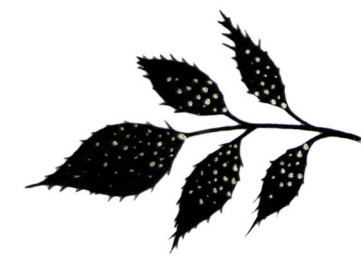

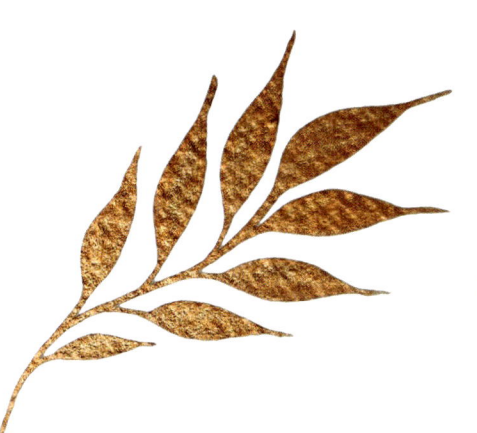

DRAGONFLY WITH FLORAL WINGS

75

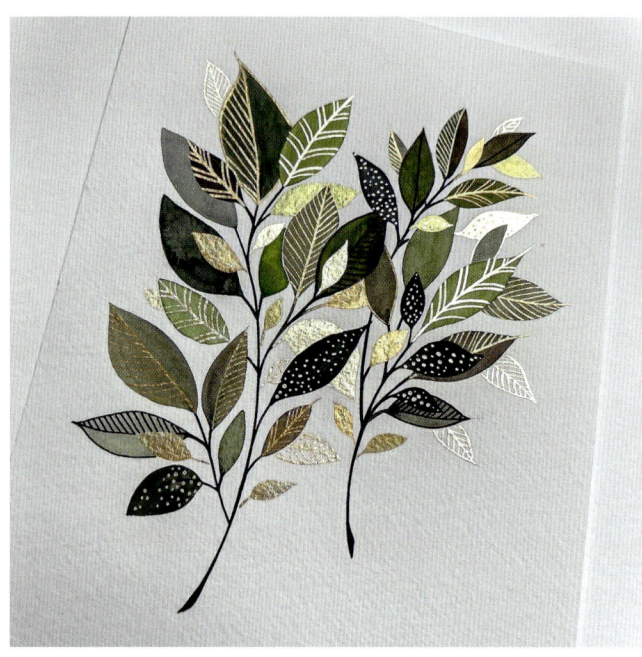

You can use some of my earlier compositions of leaves, flowers, and twigs as a source of further creative inspiration. There are no limits on what colors you can use. Why not experiment with different colors? You'll discover that the combination of different shades has a big influence on the effect of your picture. One good idea, for example, is to create a gradient from the traditional colors of the rainbow.

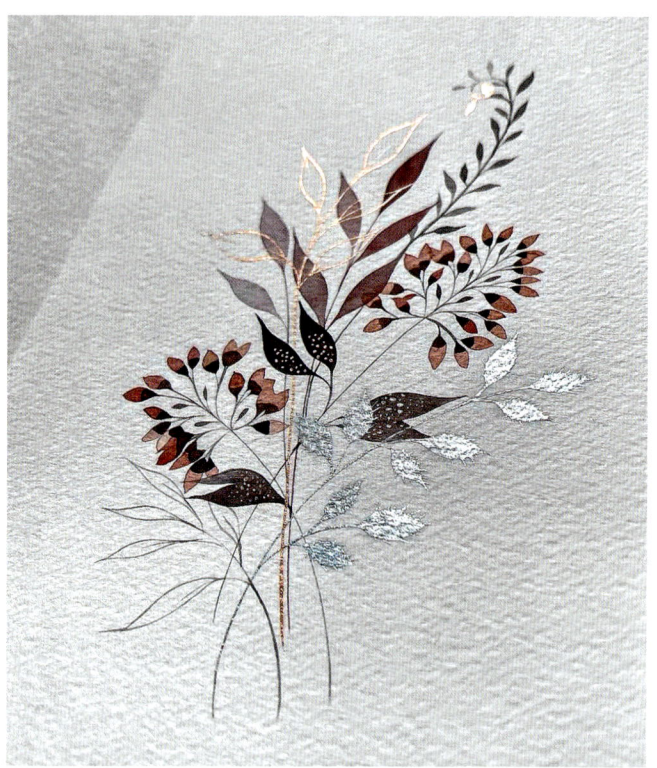

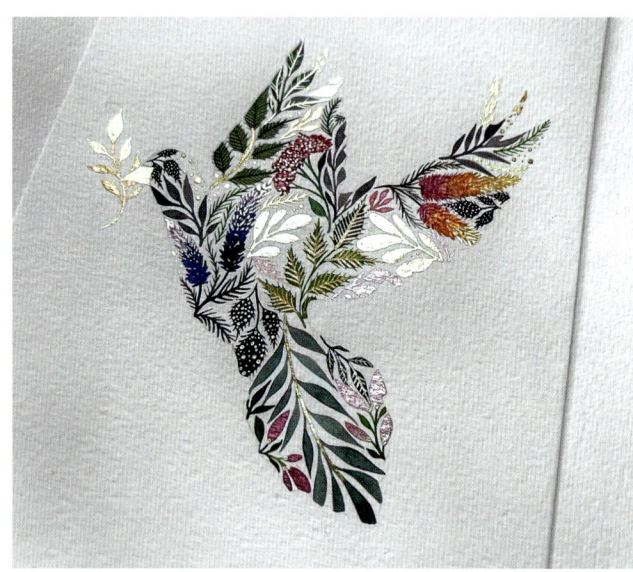

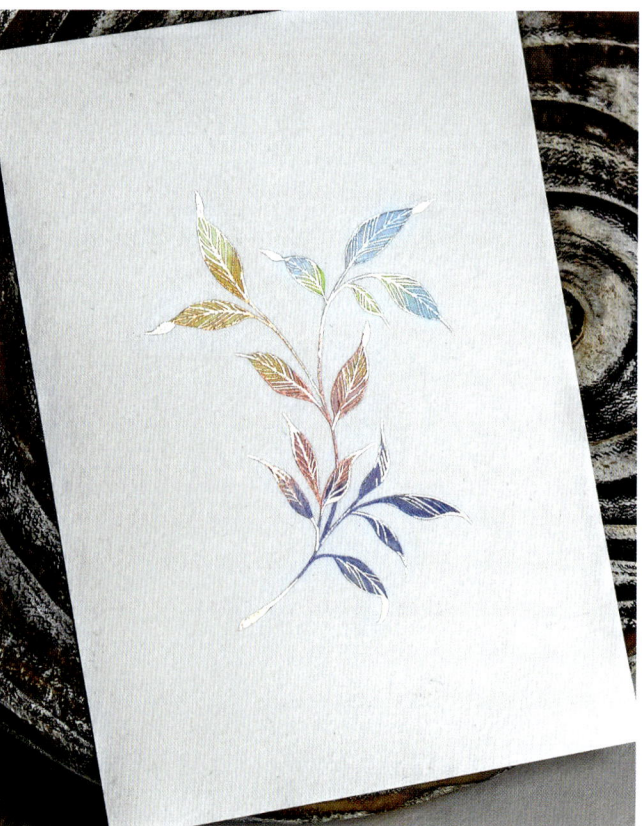

METALLIC WATERCOLOR

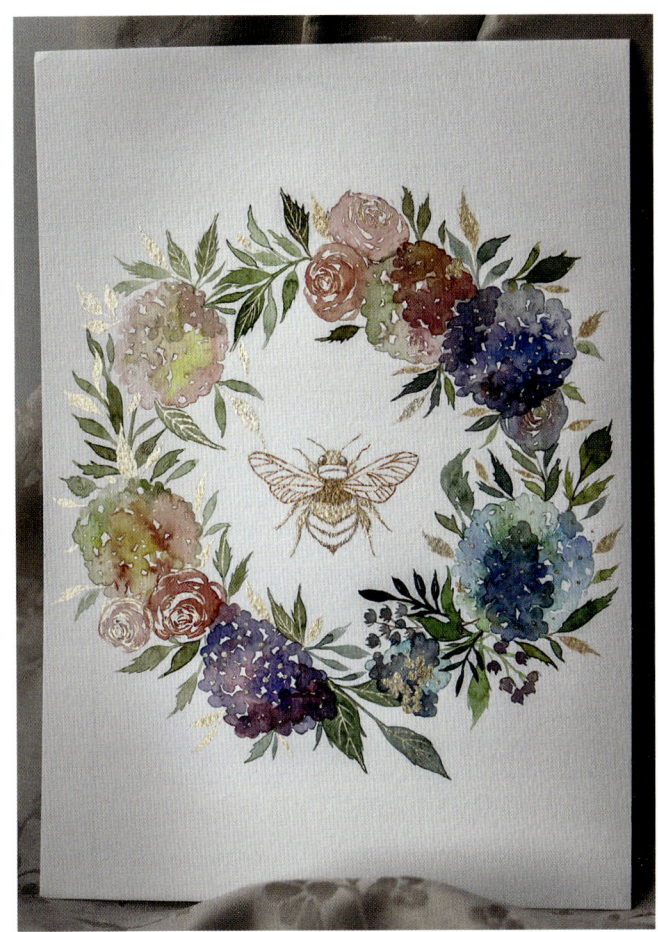

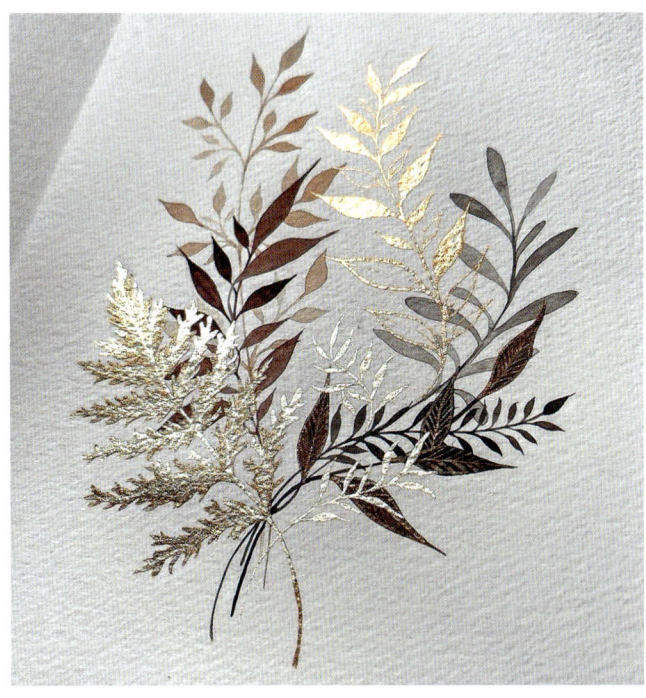

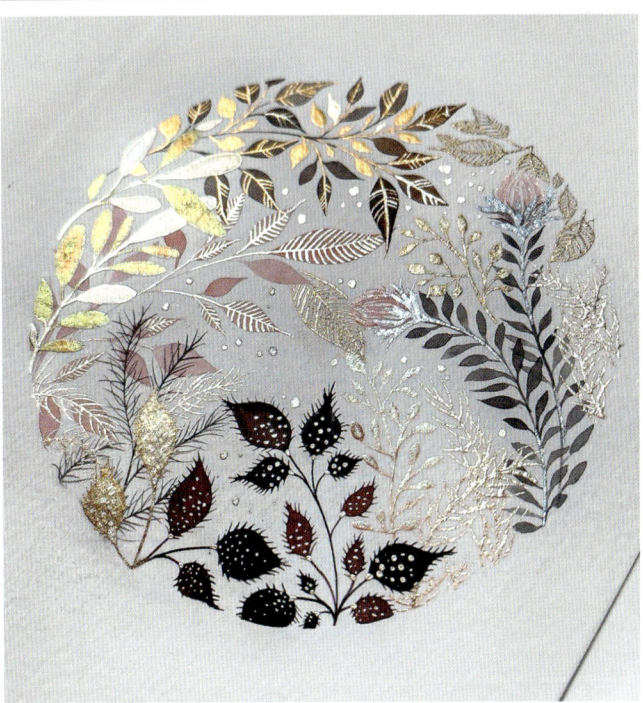

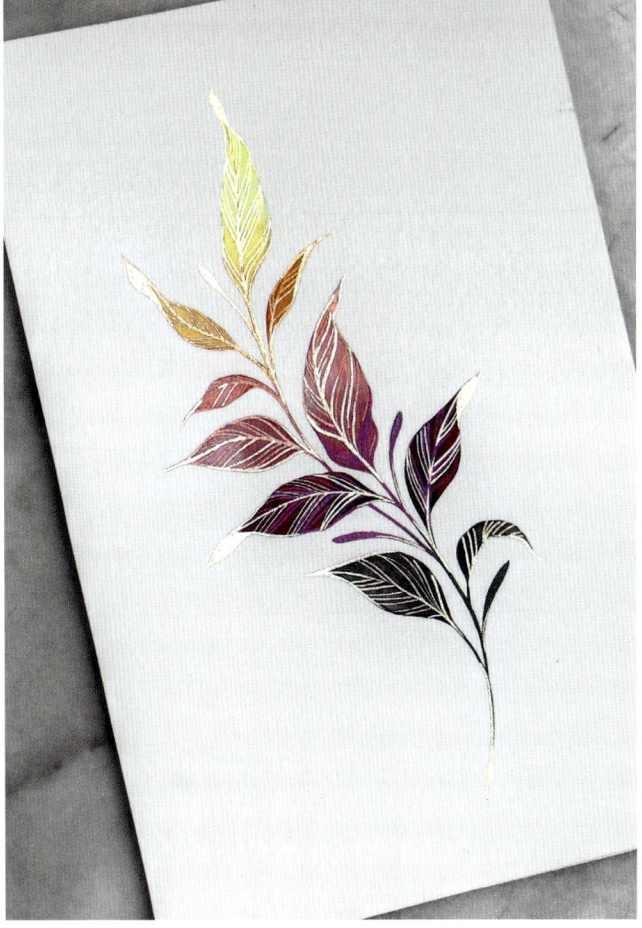

INSPIRATION: FLORALS

77

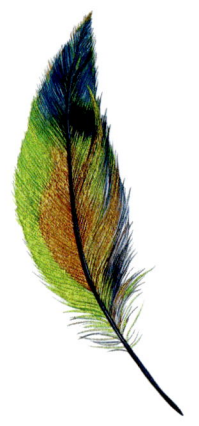

Iridescent
FEATHER

Feathers are great for combining different metallic paints and watching how they impact the motif. The finished painting looks almost like a shimmering feather from the world of birds. This iridescent feather is the first motif in the advanced category, which means that the projects are even more detailed and offer more freedom of choice.

MATERIALS
ROUND BRUSH | RIGGER BRUSH | PENCIL | WATERCOLOR PAPER

MY COLOR PALETTE

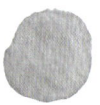 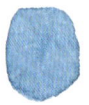  

=== METALLIC PAINTS ===

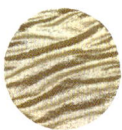  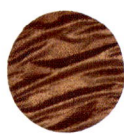 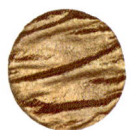 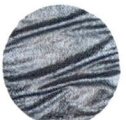

| LIGHT GOLD | SILVER | WARM BROWN | BRONZE | PALE BLUE |

METALLIC WATERCOLOR

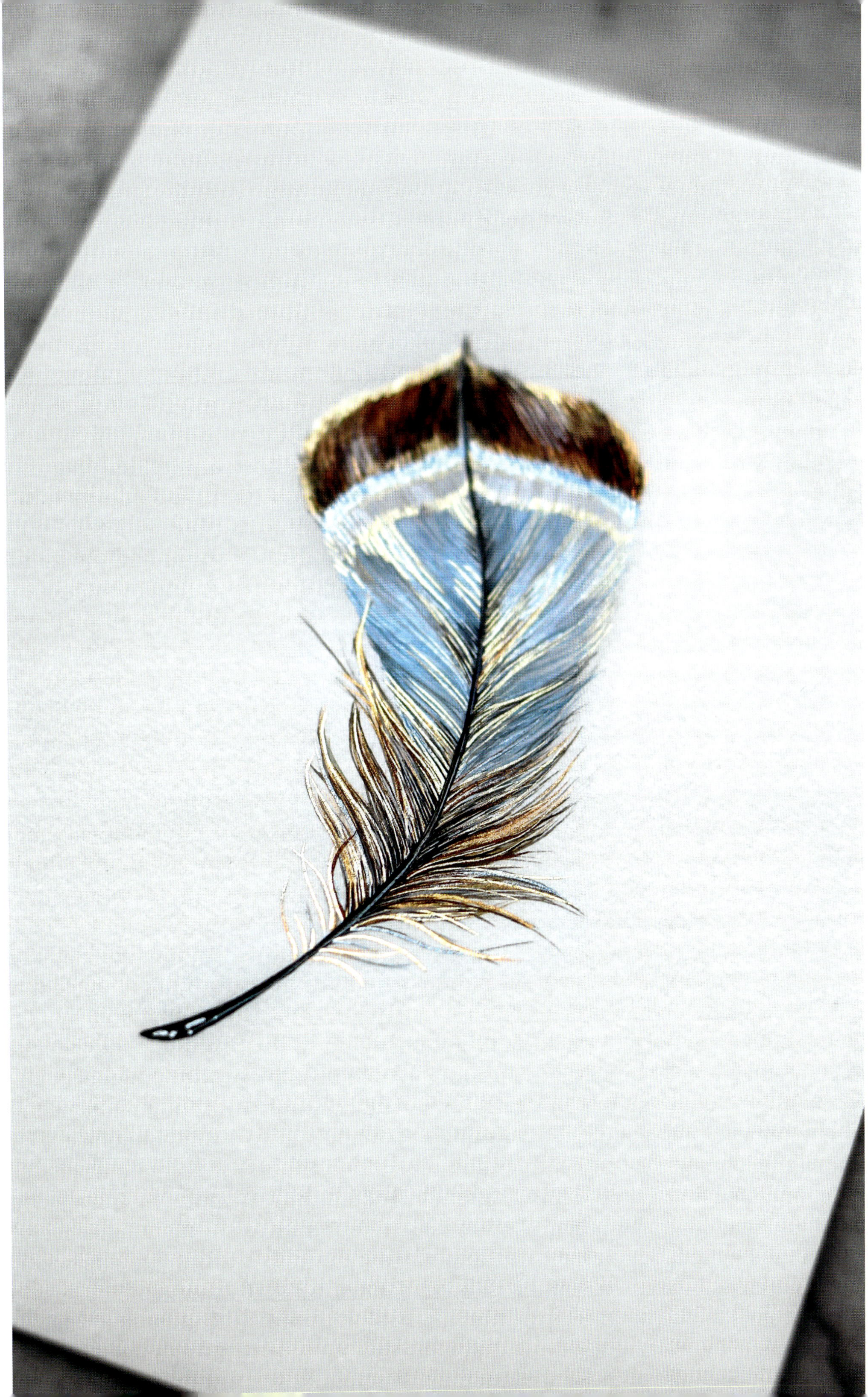

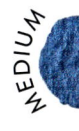

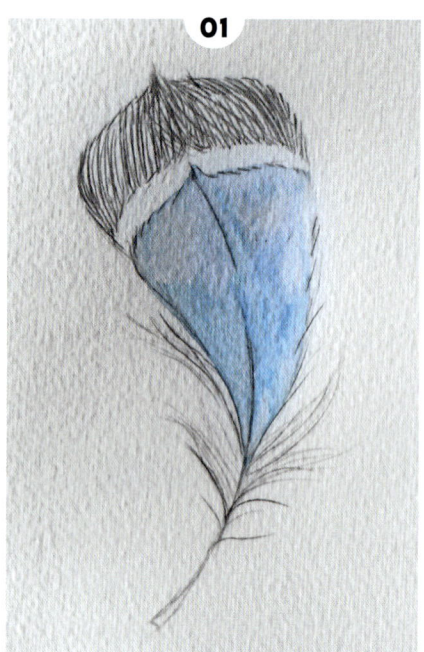

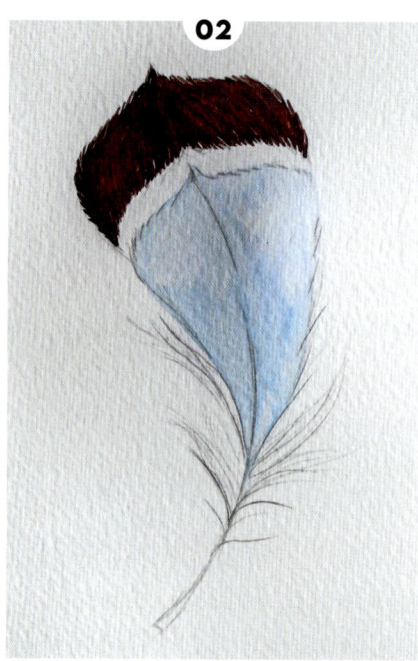

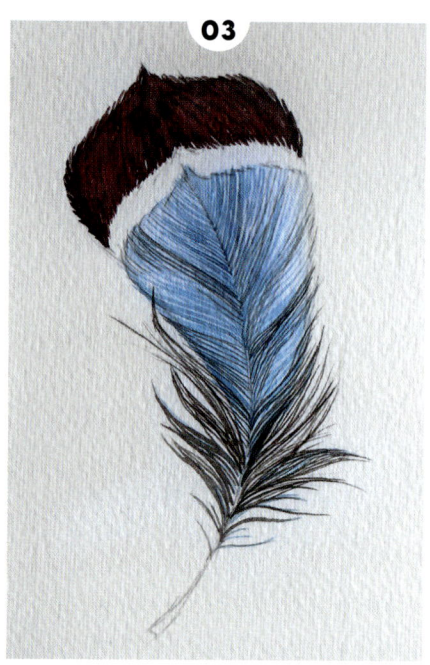

01   Draw the rough outline of the feather on your watercolor paper with a soft pencil. (You can also scan the QR code on page 31 to download a traceable sketch.) Now thin a light-blue paint with plenty of water and apply it to the middle of the feather with a round brush using the wet-on-dry technique.

02   For the tip of the feather, I've chosen a mahogany brown, which I've distributed evenly over the dry paper. Make sure at this stage to emphasize each individual strand of the feather, making their ends slightly frayed.

03   In this step, I continued with my thin rigger brush. I painted the bottom of the feather stroke by stroke in a dark brown. Let some of the strands stick out and overlap. On the feather's light-blue center, I added more strands with the brown from the bottom of the feather, as well as a darker shade. These strands start from the feather's shaft and stick out to the left and right.

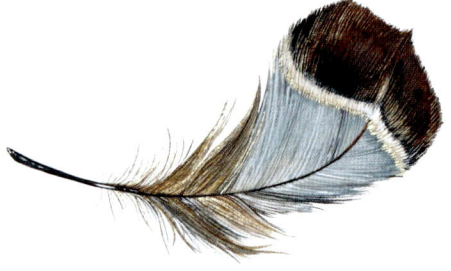

METALLIC WATERCOLOR

80

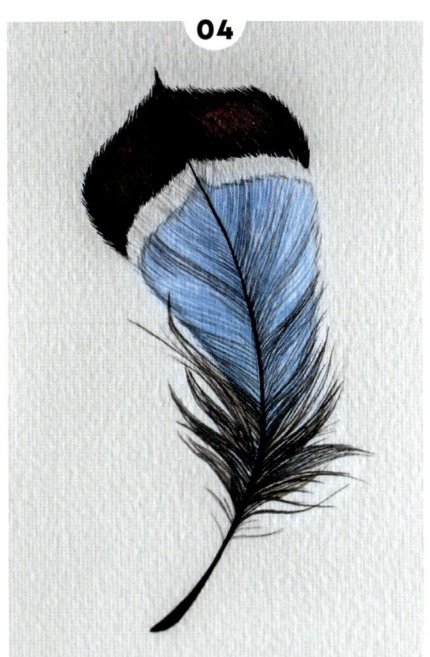

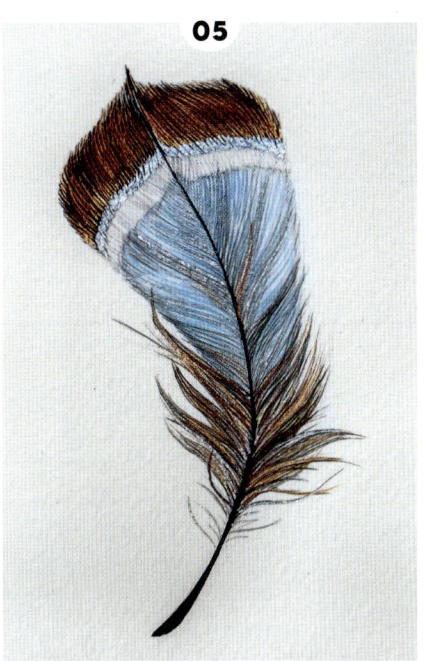

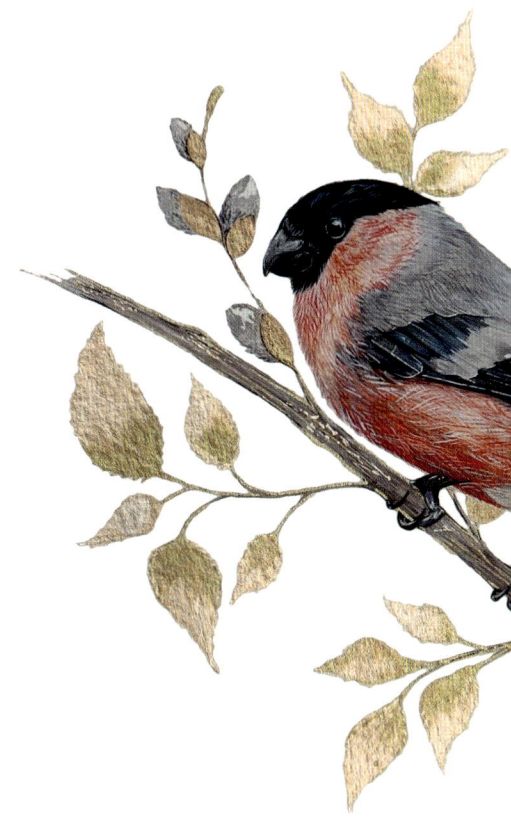

04 Using the dark-brown shade, you can now trace over the outer edges of the tips of the feathers to give them more texture. The thin rigger brush can be used to give the frayed edges more shape. You can also highlight the light-gray strands in the (still colorless) stripes between the light-blue and dark-brown parts of the feather. Once you're happy with the texture of your feather, take your thin brush and trace over the shaft of the feather in a dark shade. (I've used black.)

05 Now we're going to paint some more details using our metallic paints. I've started with the color pale blue, using it to paint a shimmering stripe below the tip of the feather and individual strands. Other individual strands are highlighted with the metallic bronze and warm-brown paints.

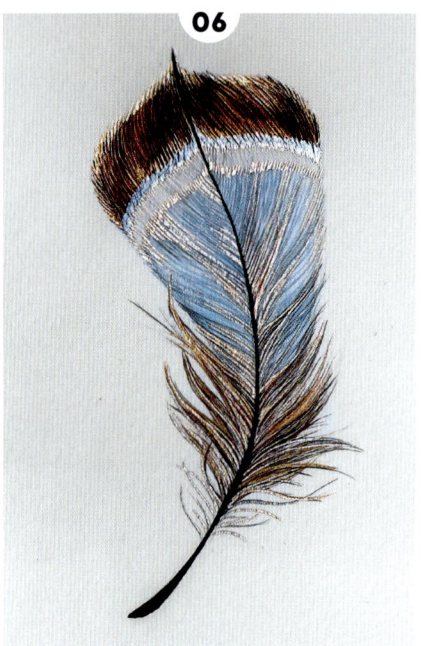 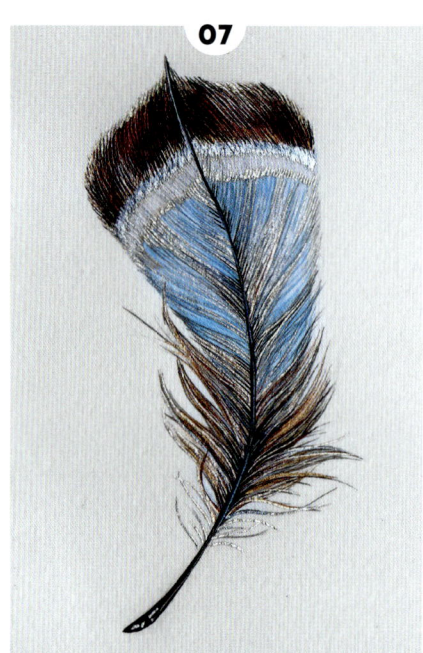 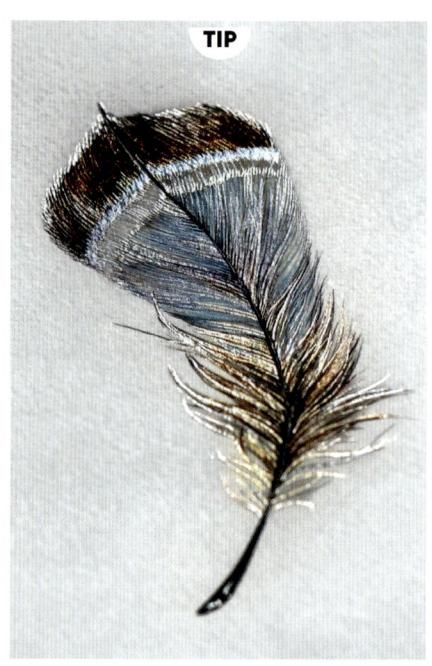

06   As with the watercolors, I like to apply the metallic accents in different layers (but always from dark to light) so that they partially overlap and merge into one another. I've painted the penultimate accents in light gold.

07   For the finishing touch, you can add some final accents and contours. In the middle, I've added some fine strands in black to make the feather's texture stand out even more. I've applied the silver metallic paint to the tips in just the same way. Lastly, I've added some white accents to the shaft of the feather. These final details add depth and three-dimensionality to the motif.

Tip

To show how striking pearlized paints look in sunlight, I've taken a photo of our feather under direct sunlight.

You can also use metallic paints to add shine to other kinds of feathers. Take your inspiration from nature and use different birds' feathers as templates for your own motifs.

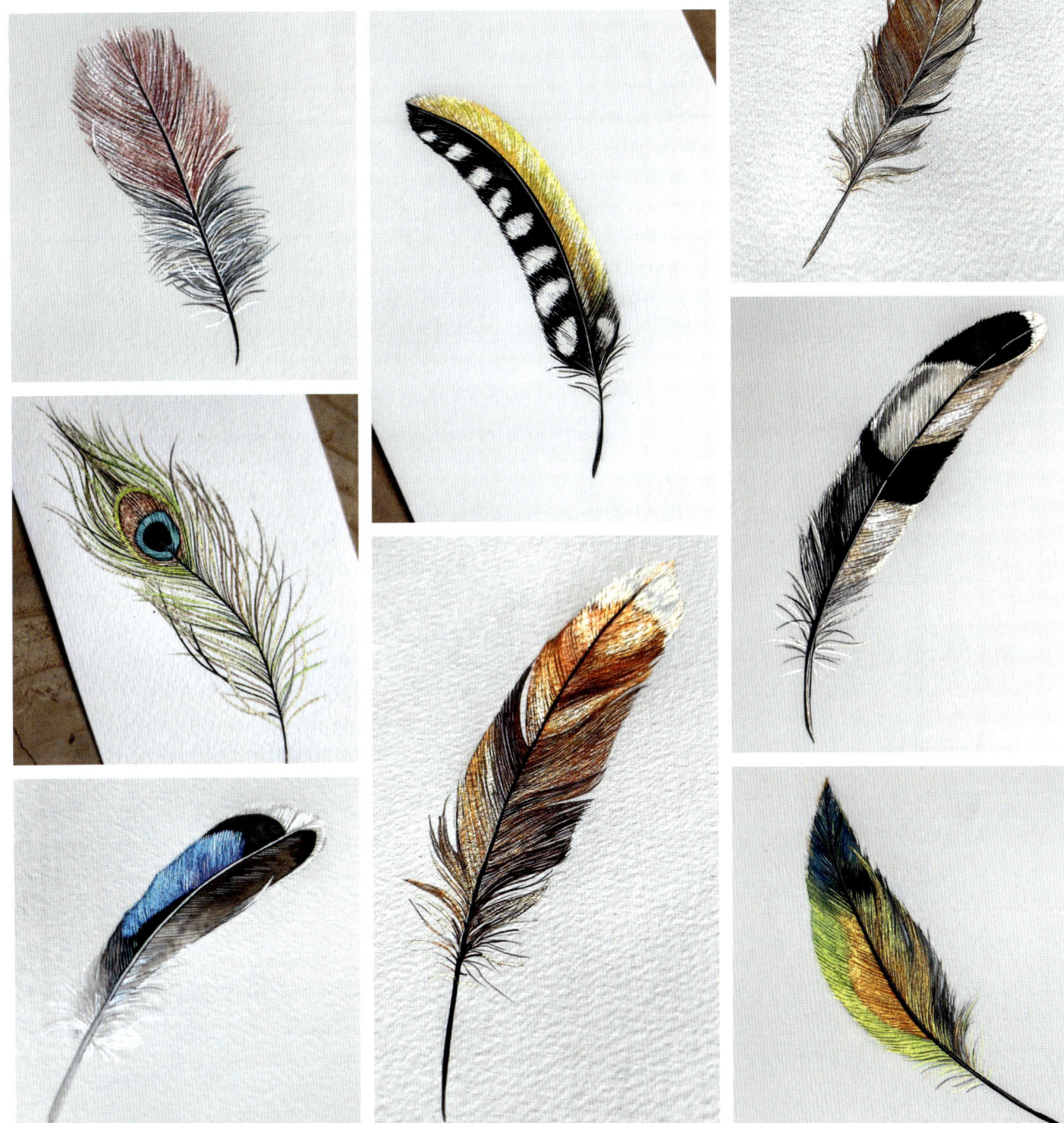

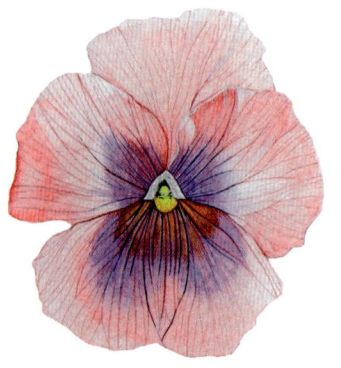

Colorful
PANSIES

I plant pansies in my garden every year! Their diverse colors and patterns make them perfect models for a delicate watercolor painting.

MATERIALS

RIGGER BRUSH | ROUND BRUSH | PENCIL | WATERCOLOR PAPER

MY COLOR PALETTE

 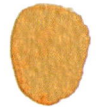 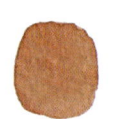 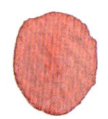   

═══ METALLIC PAINTS ═══

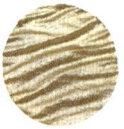 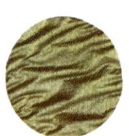 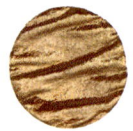

LIGHT GOLD   PALE OLIVE   BRONZE

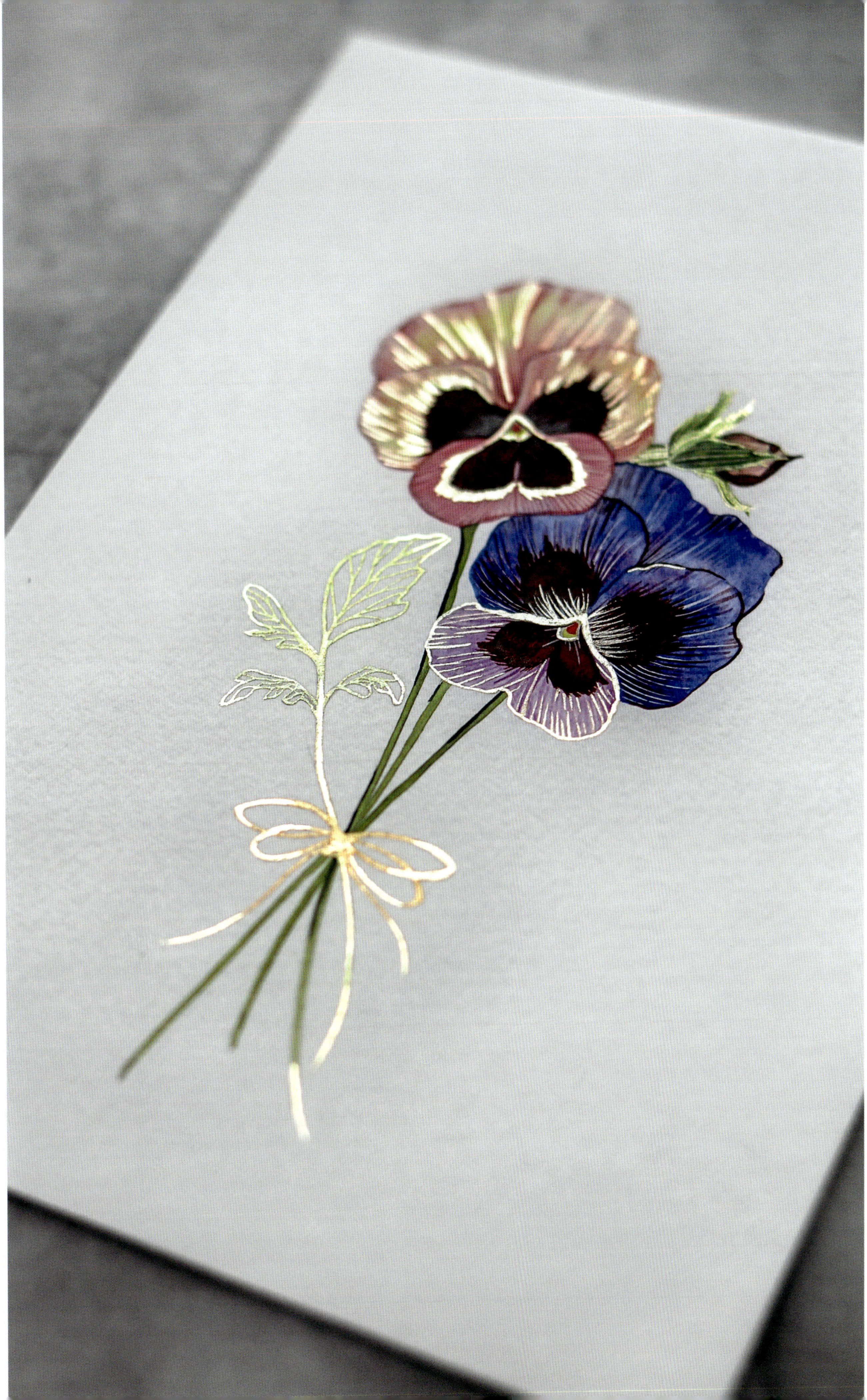

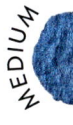

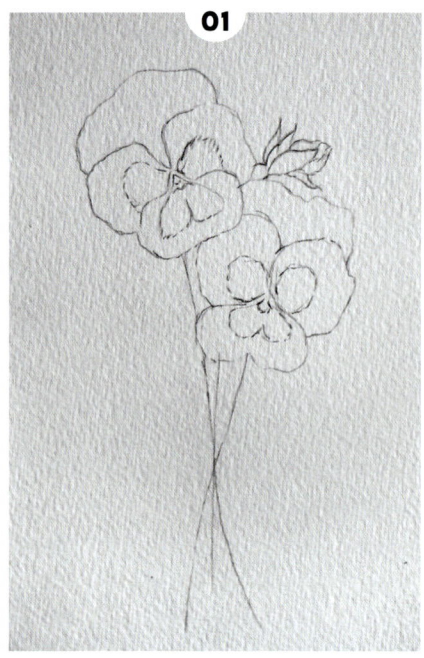

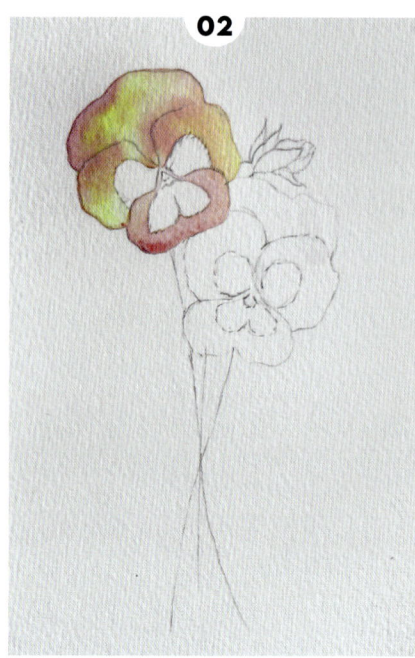

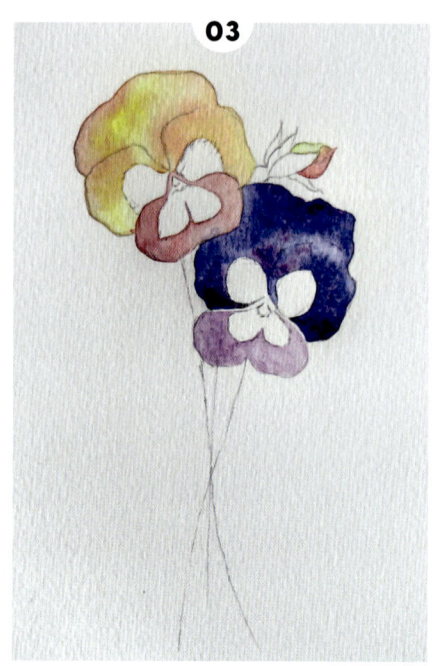

01   Sketch the outlines of both pansies and the unopened flowers with a soft pencil. (You can also scan the QR code on page 31 to download a trace-able sketch.)

02   Begin with the lighter pansy (the one on the left in my example) and prime the surface of the flower with water. Using the wet-on-wet technique, dab a soft yellow and a light pink on the outside of the flower.

03   I've chosen the same color combination for the unopened flower. The pansy on the front right is the darkest in our arrangement. I've colored it in a variety of purple tones (also using the wet-on-wet technique).

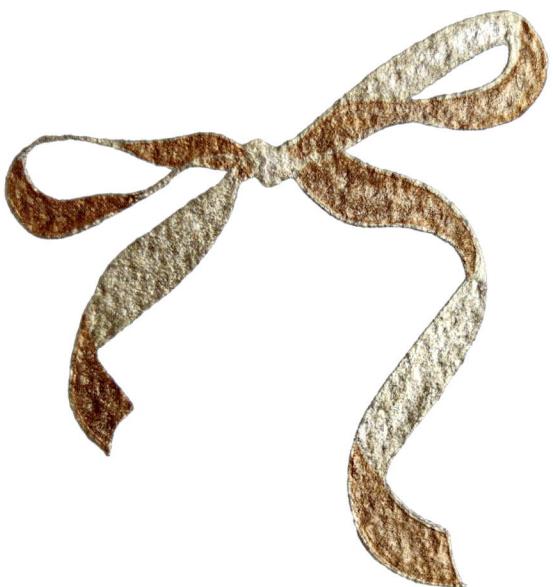

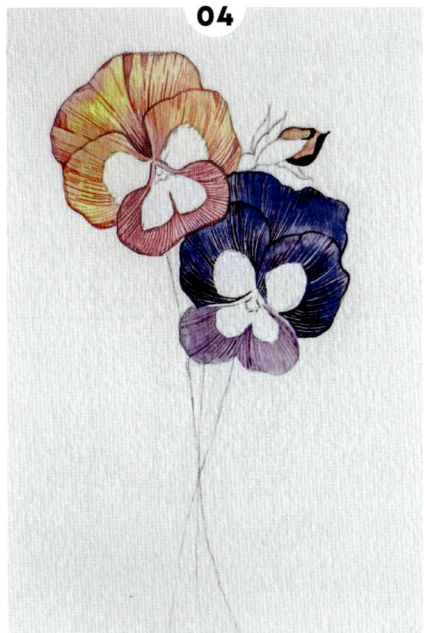

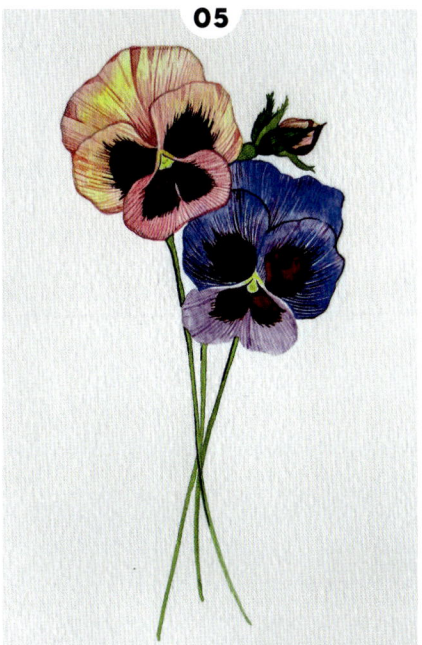

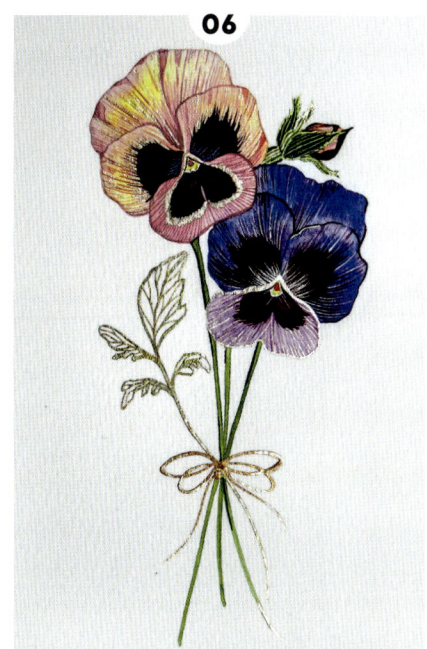

04 Once your flowers are completely dry, you can add some fine texture with a rigger brush. For the pansy on the left, I've used the pink again, while for the one on the right, I mixed a very dark purple. To create a contrast in the dark flower, some fine white lines are essential. The unopened flower is edged in a dark magenta.

05 In this step, I've colored the inside of the flowers in the same dark magenta and made the edges slightly frayed. The stem of the flower can be colored a light yellow. Choose a variety of greens for the leaves and stems.

06 Now we'll start working with our pearlized paints. First, I've added some streaks inside the flower in light gold. I've then used pale olive to add some fine veins to the leaves of the unopened flower. At this point I realized I still wasn't 100 percent happy with the three flowers I'd painted so far. So I quickly added some pale olive to another petal. In my opinion, this decision makes the bouquet look much more consistent. To round off your painting, you can add a thin bow tying together the stems of the flowers and the twigs.

A Delicate
BUTTERFLY

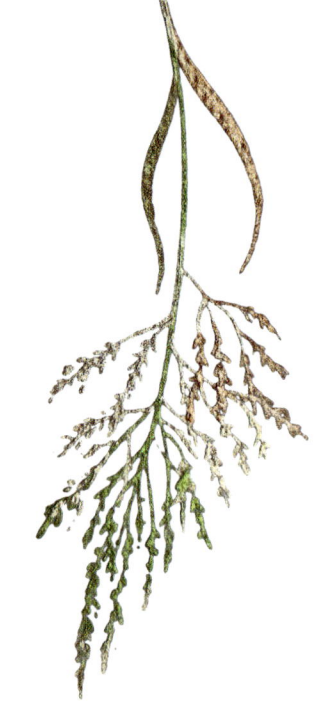

Now let's paint this enchanting butterfly on a shimmering stem of oats. In this motif, I can actually smell the scent of a field on a warm summer's evening. The butterfly's wings have been inspired by the Apollo butterfly.

MATERIALS

ROUND BRUSH | RIGGER BRUSH | MICROBRUSH | PENCIL | WATERCOLOR PAPER

MY COLOR PALETTE

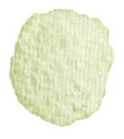    

METALLIC PAINTS

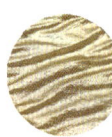 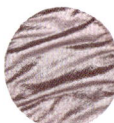 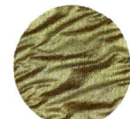 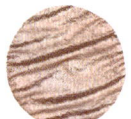

LIGHT GOLD   LIGHT VIOLET   PALE OLIVE   PALE PINK

METALLIC WATERCOLOR

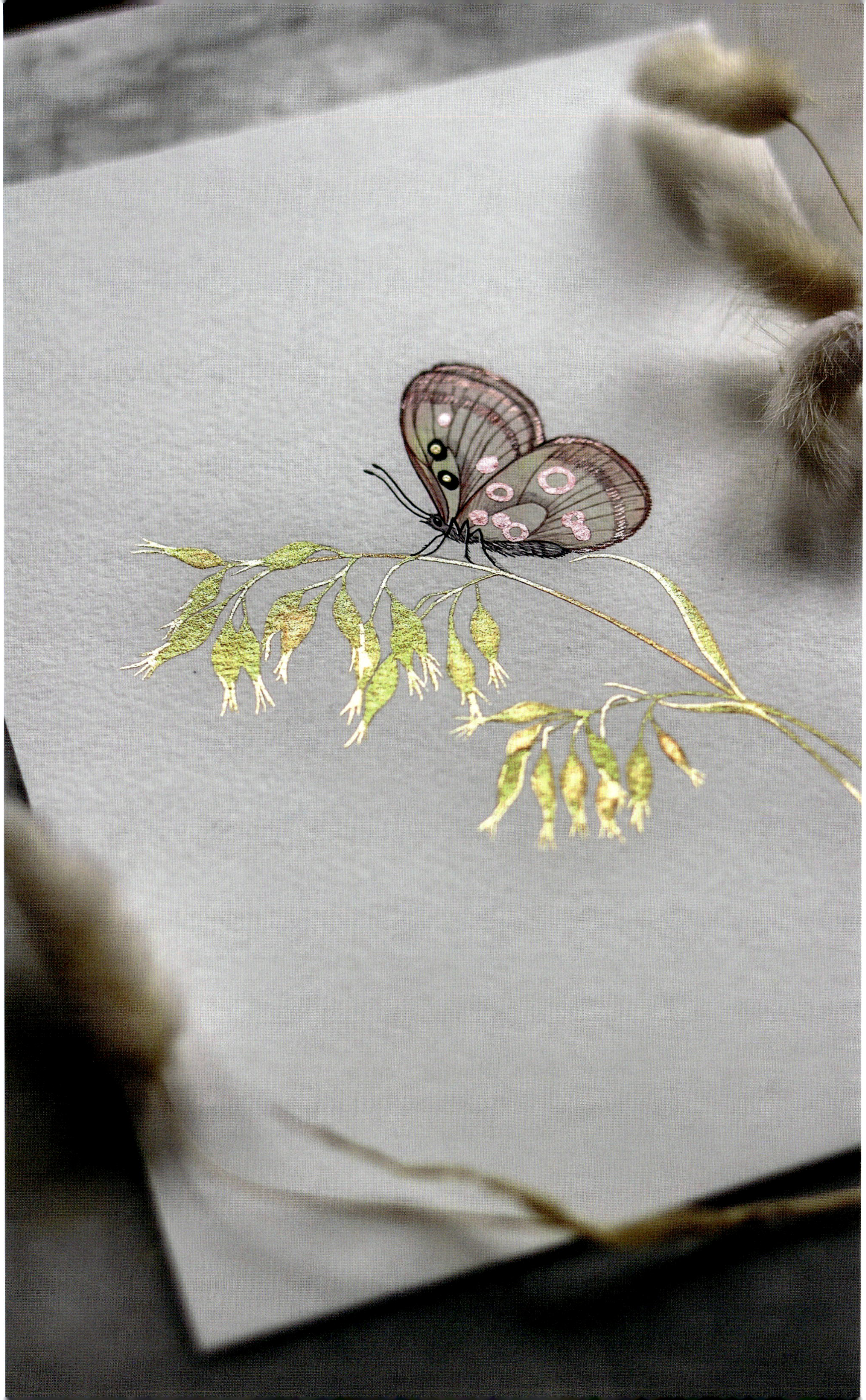

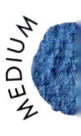

MEDIUM

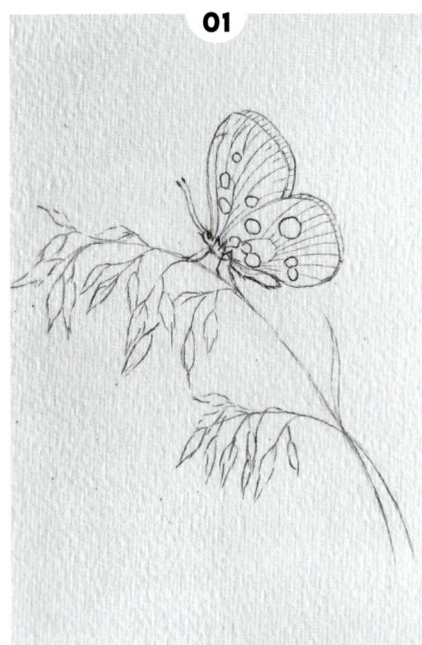
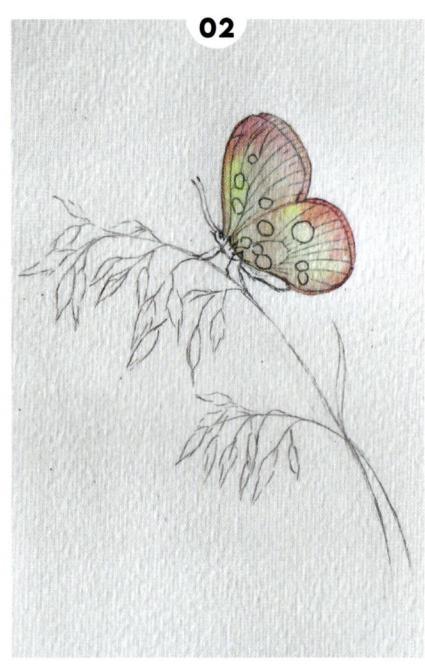
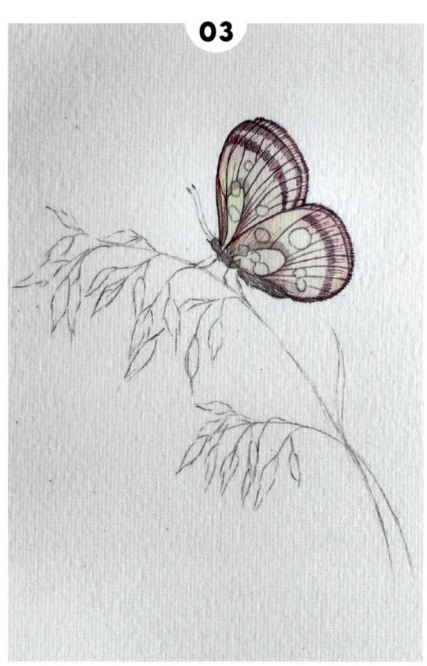

01 Draw the outline of the butterfly and stem of oats on your paper in pencil. (You can also scan the QR code on page 31 to download a traceable sketch.) Try to keep the lines of the butterfly as fine as possible.

02 We're going to keep working in the wet-on-wet technique. So prime the butterfly's wings with clean water and a size 1 round brush. Paint the damp surface using a color of your choice. I've chosen a light yellow and a delicate pink on the edge of the wings.

03 Let the paints dry sufficiently before highlighting the first contours on the wings with a microbrush. I've painted these, as well as the butterfly's body, in a light gray. Taking the light-violet paint, I've lightly outlined the wings and added some fine hairs to the gray contours. I've blended the pink used previously and the light gray to create a shade for the fine veins on the wings. I've also added some delicate hairs at the edges.

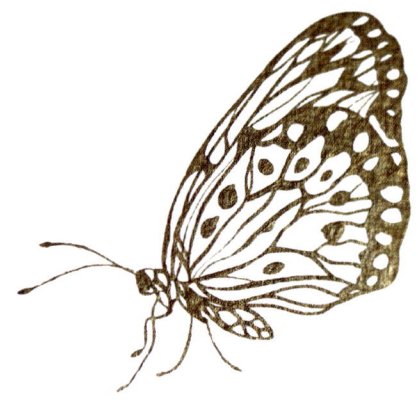

METALLIC WATERCOLOR

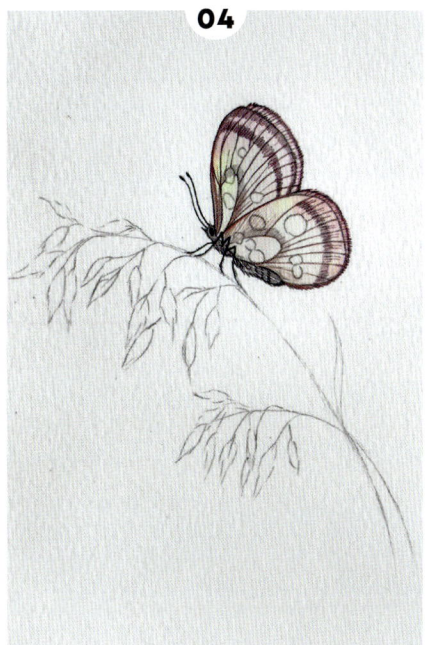

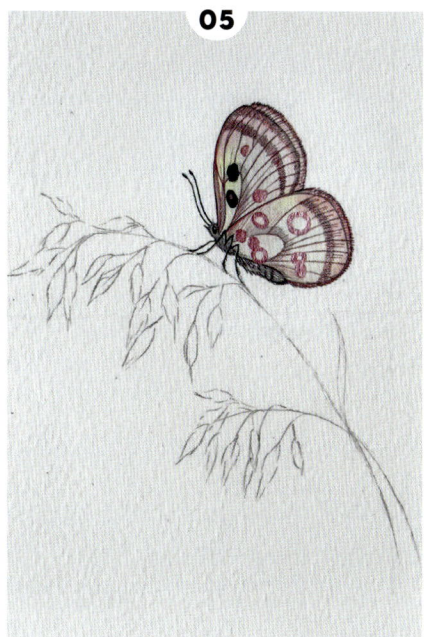

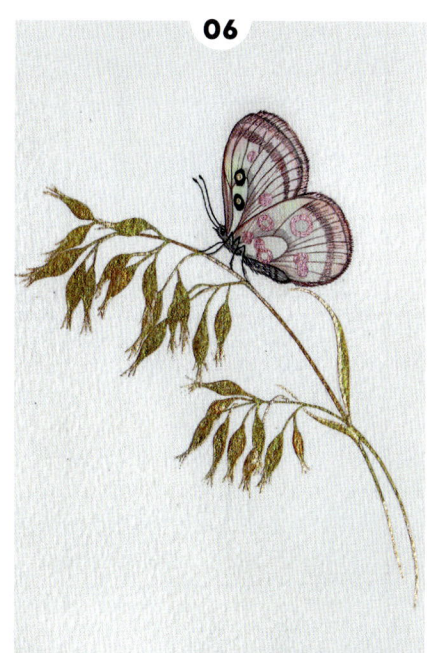

04 We're now going to add more detail to the butterfly's body with a dark gray, which looks almost black. We do this by painting its fine antennae, its thin legs, and an indication of hair.

05 You can now trace over the pattern on the wings in light violet. I've also added some more fine hairs to the edge of the wings in pale pink. Before finishing your butterfly, you can draw a little reflected light in its eye using a fine brush and the white from your paint palette. This makes it look more three-dimensional.

06 As a last step, we'll turn our attention to the oats, which I've traced over in pale-olive metallic paint using the rigger brush. I've added some final shimmering accents to the tips of the oats and the butterfly's wings in light gold.

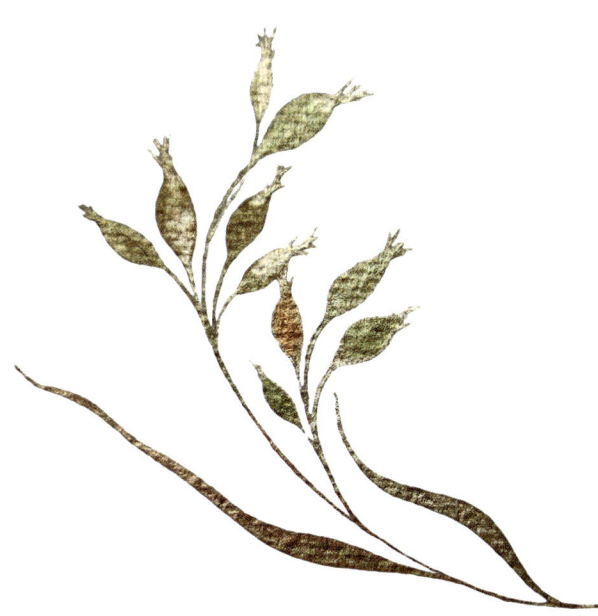

A DELICATE BUTTERFLY

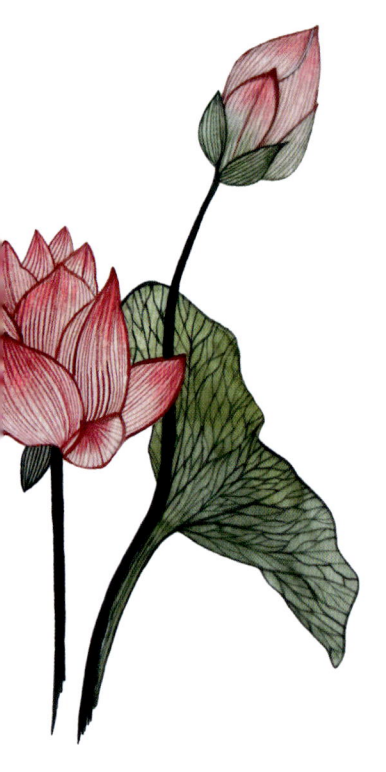

Blossoming
LOTUS FLOWER

The lotus is a wonderful, unique plant that mainly grows in muddy waters. At sunset, it closes its petals and disappears completely below the surface of the water. Once daylight returns, the lotus reemerges in all its beauty, which is why it's become a symbol of rebirth.

MATERIALS
RIGGER BRUSH | PENCIL | WATERCOLOR PAPER

MY COLOR PALETTE

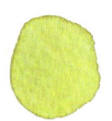 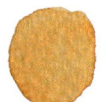 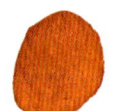  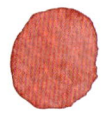 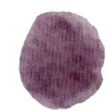 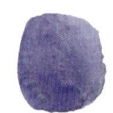 

METALLIC PAINTS

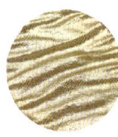 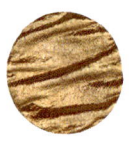  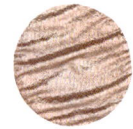 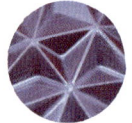

LIGHT GOLD   BRONZE   SILVER   PALE PINK   VIOLET

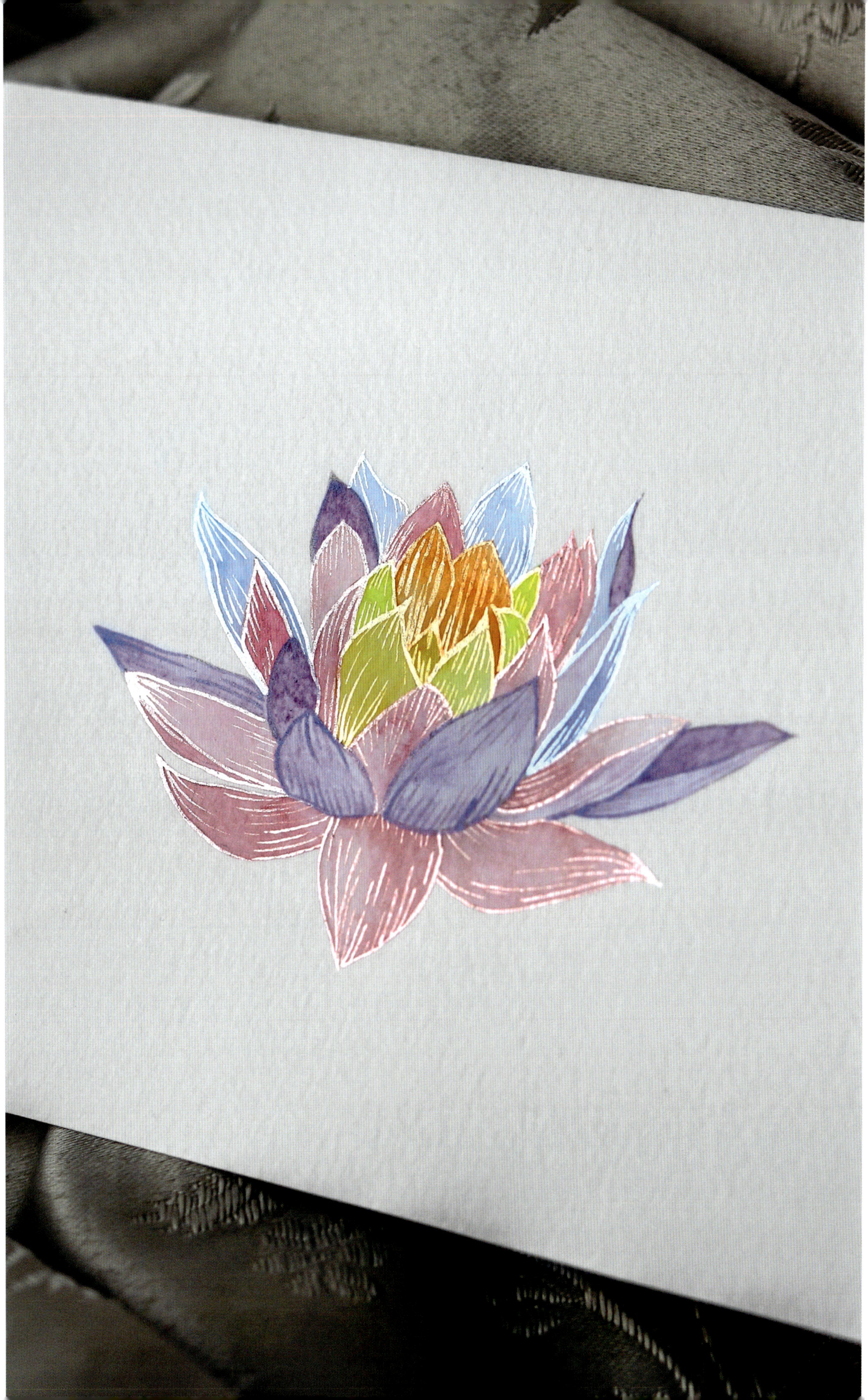

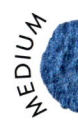

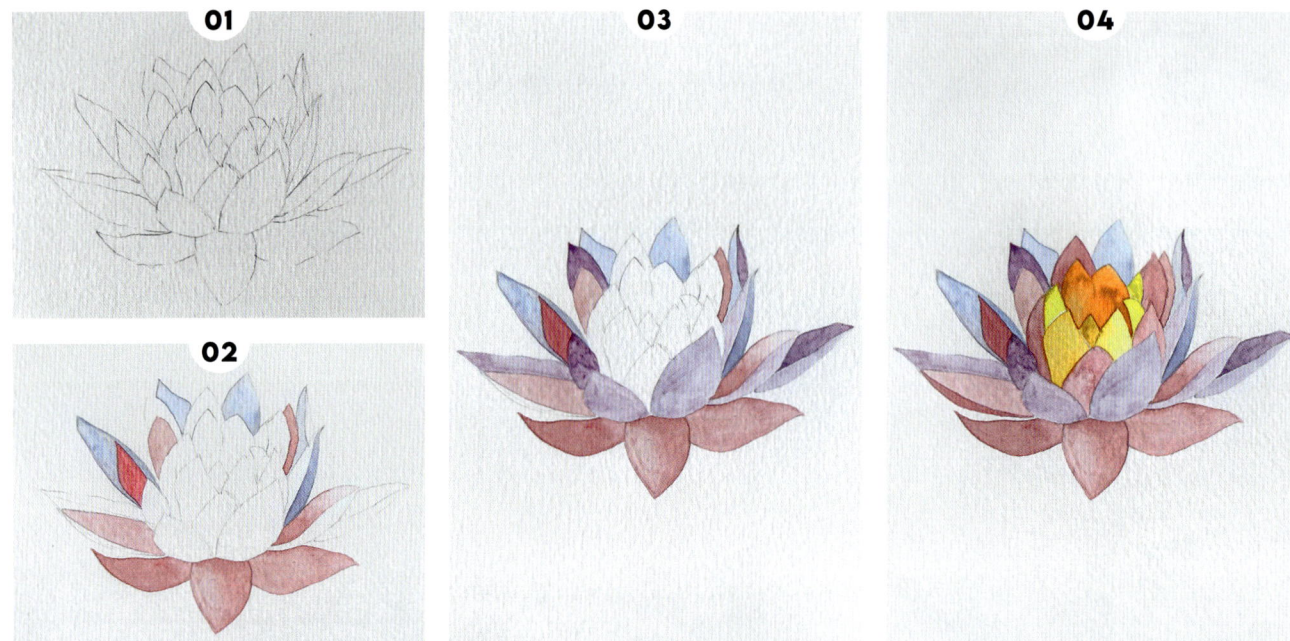

01 Paint the petals of the lotus flower on your watercolor paper with a soft pencil. (You can also scan the QR code on page 31 to download a traceable sketch.)

02 Color the blossom using a size 1 rigger brush or round brush. I've chosen a light blue for the petals at the back and a pale pink for the ones at the front. For this step, you can use either the wet-on-wet or the wet-on-dry technique. Decide which one you'd like to use. Do you want to stay in your comfort zone or practice one of the techniques in more depth?

03 I've painted the petals in the middle of the blossom in light and dark purple so the flower features lots of different shades of color.

04 I've colored the inside of the blossom in a variety of yellows and oranges. The varied color scheme makes each individual petal stand out, and the strong contrasts also give the lotus more depth. I've made the color of the petals on the inside more intense as well. This makes them stand out from the petals on the outside.

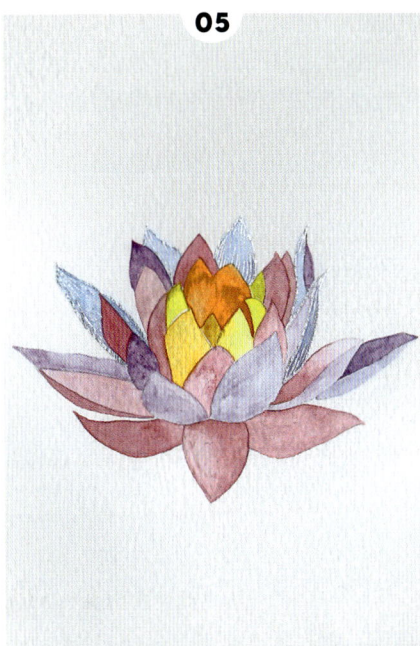

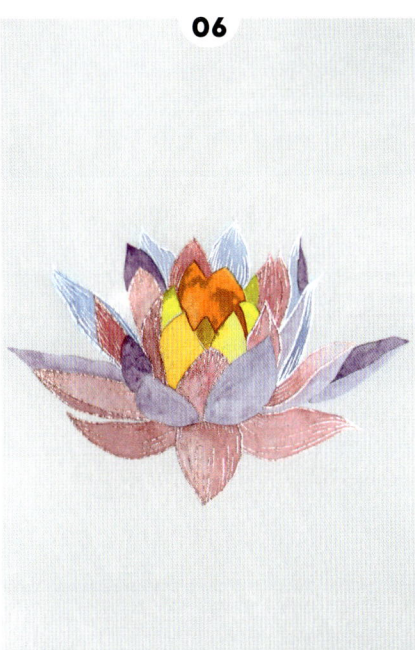

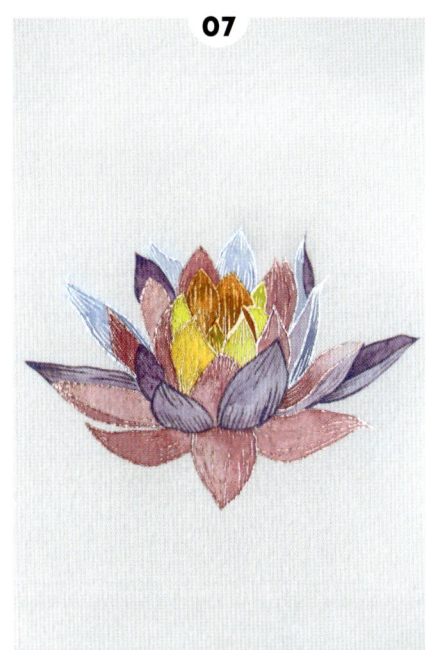

05 Now that we've finished the underpainting for our lotus, we can start adding some fine metallic accents. I've matched my choice of metallic paint to the color of the petal. I've then outlined the petal and added some fine veins. As an example, I chose silver metallic paint for the light-blue petals.

06 I've chosen pale-pink metallic paint for the pale-pink petals, making sure that the outline is as clean as possible. The more neatly you integrate the metallic accents into your painting, the more refined your finished picture will look. So take your time.

07 In this last step, I've traced around the purple-colored petals with violet metallic paint. I've used the metallic shades light gold and bronze for the rest of the petals. Now that we've finished the outlines of our lotus, you can see how beautifully they shine. You can also see how much neater a painting looks when the edges are retouched with metallic accents.

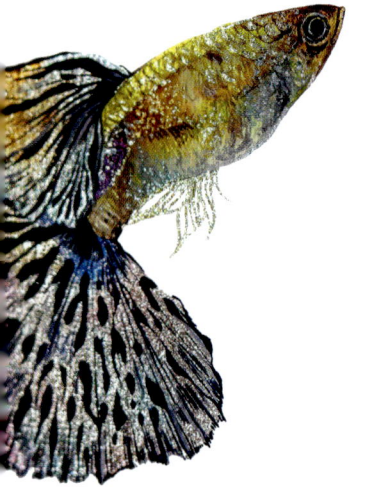

Siamese
FIGHTING FISH

In my opinion, the Siamese fighting fish (Betta splendens) is one of the most beautiful ornamental fish in the world. I have three of these graceful animals myself and I just love them. Their wonderful long fins, which come in the most beautiful color combinations, look hypnotizing as they glide elegantly through the water.

MATERIALS
RIGGER BRUSH | ROUND BRUSH | PENCIL | WATERCOLOR PAPER

MY COLOR PALETTE

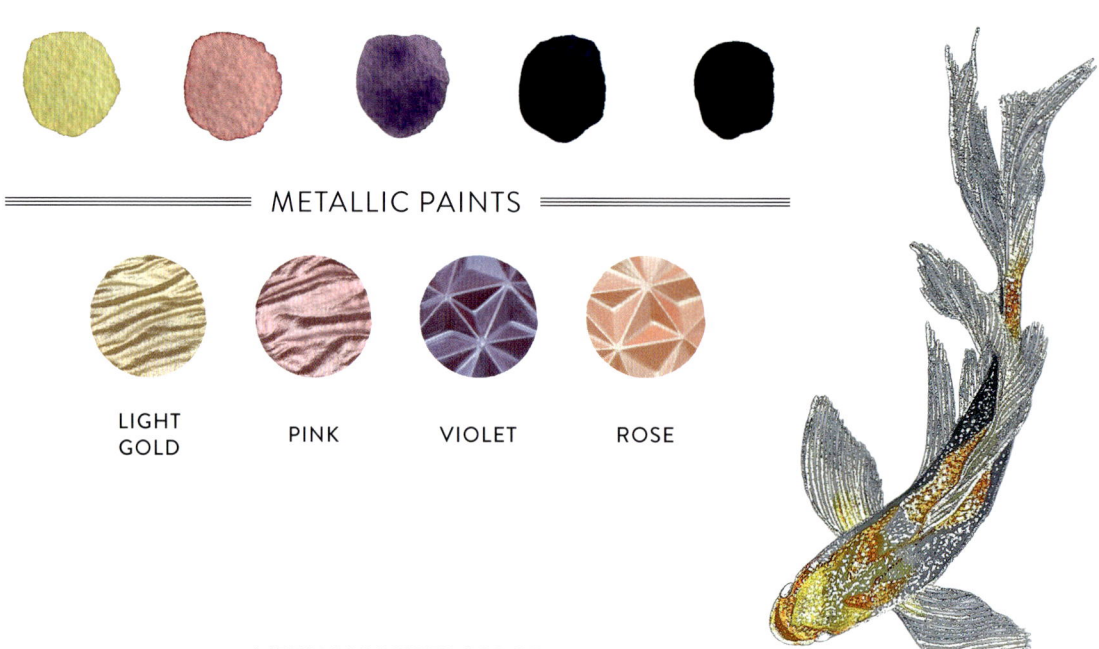

METALLIC PAINTS

LIGHT GOLD   PINK   VIOLET   ROSE

METALLIC WATERCOLOR

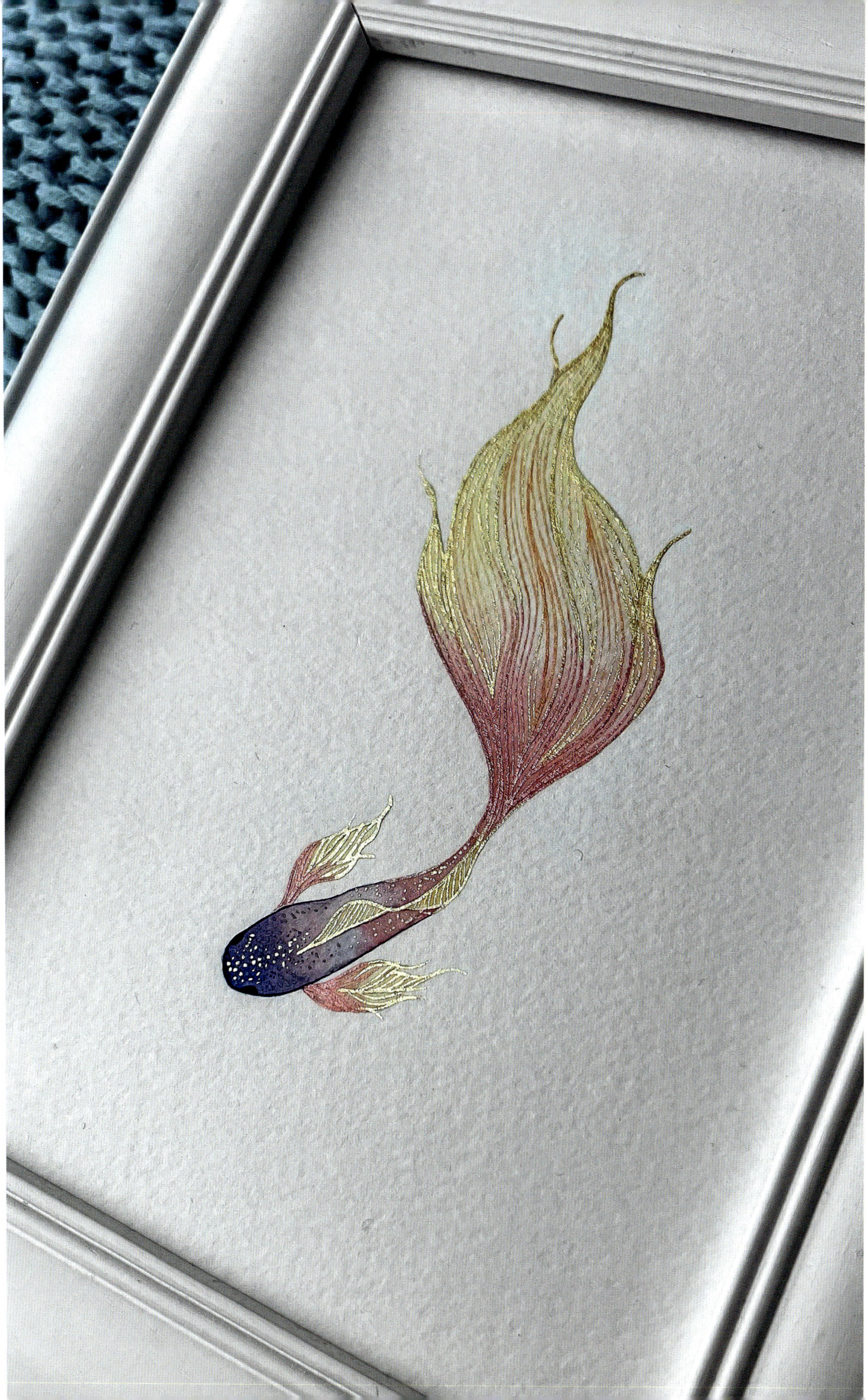

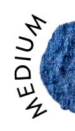

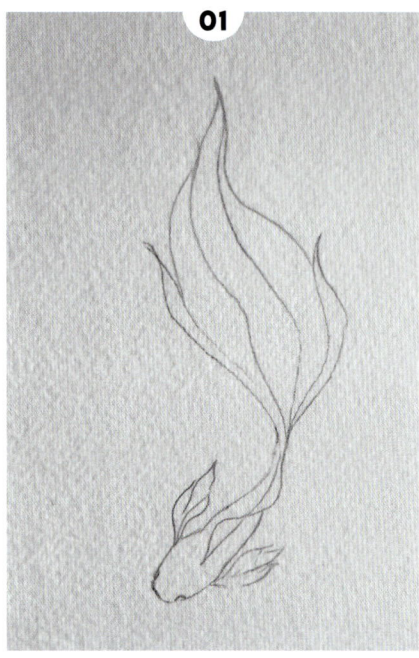

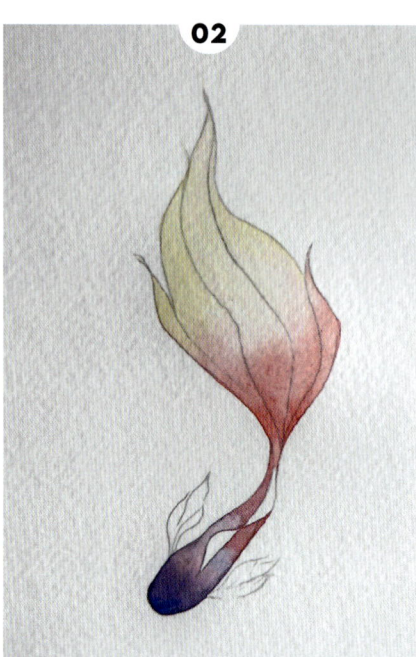

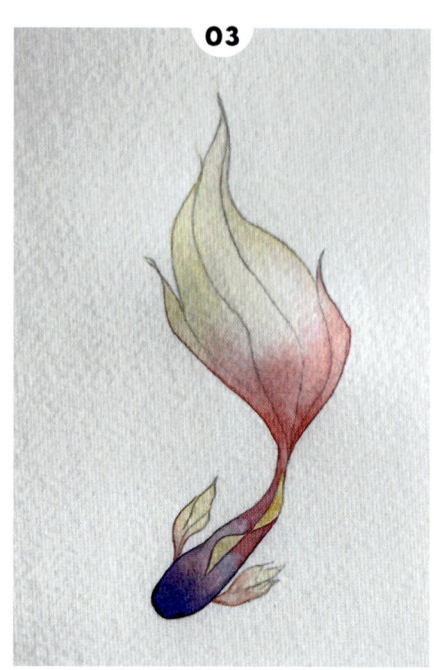

01   Trace the outlines of the fish onto your watercolor paper with a soft pencil. (You can also scan the QR code on page 31 to download a traceable sketch.)

02   Now dip your round brush into clean water and wet the body of the fish. (This is the wet-on-wet technique.) In this step, you can leave out the dorsal and pectoral fins. Now mix a purple shade and apply this to the damp body of the fish. Once you reach the tail fin, change to a pink shade, creating a flowing transition with the purple. Use the pink to color the first quarter of the voluminous tail fin and then switch to a light-yellow shade. In this priming phase, you need to work a little more quickly. That way, the paint can be distributed evenly across the damp areas of the picture, creating a soft color transition.

03   Once these areas are completely dry, you can start coloring the pectoral and dorsal fins. For this part, I used the color scheme for the large tail fin as a guide, working with the wet-on-wet technique. For small areas like this, the rigger brush or a size 1 round brush are ideal. For the head, I added some little dots in dark purple to highlight the texture of the fish. In this step, I've also drawn the little animal's mouth and eyes.

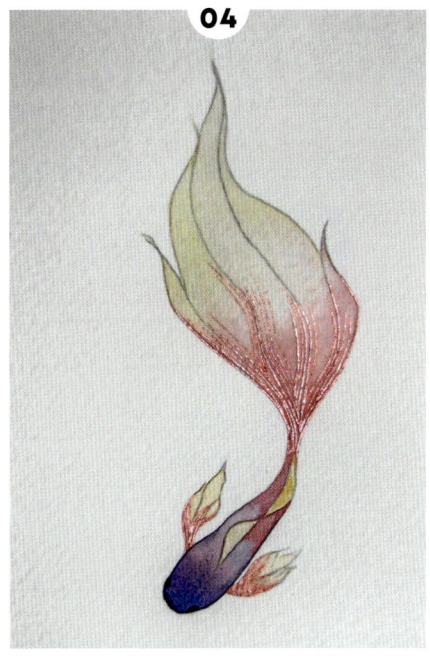

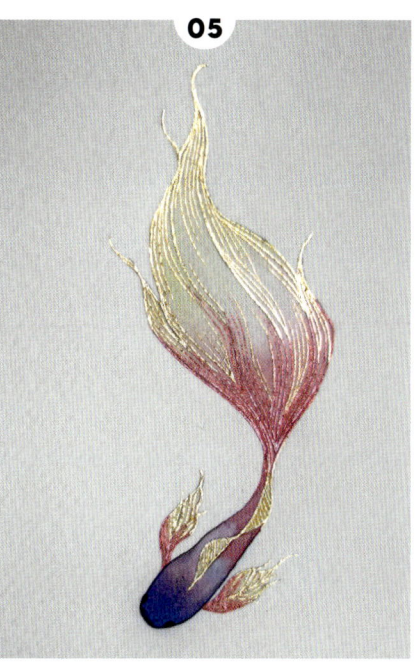

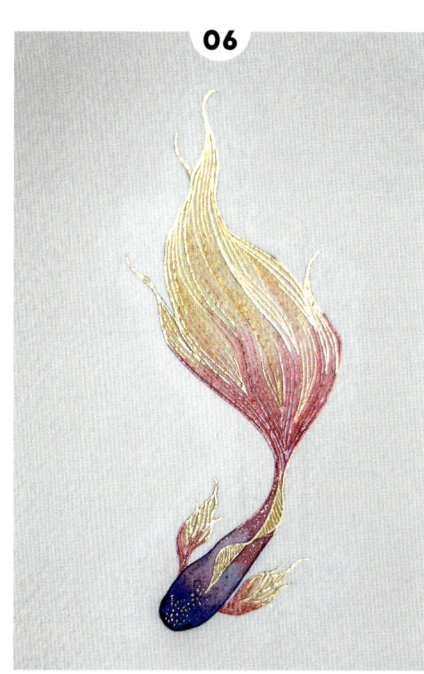

04   Like the lotus on page 92, I matched the color of my metallic accents to the colors of the underpainting. You can start with the delicate veins in the fins, carefully tracing over them with your rigger brush. For the pink sections, I opted for pink metallic paint and drew the lines as evenly as possible.

05   For the light-yellow sections of the fins, I used my favorite color of light gold to create a smooth transition to the pink-colored metallic paint. In the middle of the tail fin, I deliberately left a few areas unpainted. I then used a different metallic shade in the next step to really make the tail pop.

06   In the last step, I added delicate veins to the unpainted areas of the tail fin in rose metallic paint. I then added some small dots to the animal's body in the metallic shades of light gold, violet, and rose. Our shimmering fighting fish is now complete!

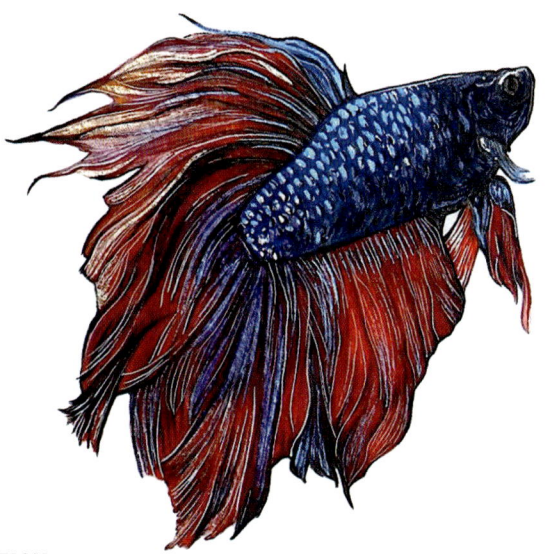

SIAMESE FIGHTING FISH

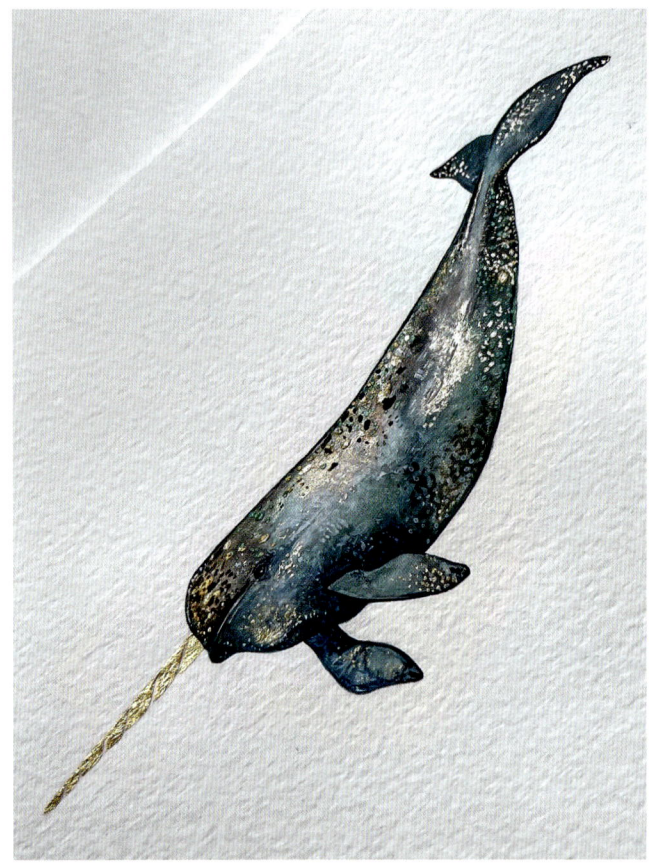

Some motifs and paintings are perfect as a set of two to four pictures. I painted a shiny crab as a companion to my seahorse, for example. It complements our motif beautifully, as they share similar metallic accents and patterns.

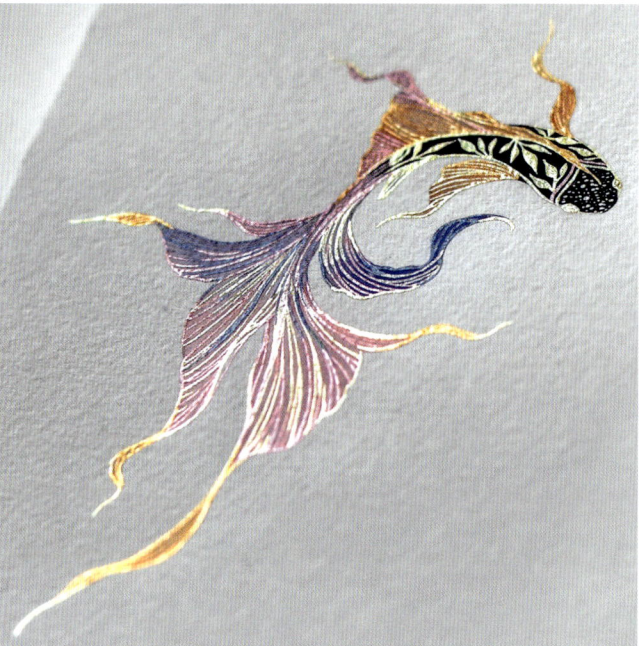

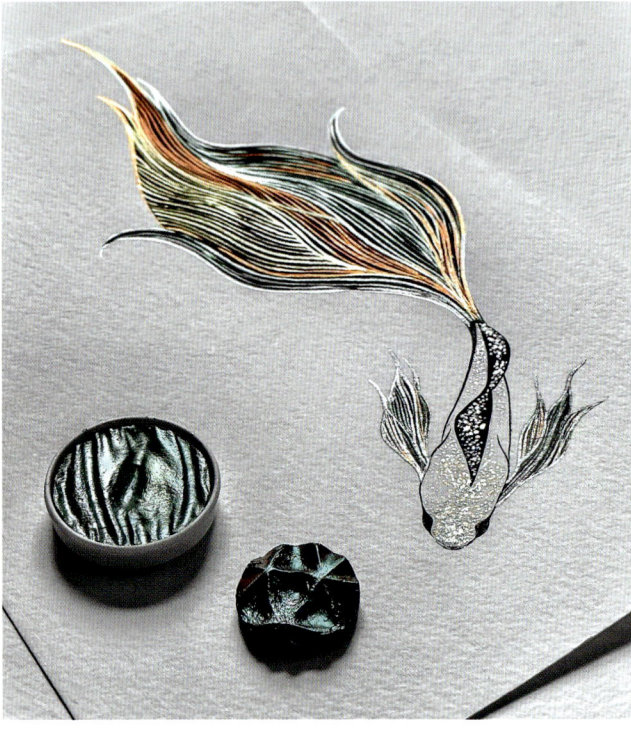

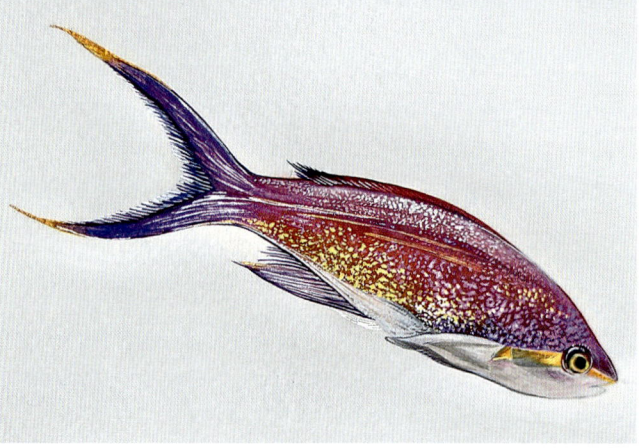

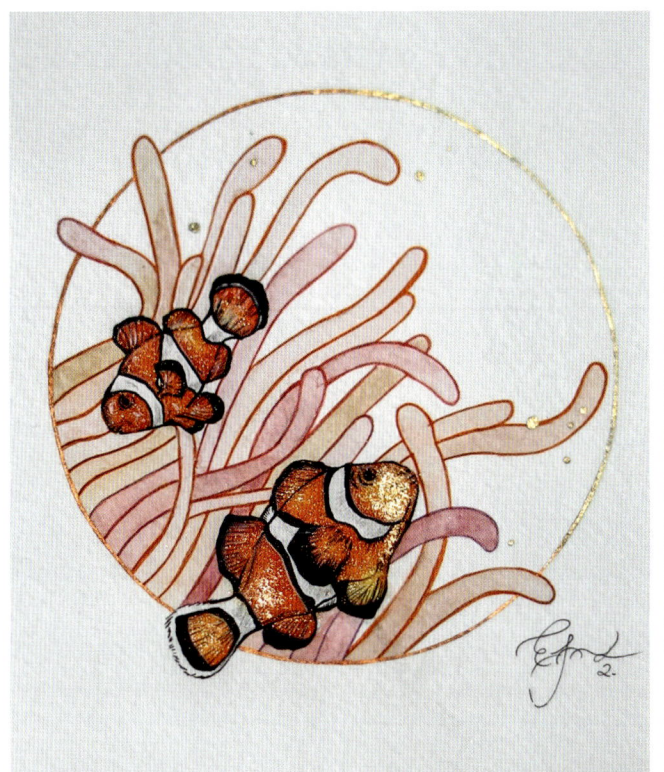
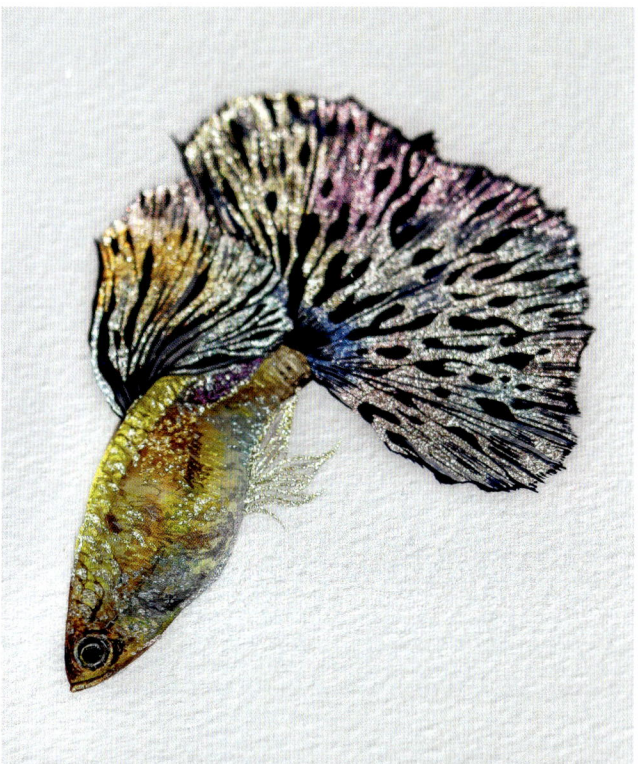
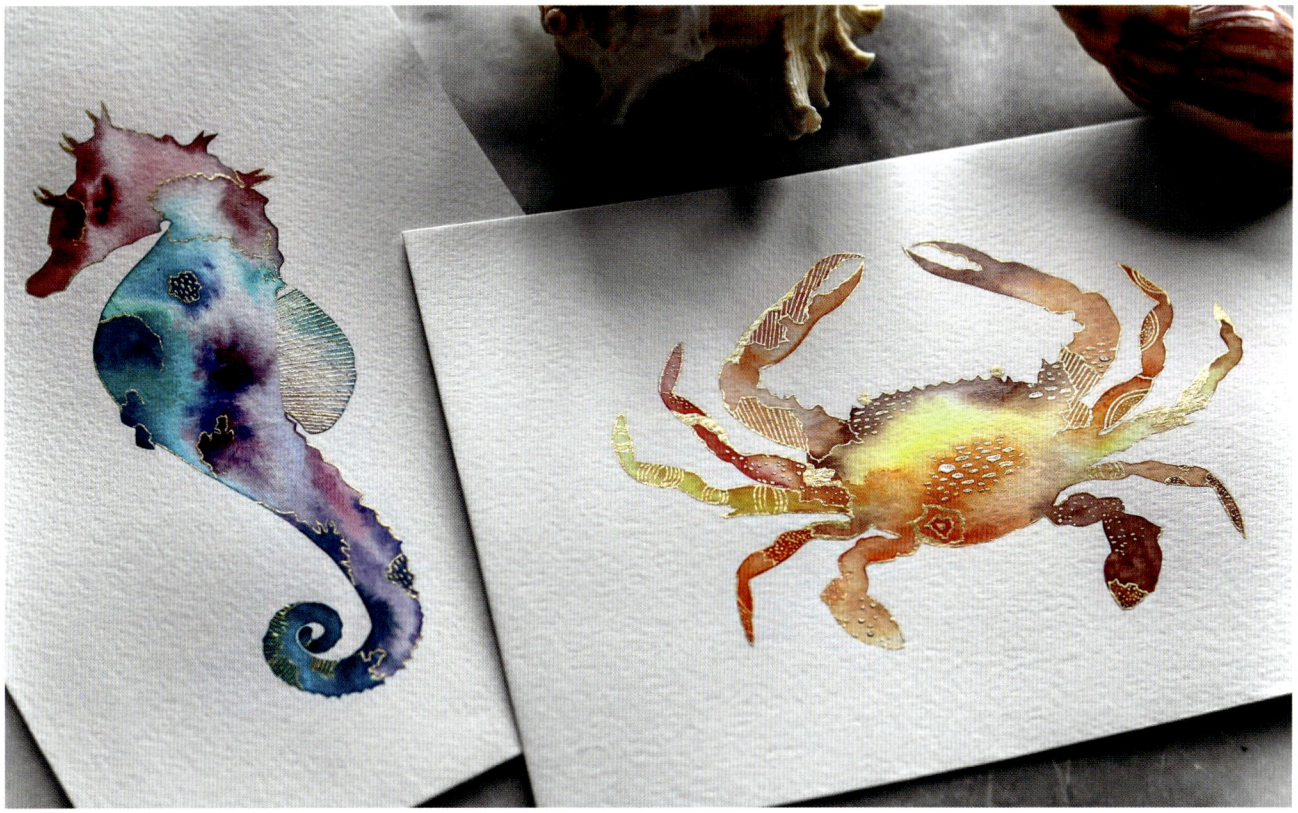

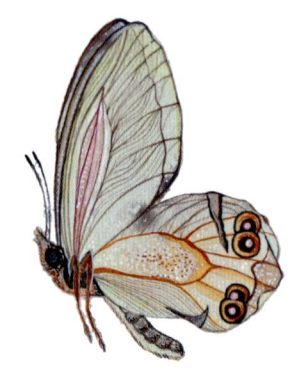

Shimmering
PEACOCK FEATHER

This beautiful shimmering peacock feather is the first motif of the most challenging difficulty level and is also one of the first pictures to be painted almost exclusively with metallic paint. That's what makes it shine so intensely. In my opinion, it more than does justice to a real-life peacock feather.

MATERIALS
RIGGER BRUSH | PENCIL | WATERCOLOR PAPER

MY COLOR PALETTE

=== METALLIC PAINTS ===

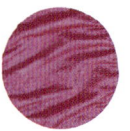 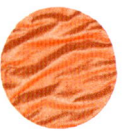 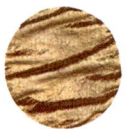 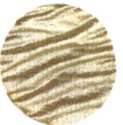 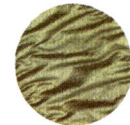 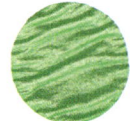 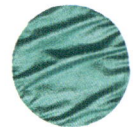 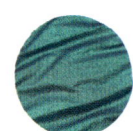

| DEEP PINK | DEEP ORANGE | BRONZE | LIGHT GOLD | PALE OLIVE | LIGHT GREEN | TURQUOISE | TEAL |

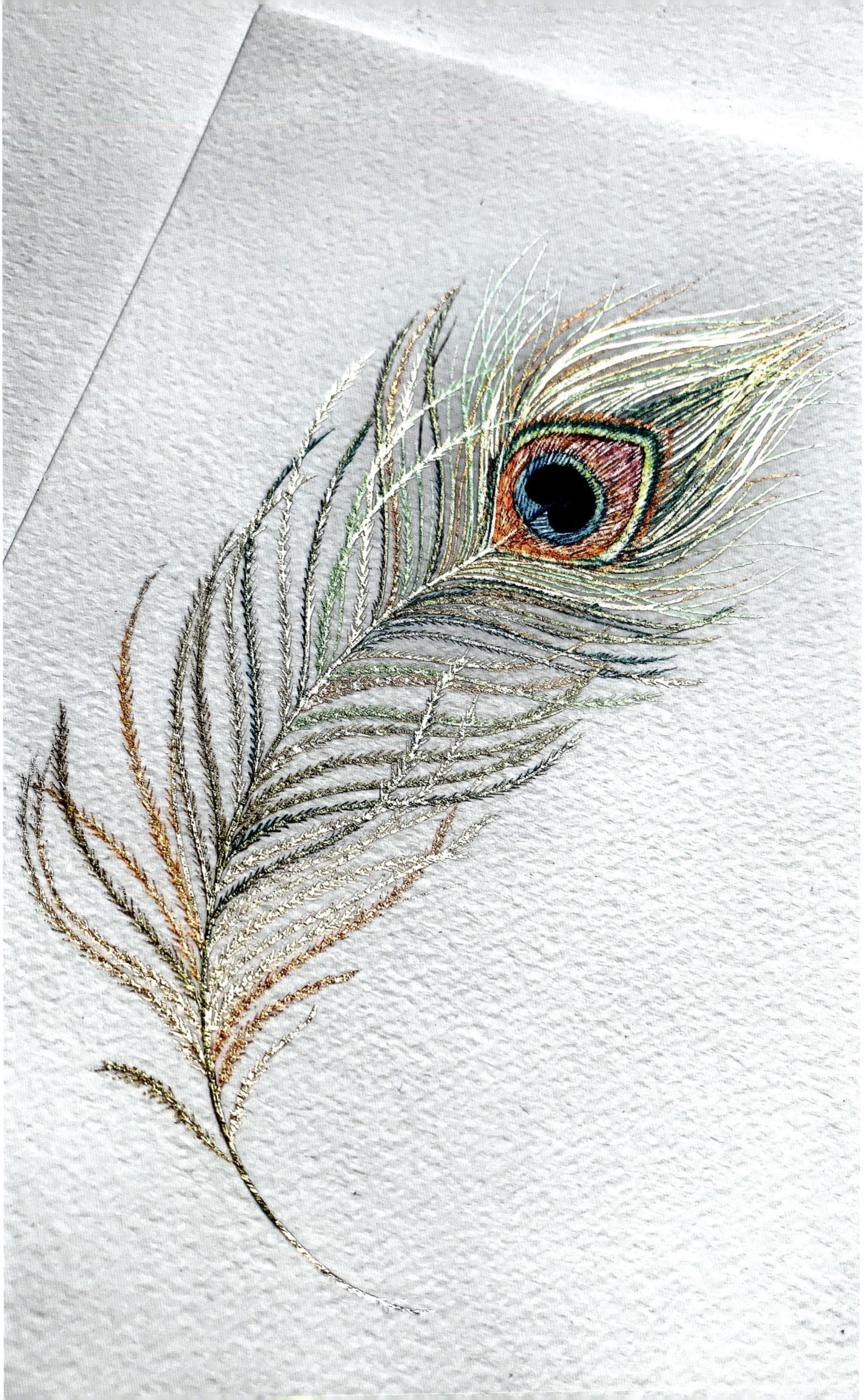

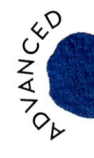

ADVANCED

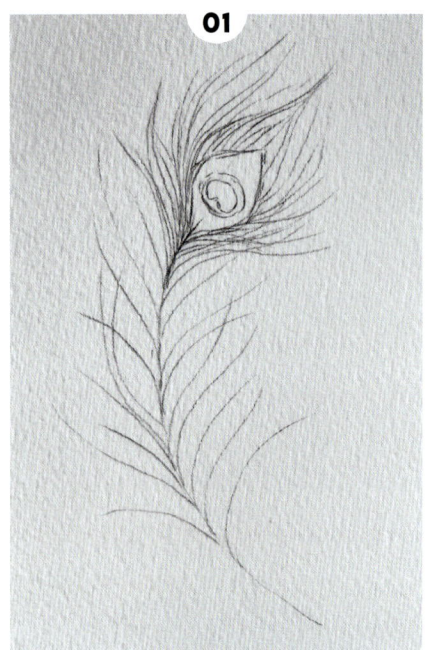

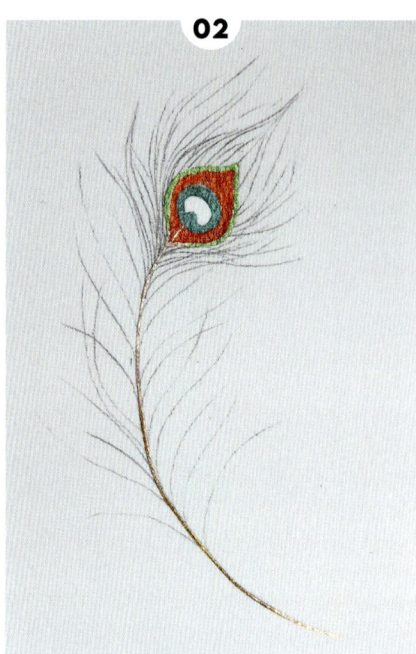

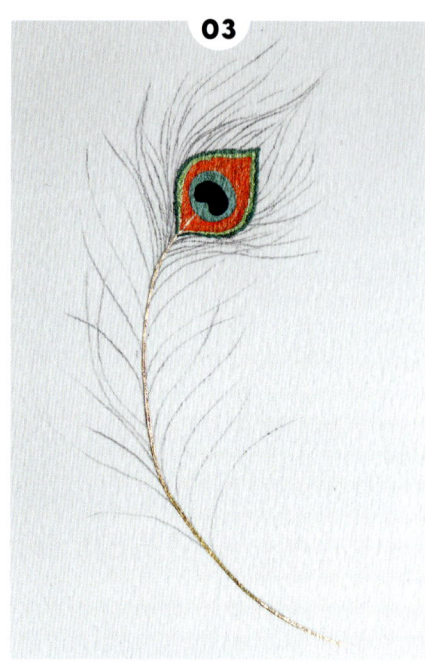

01 Trace the outlines of the peacock feather onto your watercolor paper with a soft pencil. (You can also scan the QR code on page 31 to download a traceable sketch.)

02 I painted the peacock feather almost exclusively with metallic paint, so you can activate your pans and start with the eye of the feather. Leave the center empty for now and paint the other parts of the pattern with a small round brush. I used the metallic shades of turquoise, deep orange, and light green. For the shaft of the feather, I combined the shades light gold and pale olive to create a gradient inside the shaft. I worked with my rigger brush, using even strokes.

03 After all of the colored areas have dried, outline the area previously painted in light green with the teal metallic paint. Use small strokes that look like individual strands of feather. You can then paint the center of the eye with the watercolor shade of indigo. The rigger brush is perfect for this. However, you can also use a microbrush if you prefer.

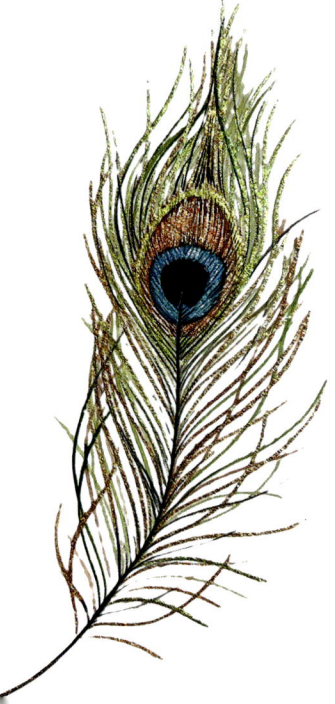

METALLIC WATERCOLOR

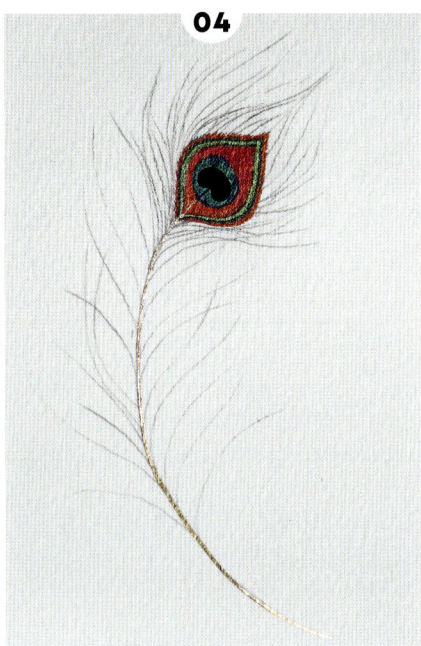

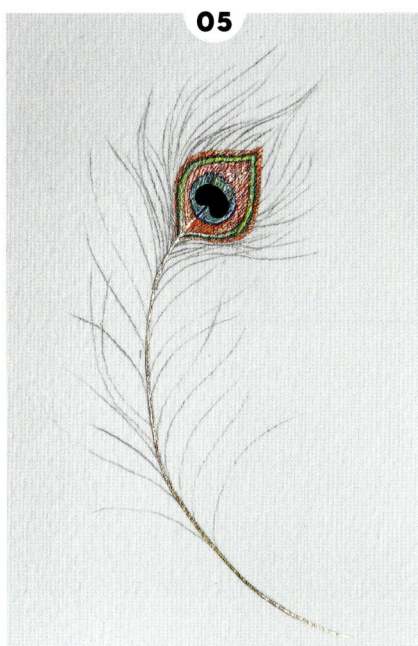

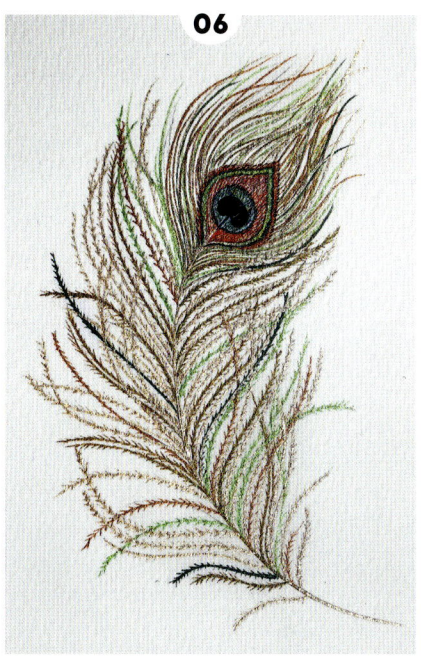

04 Using deep-orange metallic paint, I repeated the outlining process in little strands of feather. You can use the blue watercolor to add some fine strokes over the area painted with the metallic shade of teal. This will create an illusion of texture inside the feather. I've also gone over the top of the part in deep orange with deep pink. Allow everything to dry thoroughly after each step.

05 Once the metallic paints have dried completely, use your rigger brush and light gold to add fine strokes to all parts of the eye. Now our peacock feather is really starting to shine!

06 In the last step, it's time to paint the delicate strands of feather sticking out from the shaft and at the top. Here I combined the metallic paints light gold, pale olive, bronze, teal, and light green. The last two shades are only used in a few places. You can also choose your own color scheme for the feather if you wish, using my version as a guide. Just make sure that you overlap the individual strands in places and vary their orientation so that the feather looks more three-dimensional. Finally, I added some thin white strands in the indigo-colored center at the top of the feather to give it a little more texture.

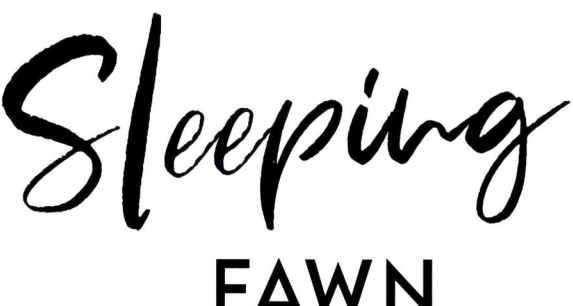

Sleeping
FAWN

"Sleeping cutie" is the phrase that immediately comes to mind when I see this little sleeping fawn circled with delicate flowers. I love painting cute motifs like this. They're perfect for decorating a kid's bedroom and make a great birthday gift.

MATERIALS

RIGGER BRUSH OR MICROBRUSH | SIZE 1 ROUND BRUSH | PENCIL | WATERCOLOR PAPER | BOWL OR COMPASS

MY COLOR PALETTE

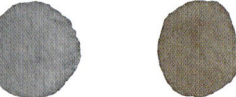 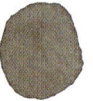   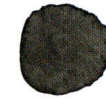

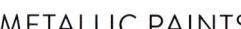 METALLIC PAINTS

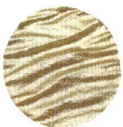

LIGHT
GOLD

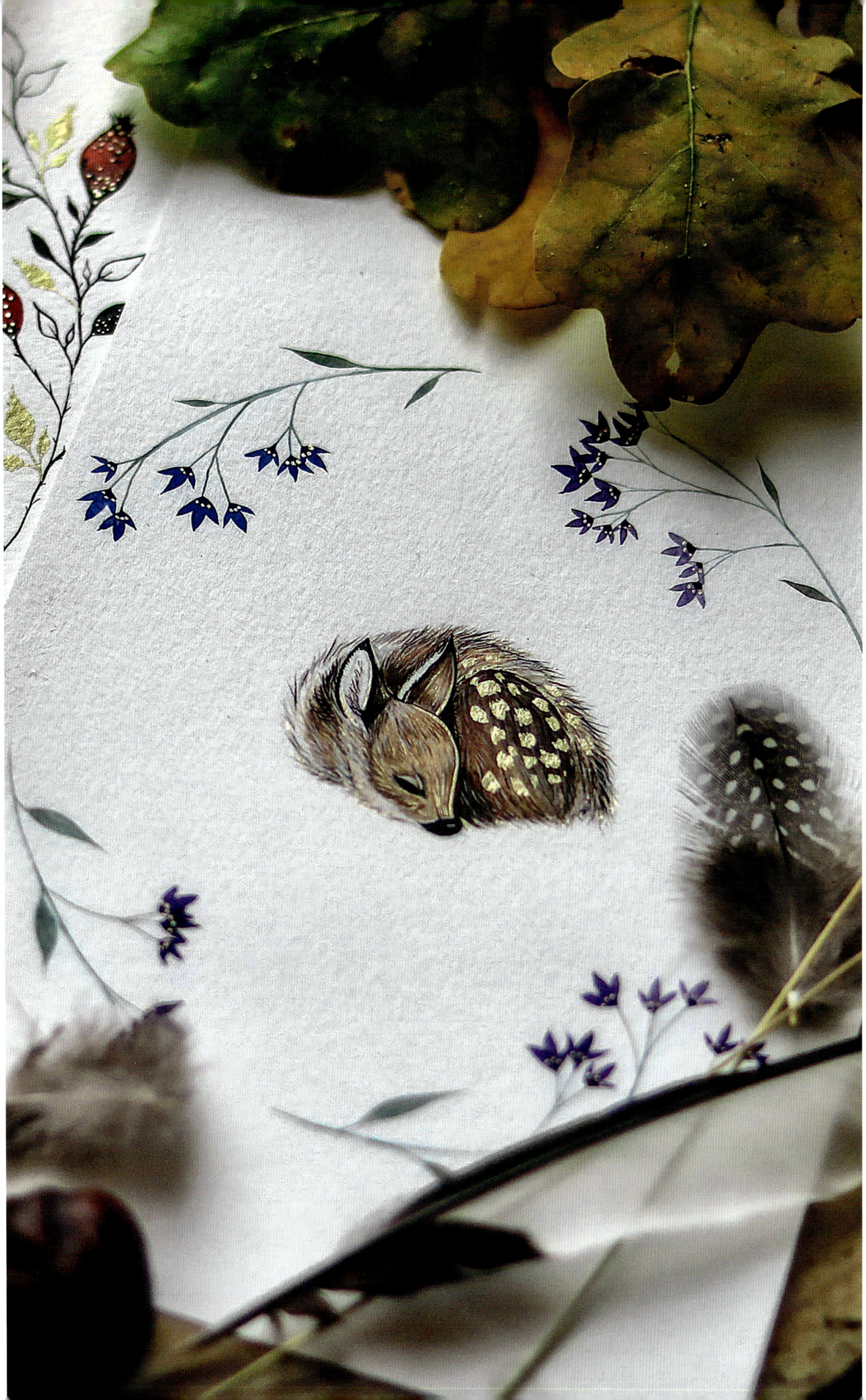

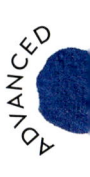

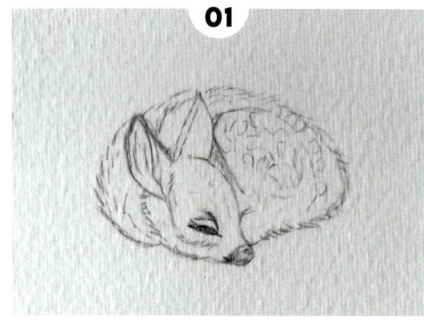

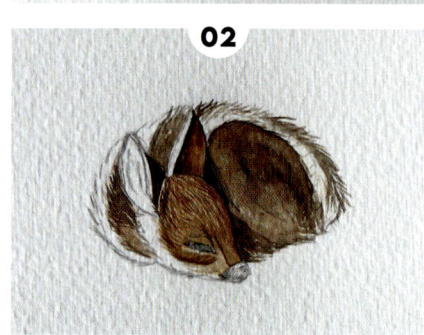

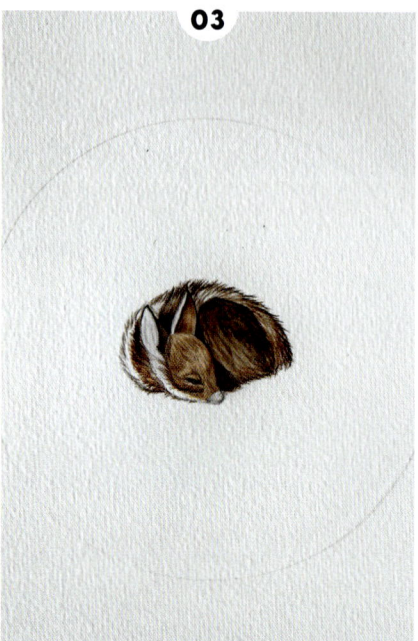

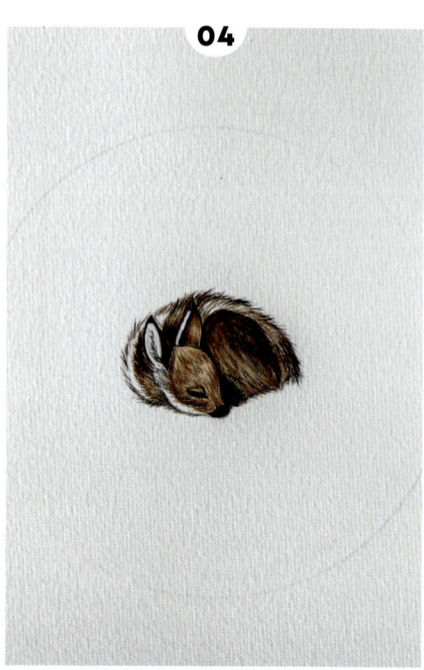

01 Take a bowl or a compass and draw the light outline of a circle on your paper. (You can also scan the QR code on page 31 to download a traceable sketch.) In the center of this circle, you can make a sketch of a sleeping fawn in soft pencil.

02 For the colored underpainting, I used my size 1 round brush and applied a light-brown shade using the wet-on-dry technique. At this stage, I left out the parts of the fawn that I wanted to make lighter or white. Once your light brown has dried, you can paint the first fine hairs of the fawn's coat with your rigger brush (or a microbrush) and a darker shade of brown.

03 Now repeat this step, working the fine textures of the animal and its facial features. Give yourself plenty of time so the transitions are as soft as possible. Just make sure that you lay down the different layers of paint from light to dark.

04 Keep painting the fine hairs in the various brown shades until you have a dark brown (almost black), using them to highlight certain areas of the coat and subtly outline the head, ears, nose, eyes, and facial features. By now, your fawn will look really cute!

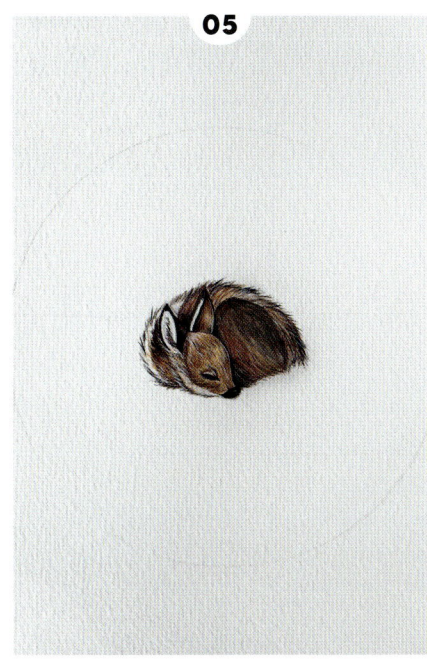

05

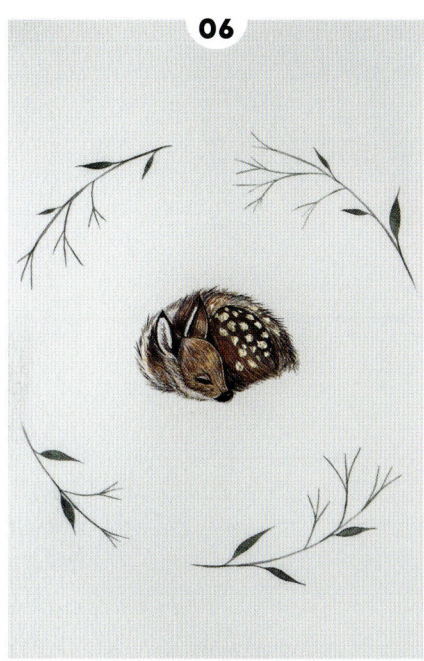

06

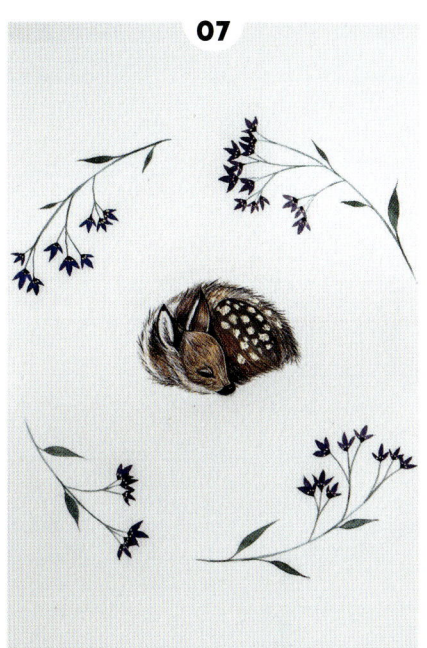

07

05   In this step, wash your rigger brush or microbrush well and activate the white in your watercolor palette. You can use this to paint some light hairs on the fawn's coat and make the colors look gentler overall. You can also use the white to add a gentle shine to the nose.

06   I've used the light-gold metallic paint for the fawn's characteristic dots and have also drawn a few golden hairs. Once you've finished painting the baby animal and the paint has dried, you can start the delicate floral border. For this, I mixed a cool green shade and drew some fine stems and leaves on the pencil circle using my rigger brush. Once this is completely dry, you can carefully rub out your reference lines. Personally, I think it looks really nice if the stems don't close the circle completely.

07   Finally, I painted lots of little flowers in various shades of purple and added a pattern of little gold dots. Your sleeping fawn is done!

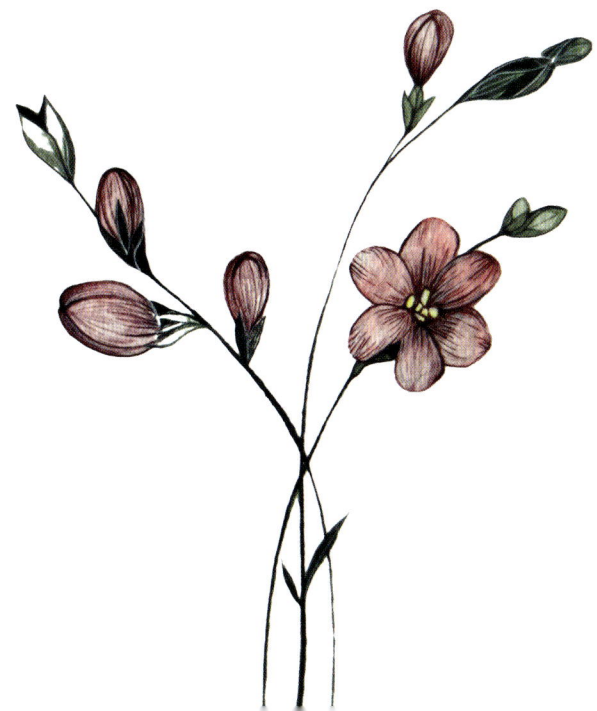

SLEEPING FAWN

Owl
MADE FROM LEAVES

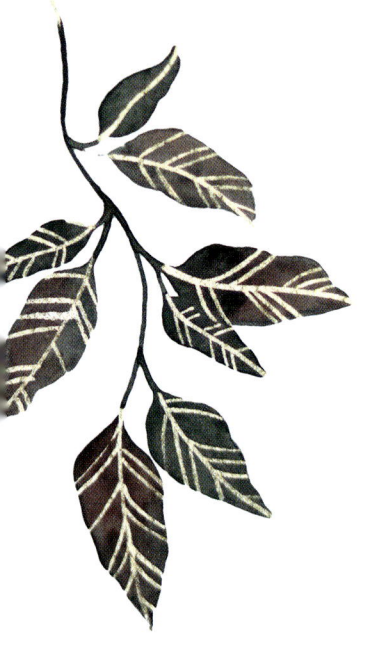

The silhouette of an animal filled with glittering flowers and leaves is great for experimenting with patterns and metallic paints. I always find pictures like this relaxing, as I let my intuition guide me. There are no limits to what you can do. Here I want to show you how to work with these sorts of motifs with the example of this shimmering owl.

MATERIALS
RIGGER BRUSH | PENCIL | WATERCOLOR PAPER

MY COLOR PALETTE

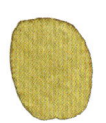 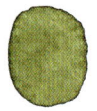 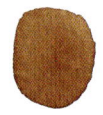 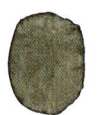 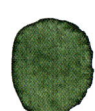  

— METALLIC PAINTS —

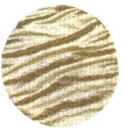 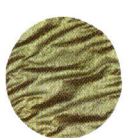 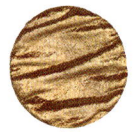 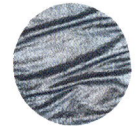 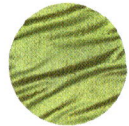

MOON GOLD   GOLDEN OLIVE   BRONZE   BLUE SILVER   APPLE GREEN

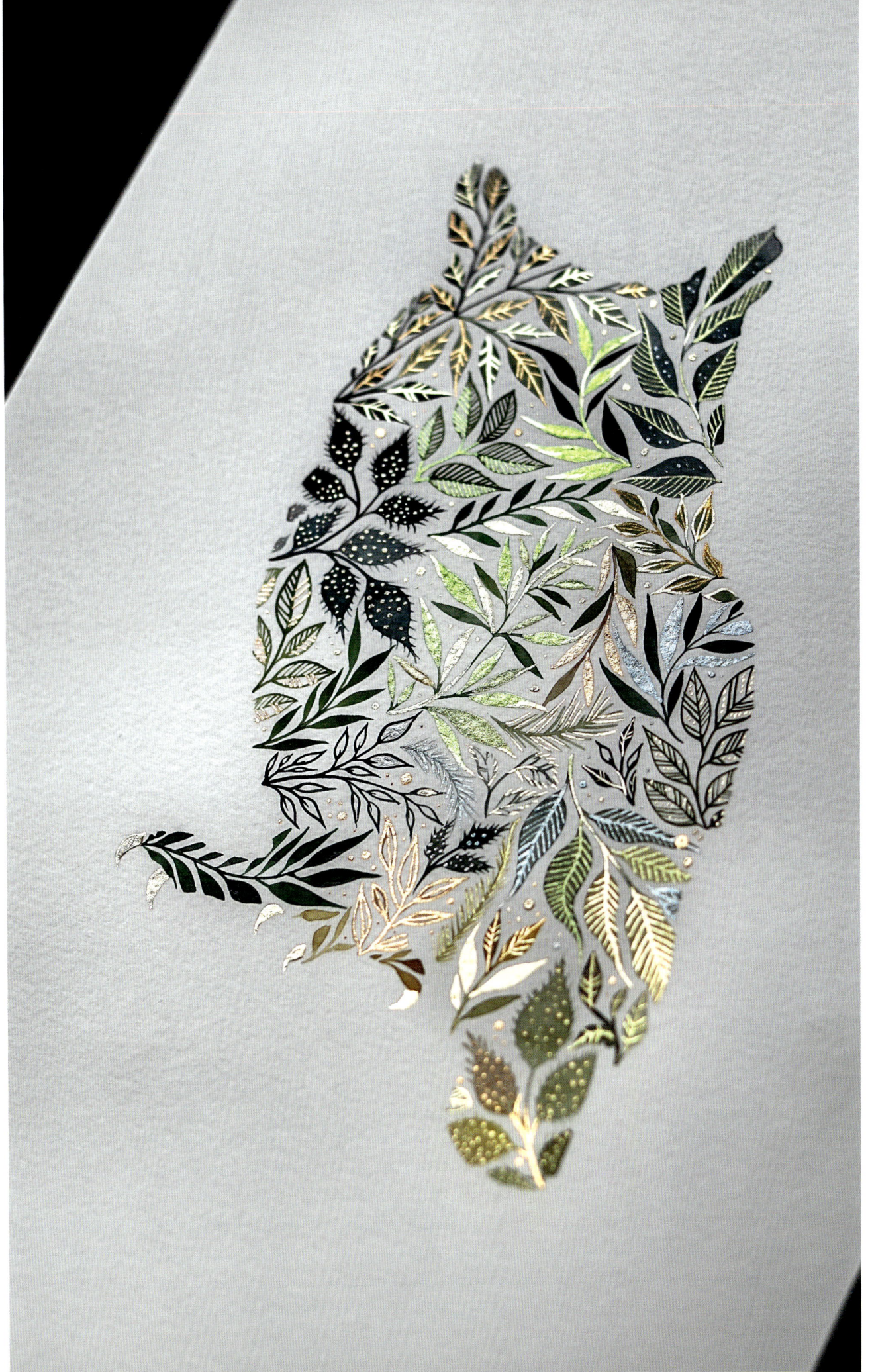

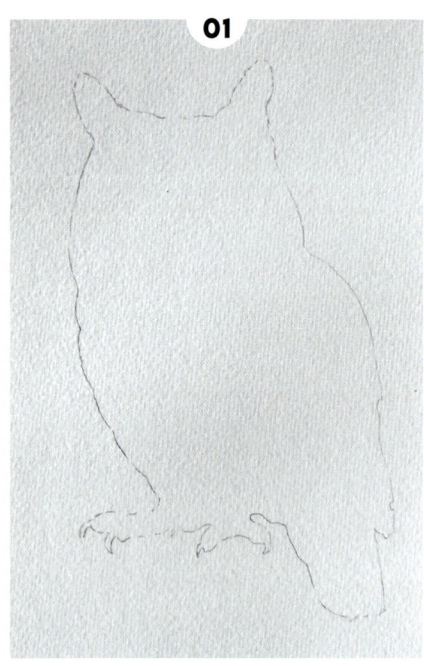

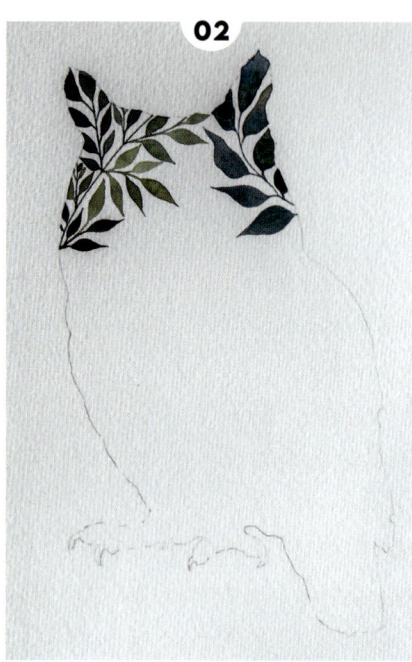

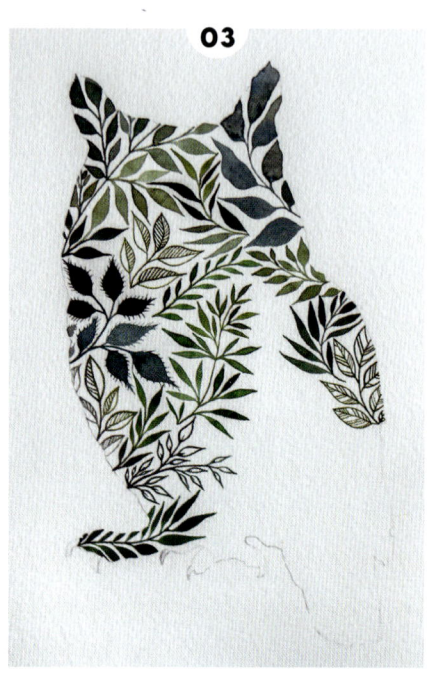

01 Using a soft pencil, draw the outline of an owl or another animal of your choice on your watercolor paper. (You can also scan the QR code on page 31 to download a traceable sketch.) As a template for silhouettes like this, I like to use photographs of nature that I find in books or online.

02 You can now fill your animal's silhouette with lots of different leaves. Use your rigger brush for this. As far as the shape and color are concerned, there are no limits. Follow your intuition! Just make sure that you can still see the animal's shape clearly through the leaves.

03 Little by little, you can design the empty areas inside your silhouette however you like. However, I'd suggest trying out as many different patterns and variations as possible. It's always a nice idea to just draw the texture and some leaf fibers in a few of the leaves instead of filling them in. This will make your watercolor look more delicate.

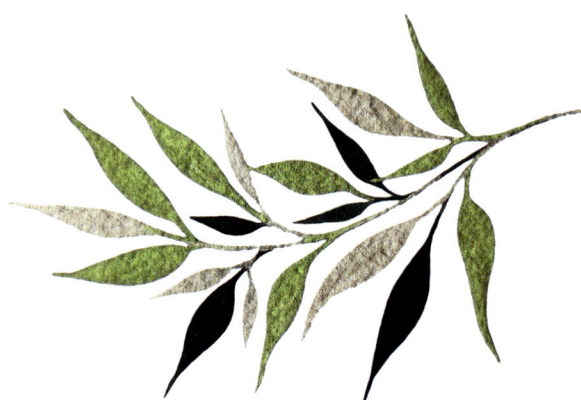

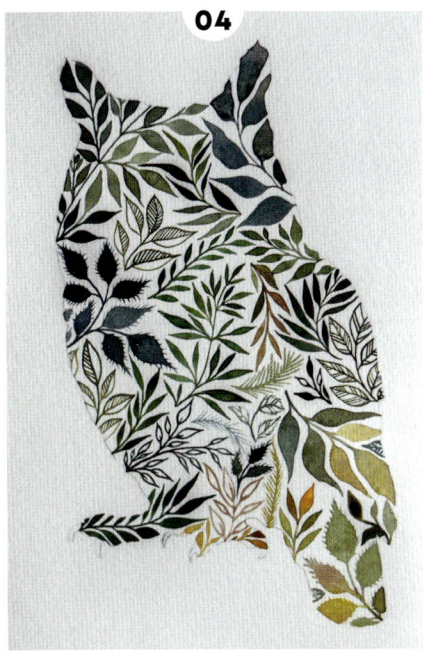

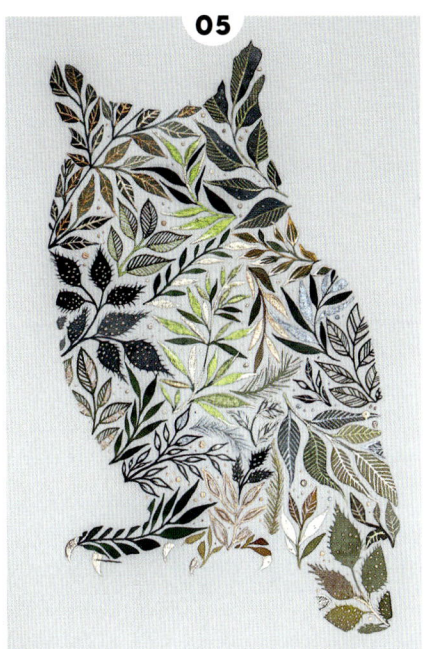

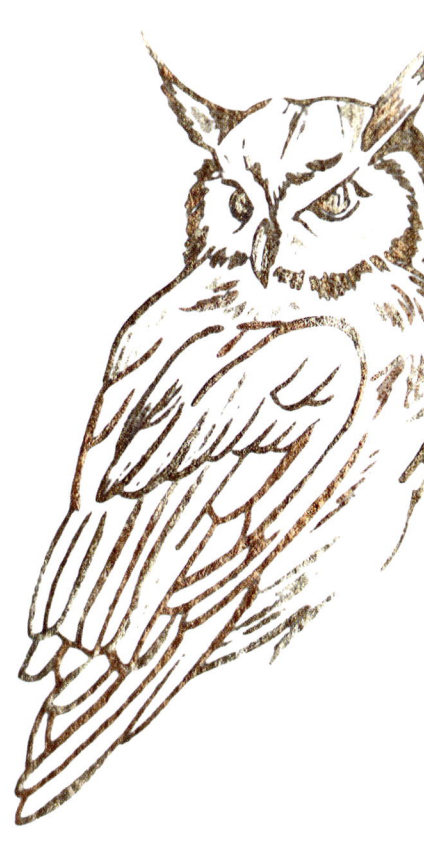

04 Another option is to experiment with gradients. Referring to my owl as an example, you can see that I've painted the underpart of the tail and feet in a warmer shade. The colors in the body transition beautifully into the cooler shades of the owl's head.

05 Once the watercolor is completely dry, you can add your fine metallic accents. I've matched my choice of shades to the color of the leaves so that the finished picture doesn't look too jarring or garish. As in step 3, I've tried out different patterns and variations. Experiment with your metallic paints! A mixture of filled metallic leaves and individual iridescent accents is the perfect way to round off your motif. Finally, I added little shimmering dots in the gaps between the twigs and painted the owl's claws entirely in light gold. Once your watercolor is completely dry, you can carefully rub out the fine pencil lines of the outline.

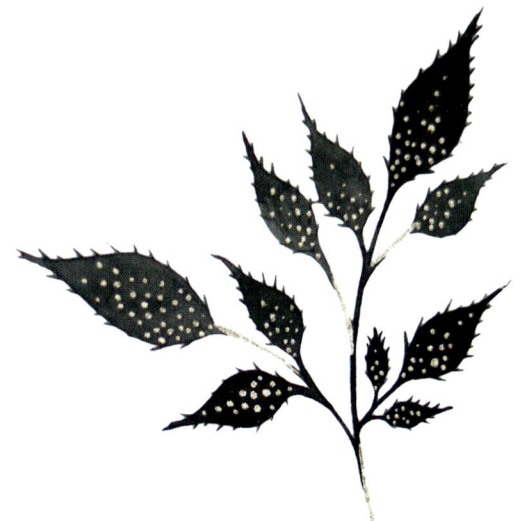

OWL MADE FROM LEAVES

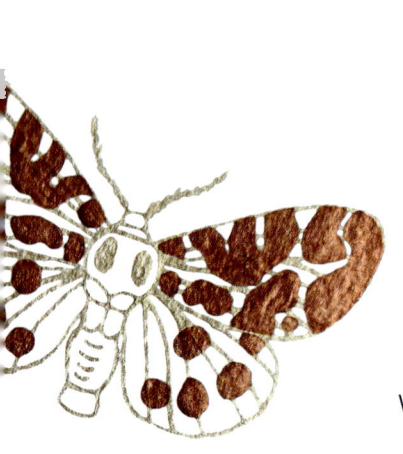

Ornamental
MOTH

With their symmetrical patterns and fine details, butterflies and moths hold a special appeal for me. With every picture I paint, I set myself the goal of getting the delicate texture of the wings even more precise. This is also why I like using these fascinating creatures to develop my drawing skills.

MATERIALS

RIGGER BRUSH OR MICROBRUSH | SIZE 1 ROUND BRUSH | PENCIL | WATERCOLOR PAPER

MY COLOR PALETTE

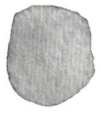   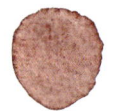 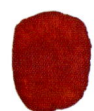  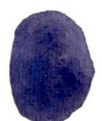

=== METALLIC PAINTS ===

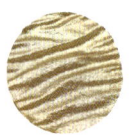 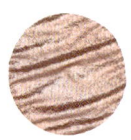 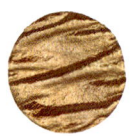

LIGHT GOLD   PALE PINK   BRONZE

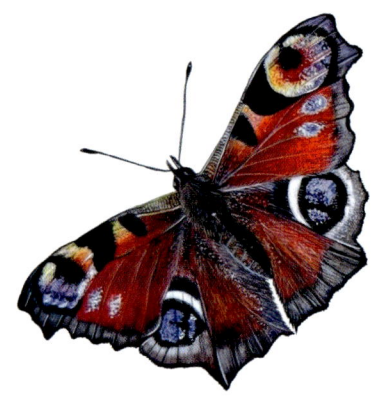

METALLIC WATERCOLOR

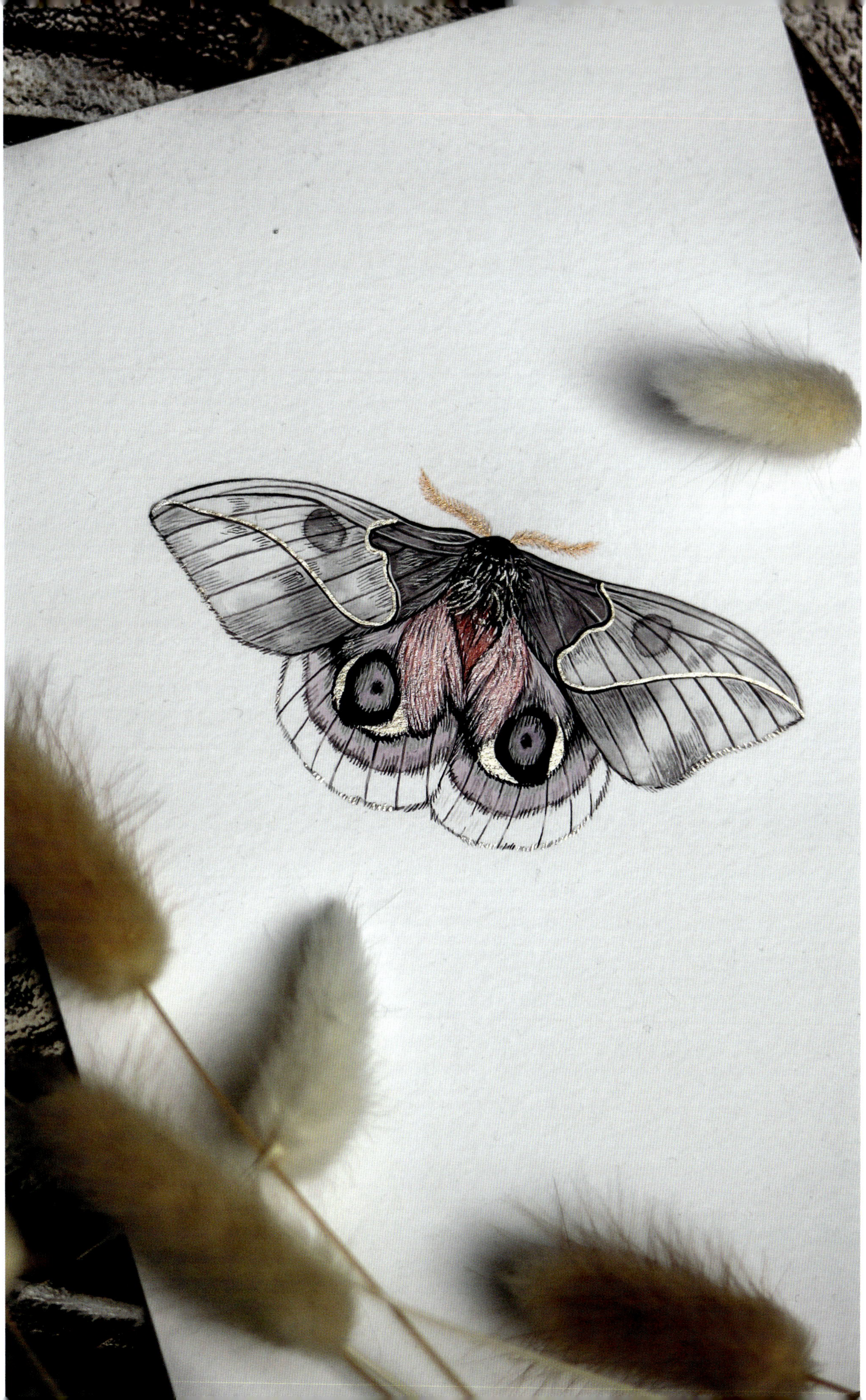

ADVANCED

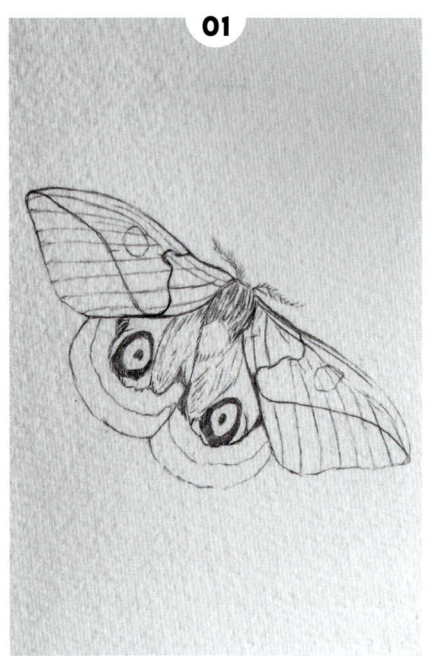

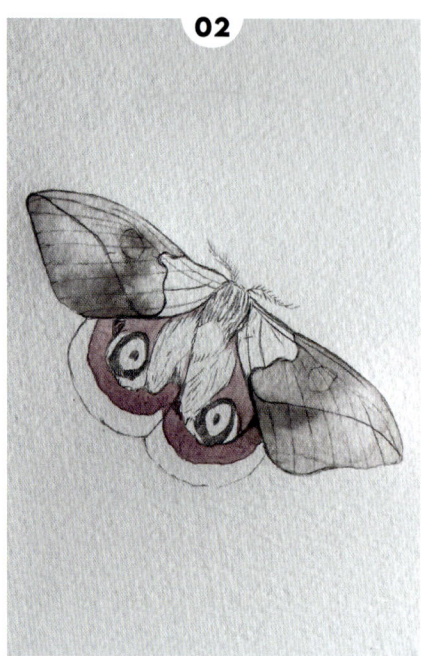

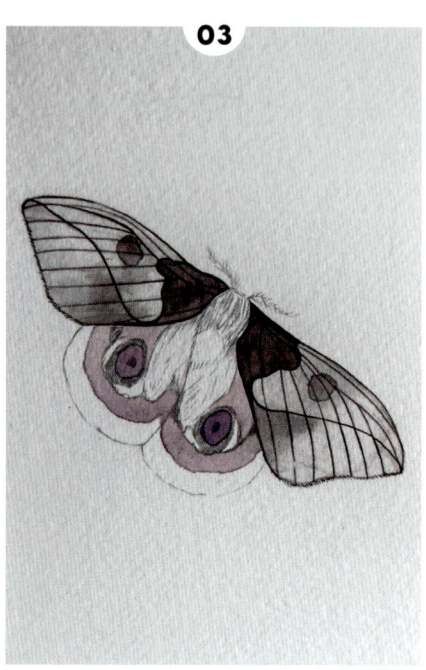

01 Sketch the outline of the moth on your water-color paper with a soft pencil and add the pattern to the wings. (You can also scan the QR code on page 31 to download a traceable sketch.)

02 Taking a small round brush and clean water, dampen the first parts of the paper in the top and bottom wings, then use the wet-on-wet technique to apply a light gray and a dusky-rose shade. The colored areas will need to dry out.

03 Now you can add the darker parts inside the wings. Once sufficiently dry, you can add fine veins in a darker gray. For this step, I've used my rigger brush to draw delicate hairs on the outside of the wings.

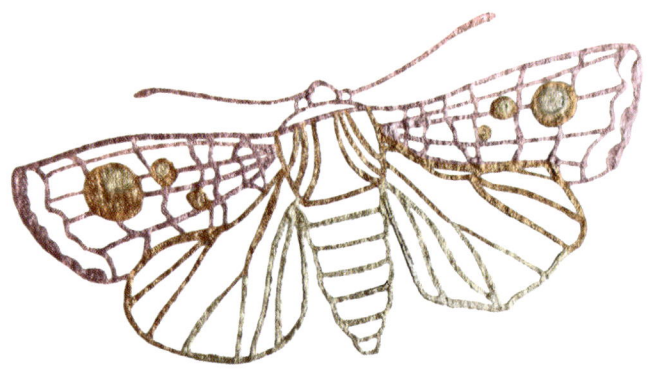

METALLIC WATERCOLOR

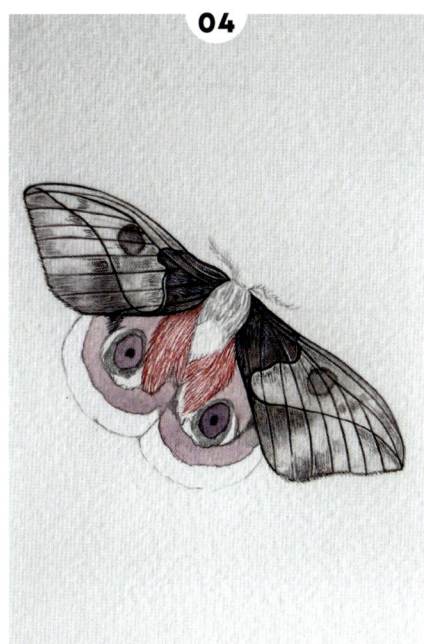

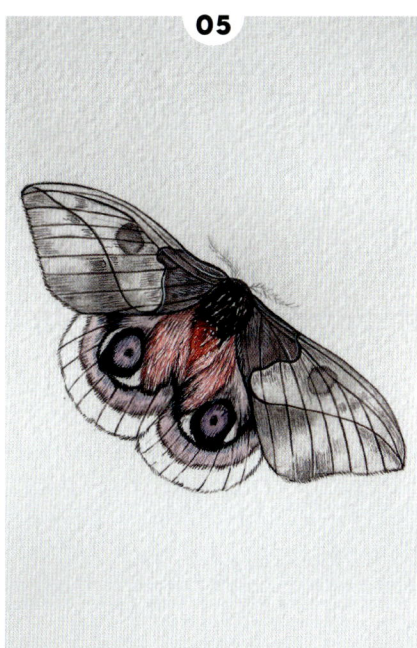

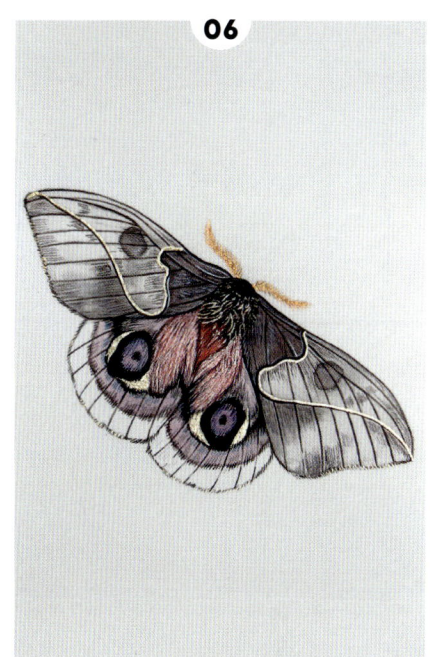

04 Once all parts have dried, you can add subtle textures on the wings with the rigger brush and a darker gray, refining them by adding more white strokes. For the bottom part of the wings, I mixed a bright pink and used it to paint the delicate little hairs on the moth.

05 In this step, I focused on the moth's hairy body and the fine textures of the lower wings. First, I went over the fine veins and hairs in the upper wings with the gray shade and then the fine textures on the surface using individual strokes. I also added a few dark hairs in the bright-pink area. To make the symmetrical pattern on the lower wings look even more striking, I outlined it with the black from my watercolor palette. The moth's body is composed of a dark gray and pink hairs.

06 In the last step, I added the metallic details, giving our moth a unique shine. I added most of the accents in light gold in the space surrounding the pattern on the lower wings and as individual shimmering hairs on the moth's body. I also outlined the upper wings on the right and left in gold. Pale-pink metallic paint is used for the pink-colored hairs of the lower wings too. I added the moth's feathery antennae in bronze.

Crafty
FOX

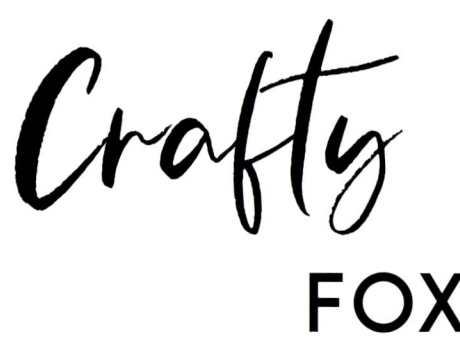
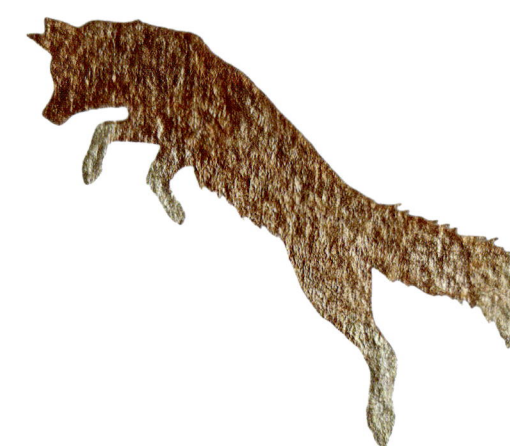

This cheeky little fox is the final motif in the book and I hope you find it as cute as I do. Foxes are some of my all-time favorite animals and I love drawing them in a realistic style. Lifelike watercolor paintings shimmer beautifully with the addition of fine metallic accents.

MATERIALS

RIGGER BRUSH | MICROBRUSH | ROUND BRUSH |
PENCIL | WATERCOLOR PAPER | WASHI TAPE

MY COLOR PALETTE

METALLIC PAINTS

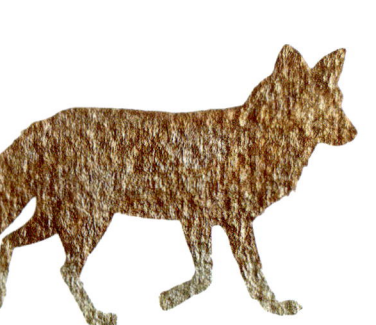

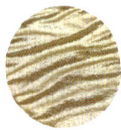 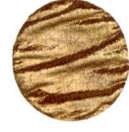 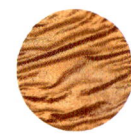

LIGHT
GOLD   BRONZE   ORANGE

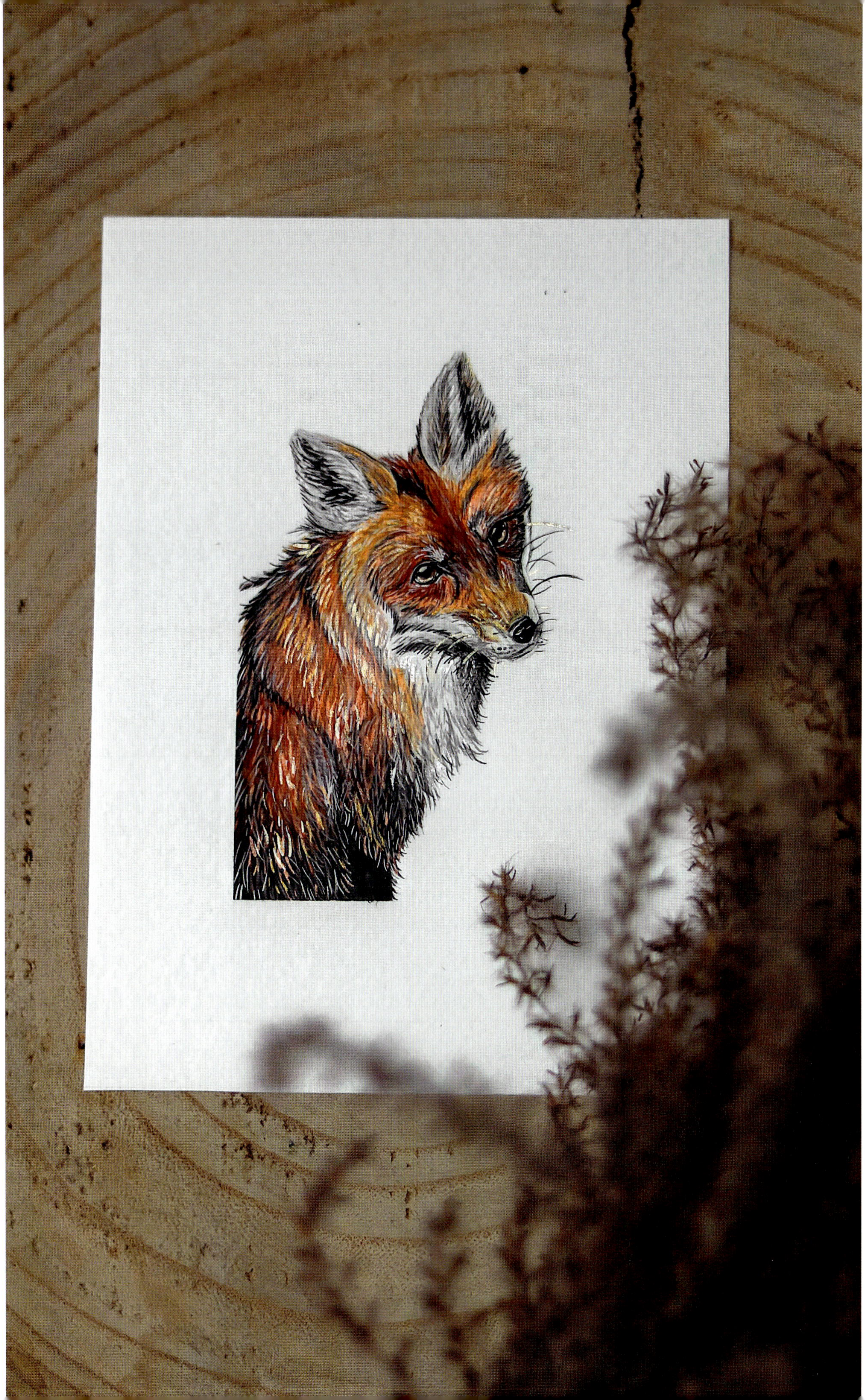

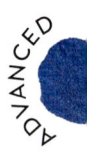

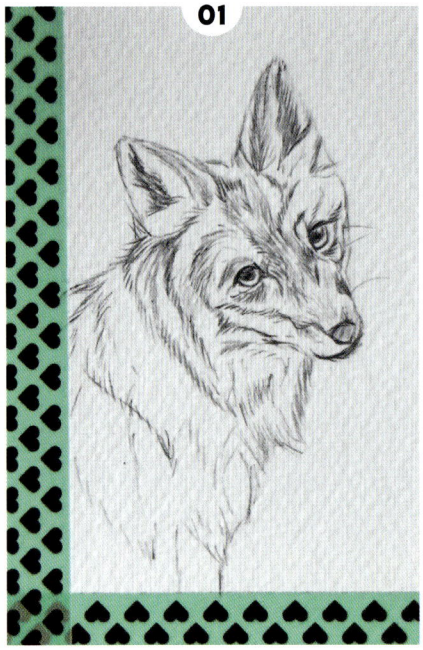

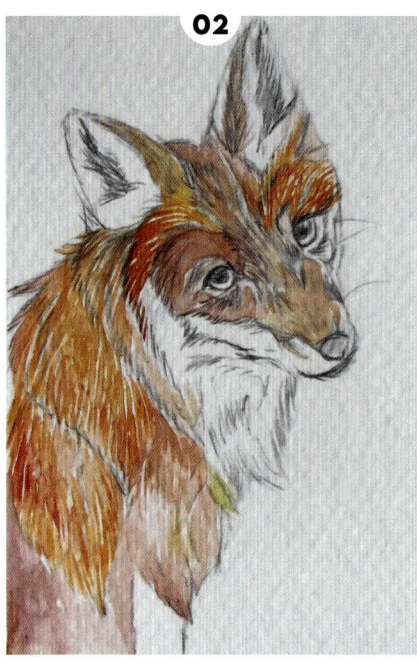

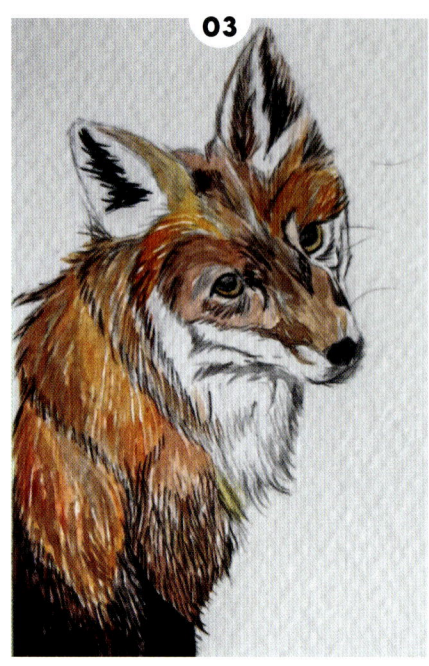

01   For the fox motif, we're going to use washi tape to get a clean edge along the bottom of our watercolor. Washi tape is a sticky tape that's easy to remove when you're finished. Once you've sketched the animal onto your paper in soft pencil, you can stick down the washi tape to form a right angle. When sketching, I shade some areas of the animal more darkly to create reference lines for the watercolors. (You can also scan the QR code on page 31 to download a traceable sketch.)

02   With a round brush (size 1) and a variety of different shades of orange, you can lay down the initial textures for your fox. Rather than filling the areas, I painted the surface of the fur using lots of individual strokes. In this motif, we also work in several layers, applied one after the other. These layers make the watercolor look increasingly refined.

03   For this step and layer, we'll continue working the pattern of the fur and the fox's outline in two darker shades of brown. I've used both shades to color the beginning of the legs and ears too. You can also start preparing the colored underpainting for the eyes.

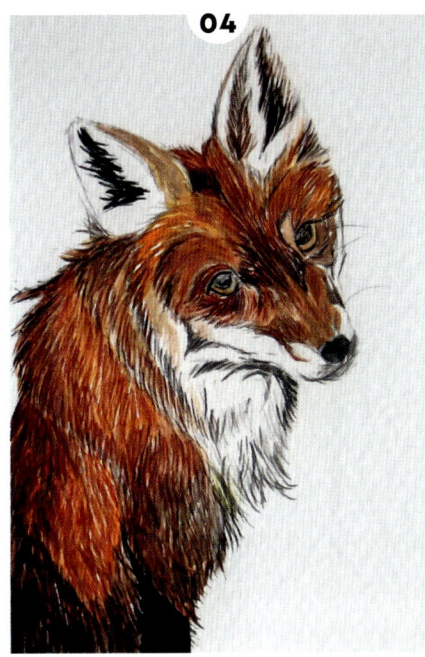

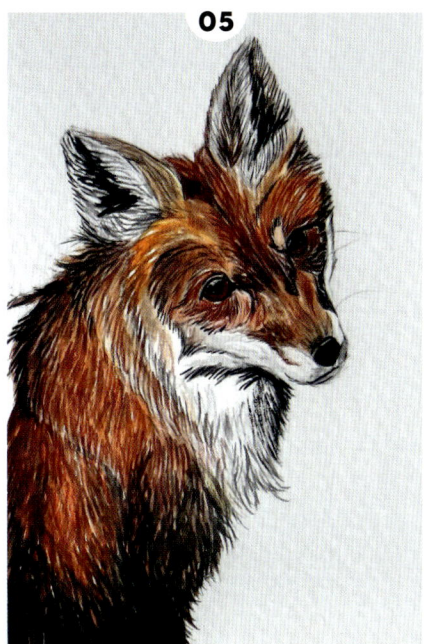

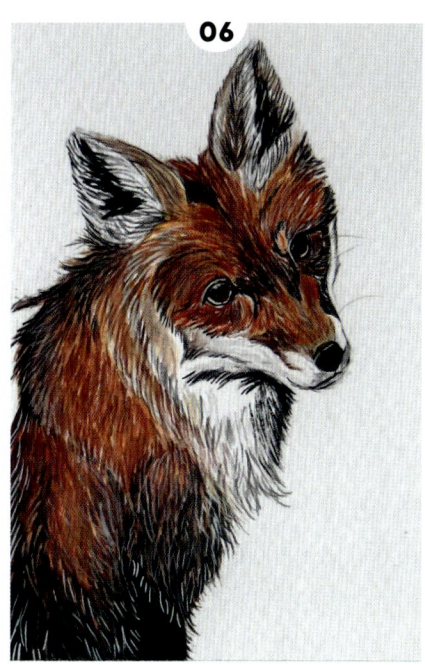

04   In this layer, we'll use two different shades of red, in lots of little lines that give the fur more texture. By now, you'll be able to see a big difference between this layer and the first one. Our fox is looking more and more detailed.

05   In this step, I put my round brush to one side and swapped to my microbrush. A rigger brush would also do. The fine tip makes it easier to work the additional details. You can start going over the fox's eyes in black. I also added fine contours and shadows in black to the fur and the head. Remember to try to keep the darker strokes as thin as possible so they don't dominate your watercolor.

06   Now we can make the picture look more vibrant and three-dimensional by adding some fine accents in a lighter shade of paint. I used the white from my watercolor palette, mixed with the shades I'd used already, applying them with a microbrush.

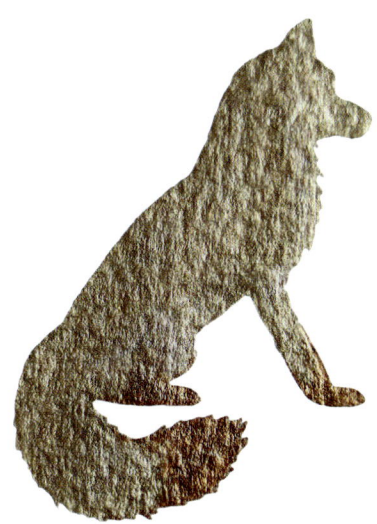

CRAFTY FOX

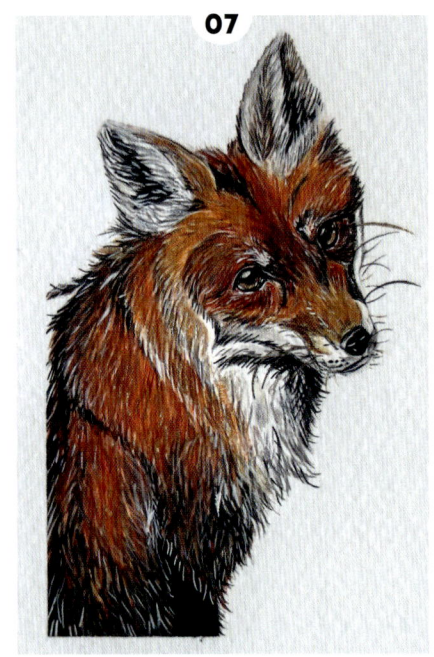

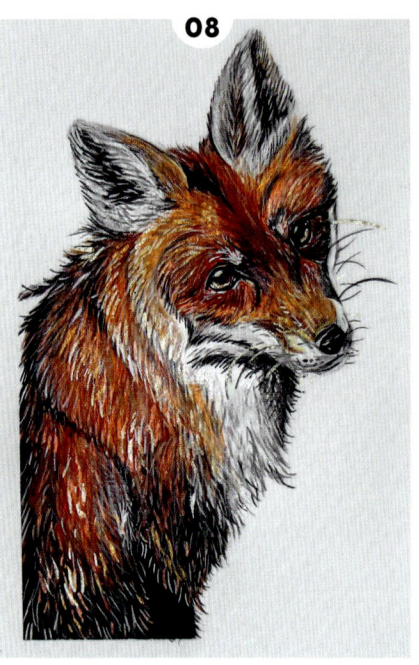

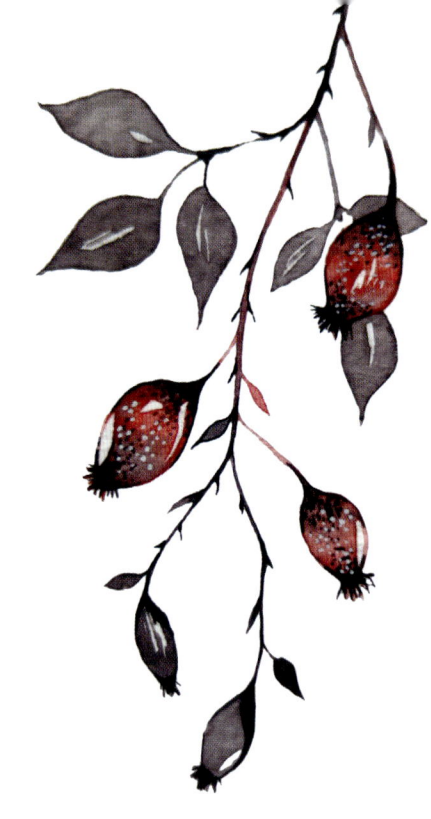

07   In this second-to-last step, I laid down the white straight from the pan using my microbrush to create the last few white details in the fur and eyes. You can then paint the fox's fine whiskers in black. I've already removed the washi tape so you can see the clean edge it makes. However, you can also remove the tape after your painting is finished.

08   Our fox painting is done and I've added a few fine metallic accents in bronze, light gold, and orange. You can only see them if you hold the watercolor at a slight angle, which lends your realistic painting a subtle elegance.

Tip

You can also draw the fox minus the metallic accents for a more natural look.

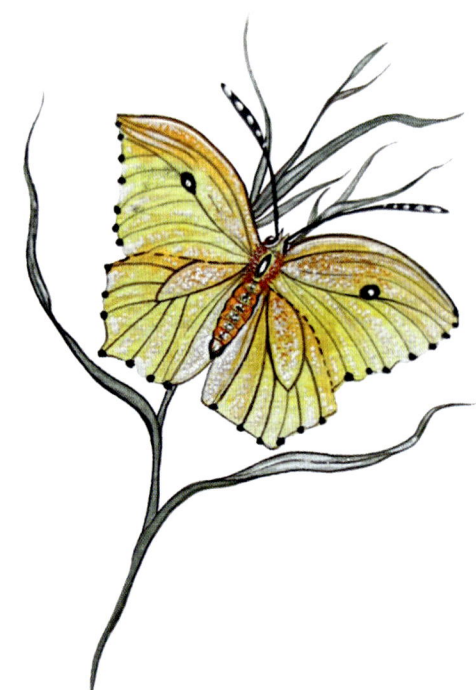

METALLIC WATERCOLOR

Woodland Creatures

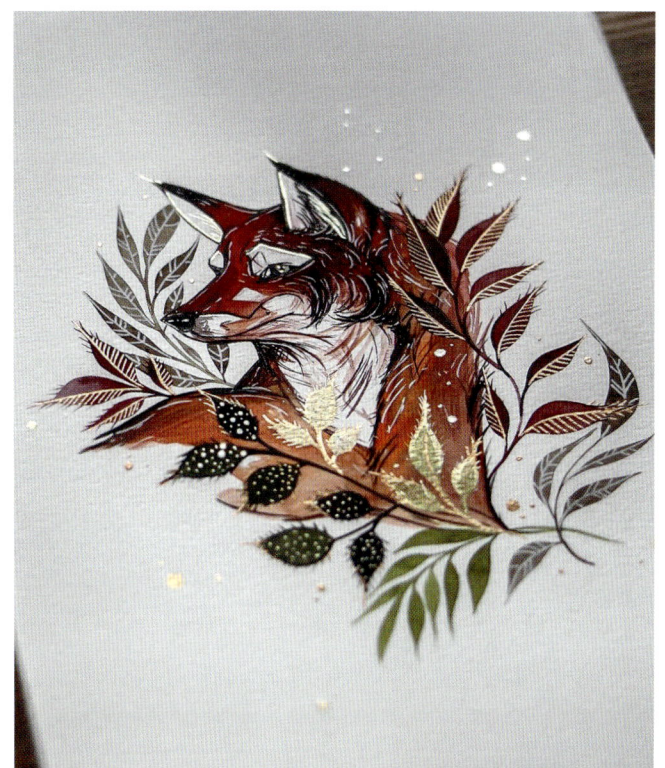

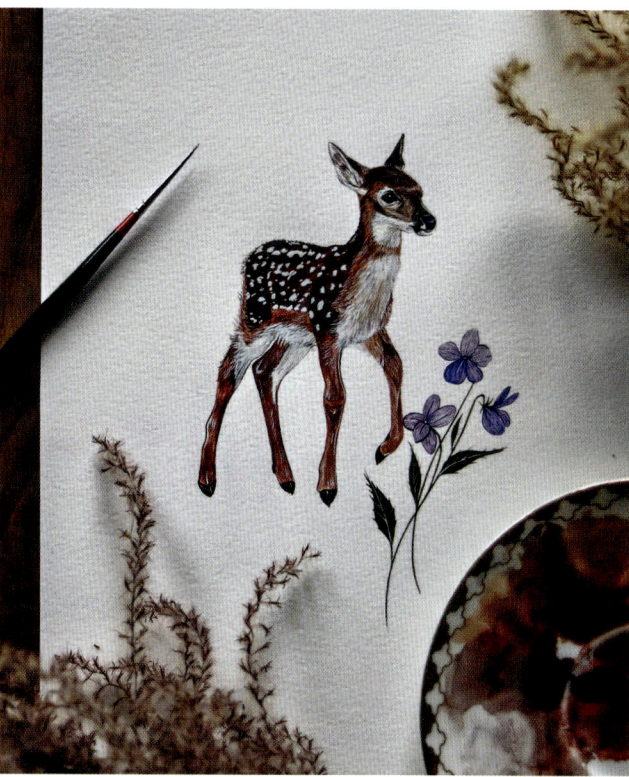

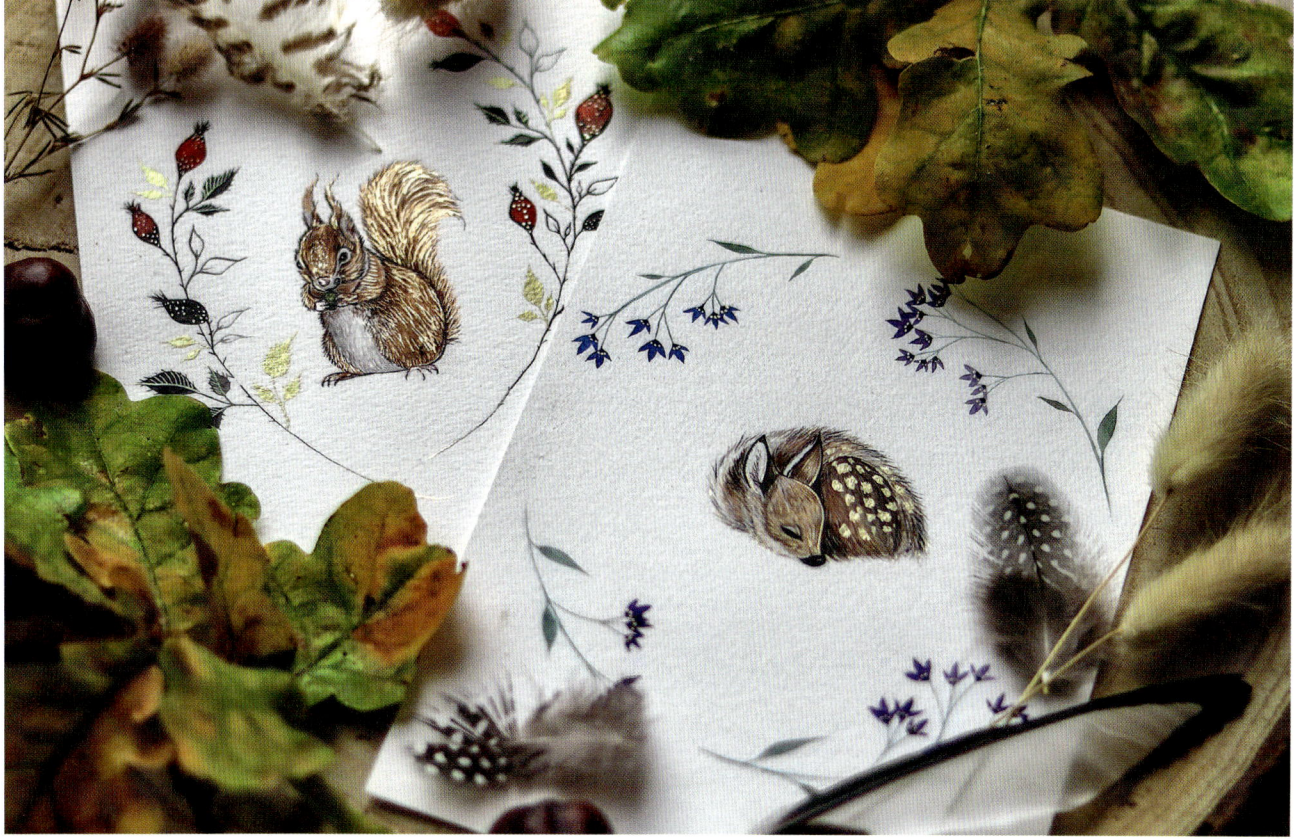

Expressive Birds & Moths

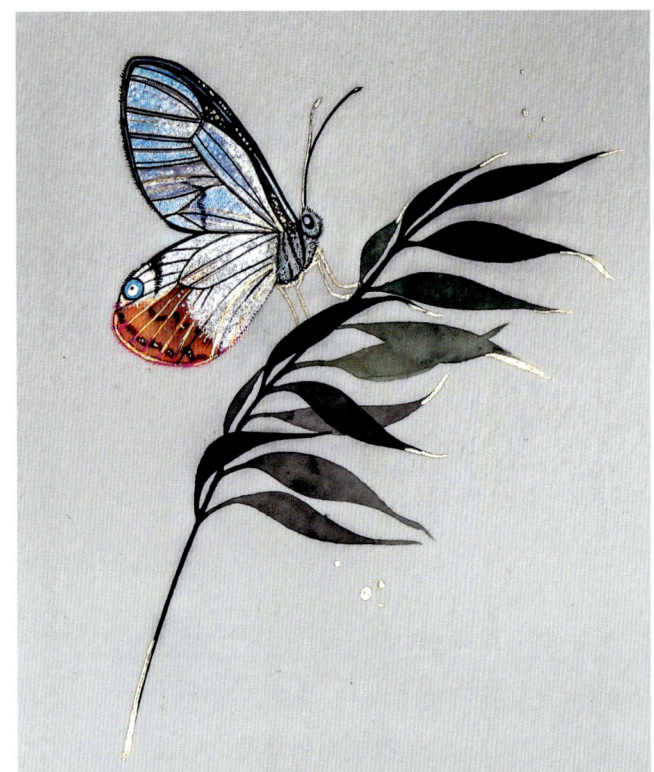

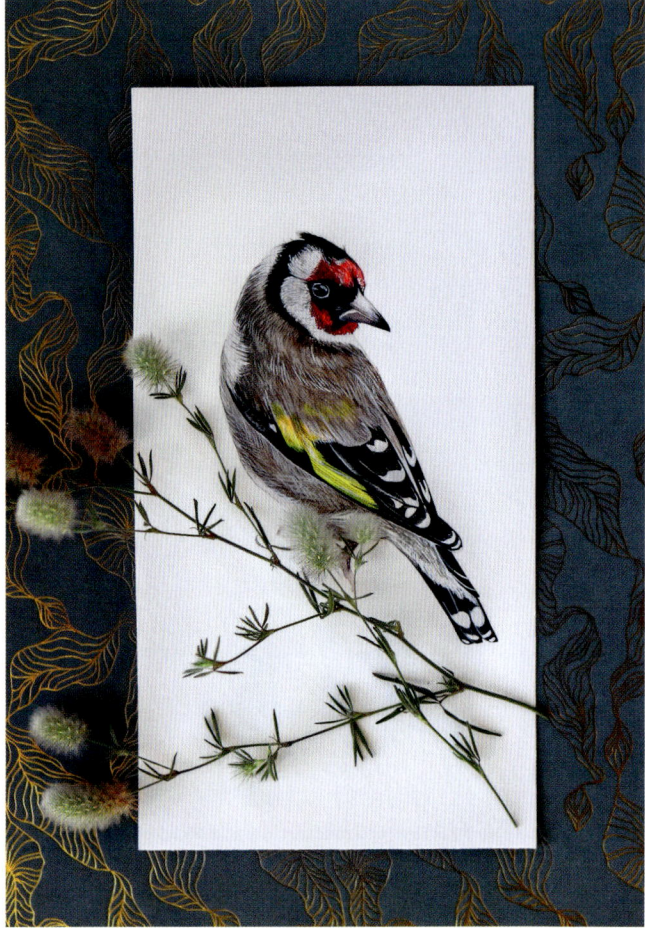

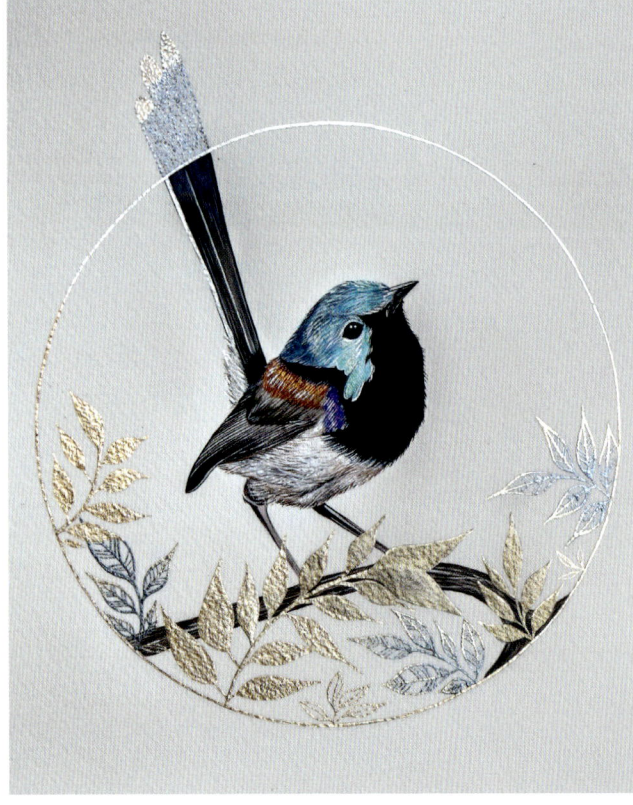

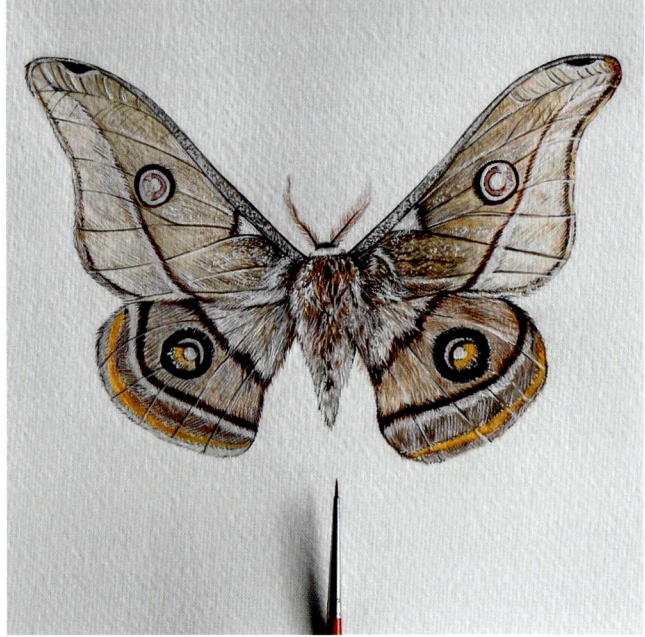

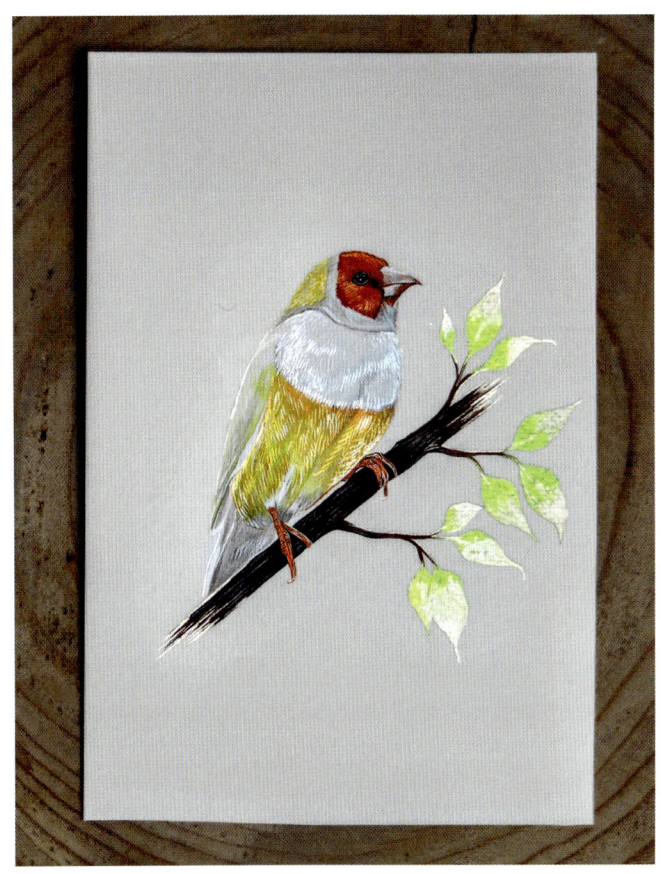

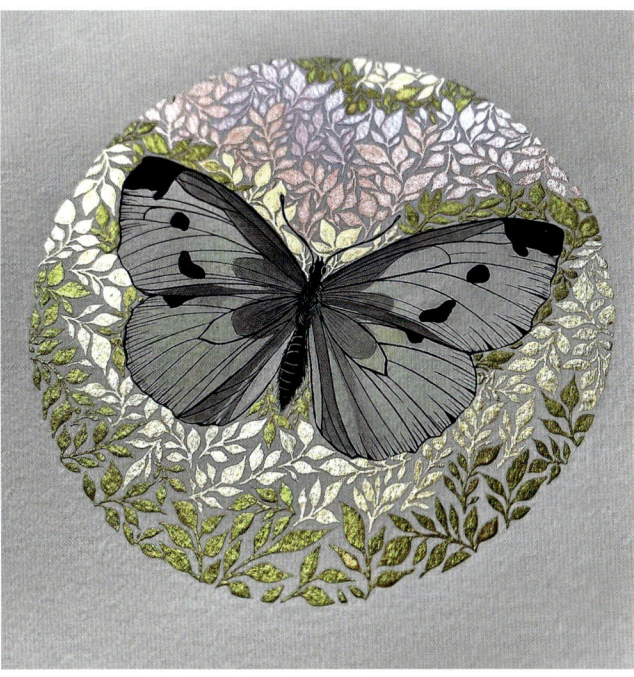

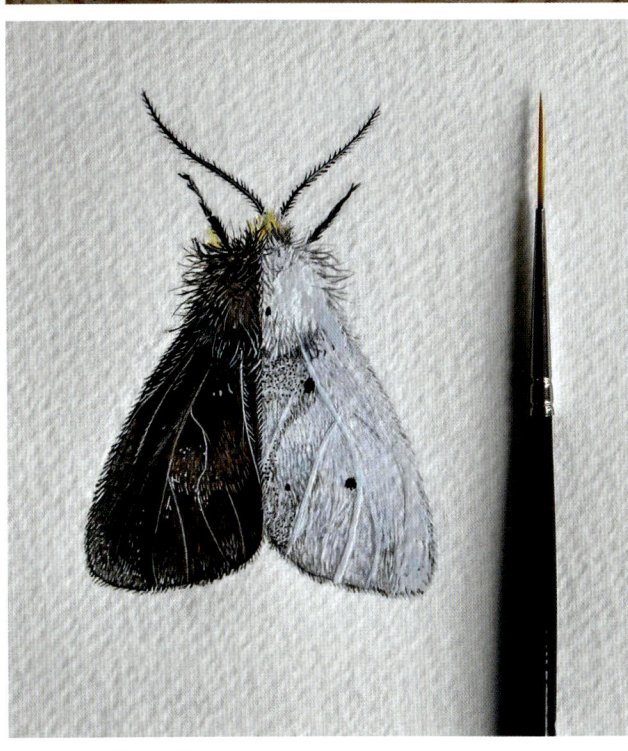

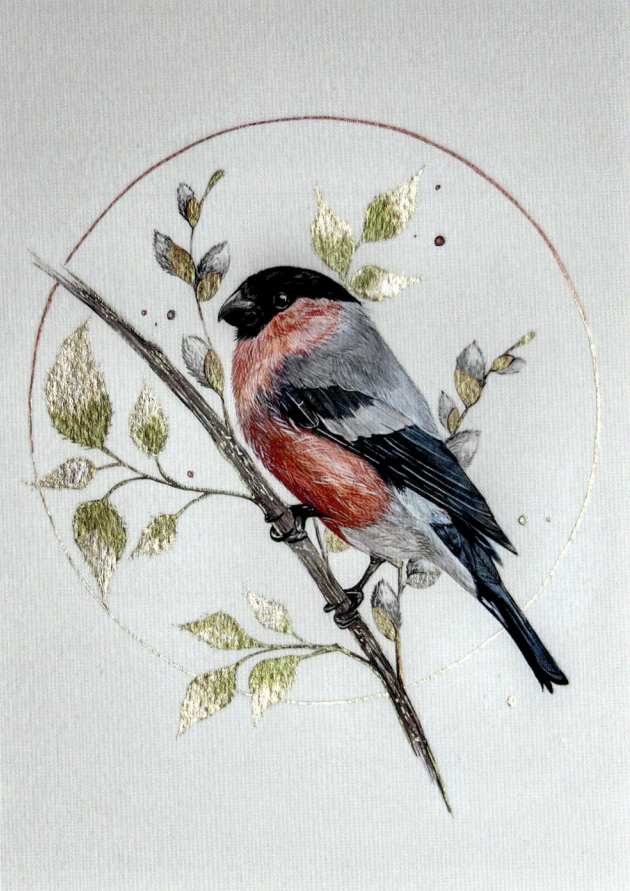

About
THE AUTHOR

Elisabeth Götz is a freelance artist and psychologist from Germany. Her studies in Berlin were very scientific, so her paintings gave her a way to not only finance her professional education, but to achieve a creative balance. She shares her pictures on Instagram under the handle @lisilinka, takes commissions, and teaches a watercolor course on the artists' platform Domestika.

Her watercolors are known for their filigree appearance and love of detail. Her use of metallic accents makes her delicate motifs shine.

Online-Shop: *www.TheClassyWay.com*

Instagram: *Lisilinka*

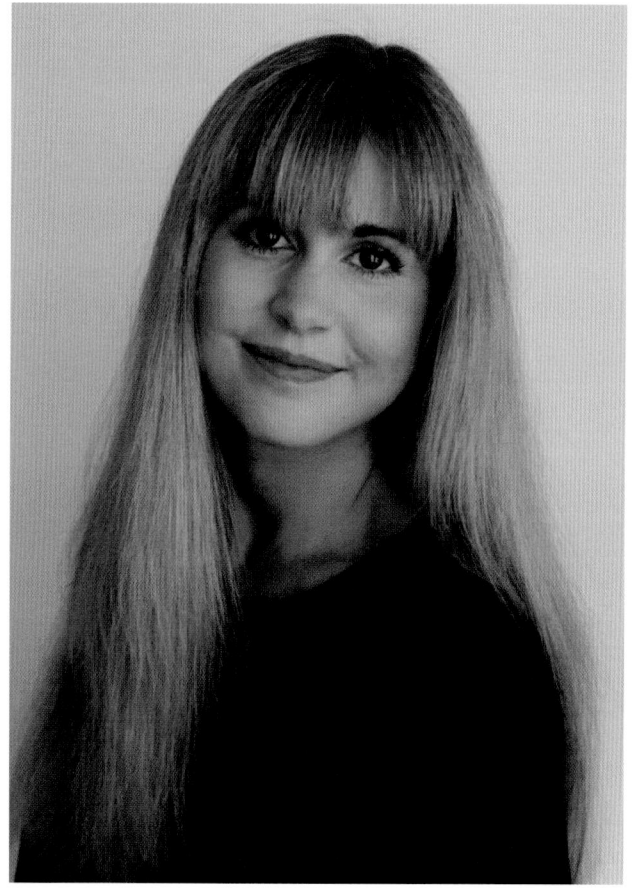

Acknowledgments

My special thanks go to EMF Verlag and, in particular, my editor Saskia Hauck, who accompanied me on this exciting journey and gave me such great advice. Thanks for always being there to answer my questions and listen to my dreams! I'd also like to thank Silvia Keller for creating such a beautiful layout and all of her creative ideas. They have made this book a real feast for the eyes!

This book would never have been possible without the support of my family. They had my back every step of the way and encouraged me to make this unbelievable opportunity a reality. Thank you for sharing in my excitement and believing in me! Finally, my thanks go to all those who get such joy from my art! It's your enthusiasm for my pictures that has made this dream come true.

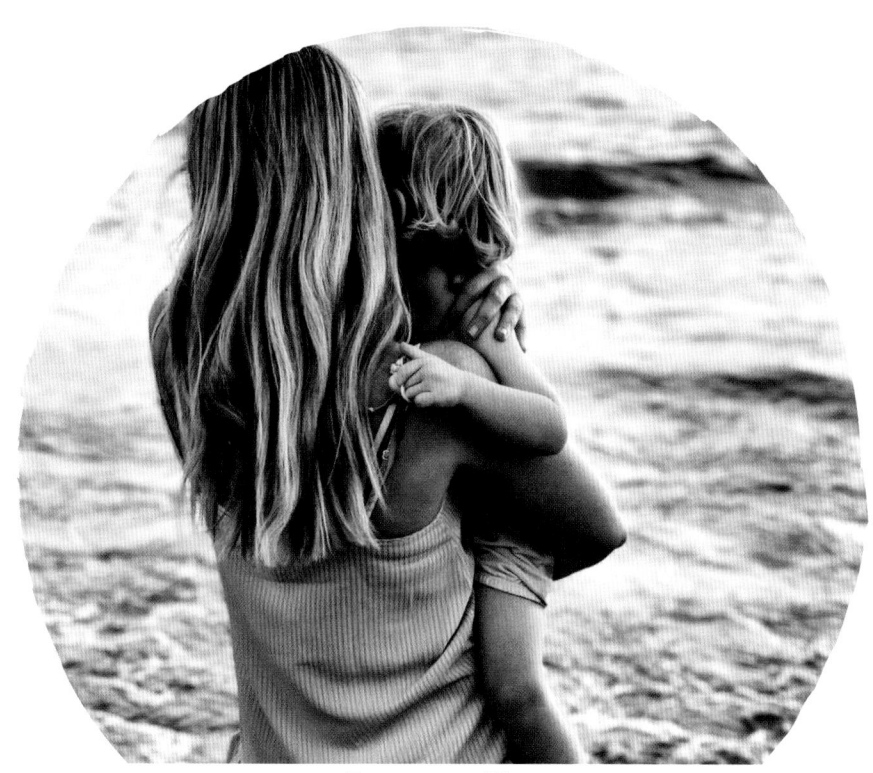

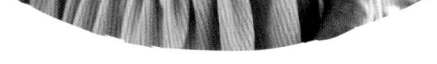

For my son, Flynn
Believe in yourself and your dreams

Quarto.com

© Edition Michael Fischer GmbH, 2022

www.emf-verlag.de

This translation of SHINY WATERCOLOR: LEUCHTENDE MOTIVE AUS FLORA UND FAUNA first published in Germany by Edition Michael Fischer GmbH in 2022 is published by arrangement with Silke Bruenink Agency, Munich, Germany.

Translation and template illustrations © 2025 Quarto Publishing Group USA Inc.

First Published in USA in 2025 by Quarry Books, an imprint of The Quarto Group,

100 Cummings Center, Suite 265-D, Beverly, MA 01915, USA.

T (978) 282-9590 F (978) 283-2742

Quarry Books titles are also available at discount for retail, wholesale, promotional, and bulk purchase. For details, contact the Special Sales Manager by email at specialsales@quarto.com or by mail at The Quarto Group, Attn: Special Sales Manager, 100 Cummings Center, Suite 265-D, Beverly, MA 01915, USA.

10 9 8 7 6 5 4 3 2

ISBN: 978-0-7603-9259-1

Digital edition published in 2025

eISBN: 978-0-7603-9260-7

Library of Congress Control Number available

Translation: Jessica West

Design: Lena Albert, Silvia Keller, and Sporto

Cover Illustration: Elisabeth Götz

Page Layout: Sporto

Photography: © Elisabeth Götz, ausgenommen Metallicfarben der Farbpalette: © coliro GmbH

Template Illustrations (based on author's original drawings): Melissa Washburn

Printed in the USA

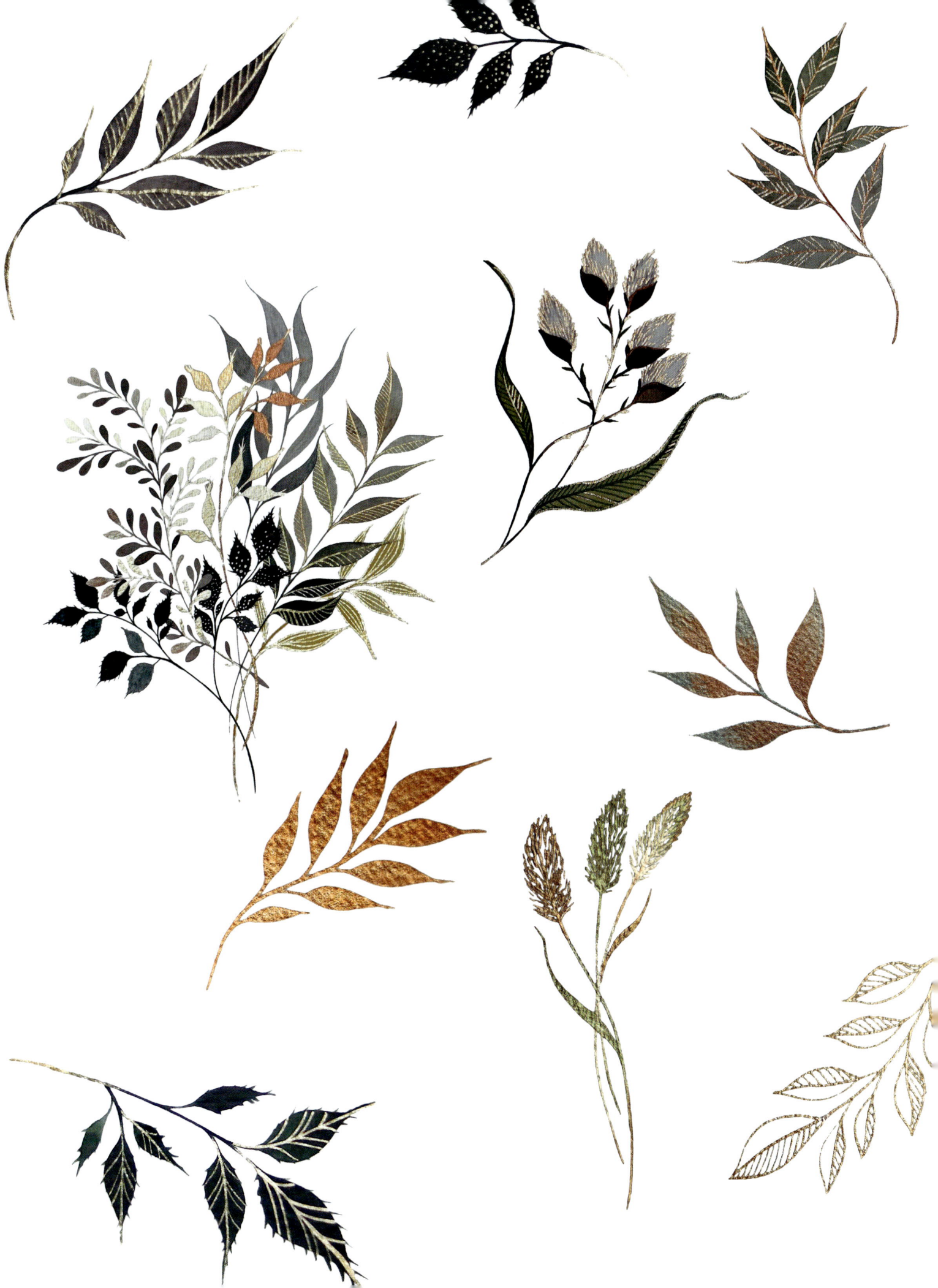

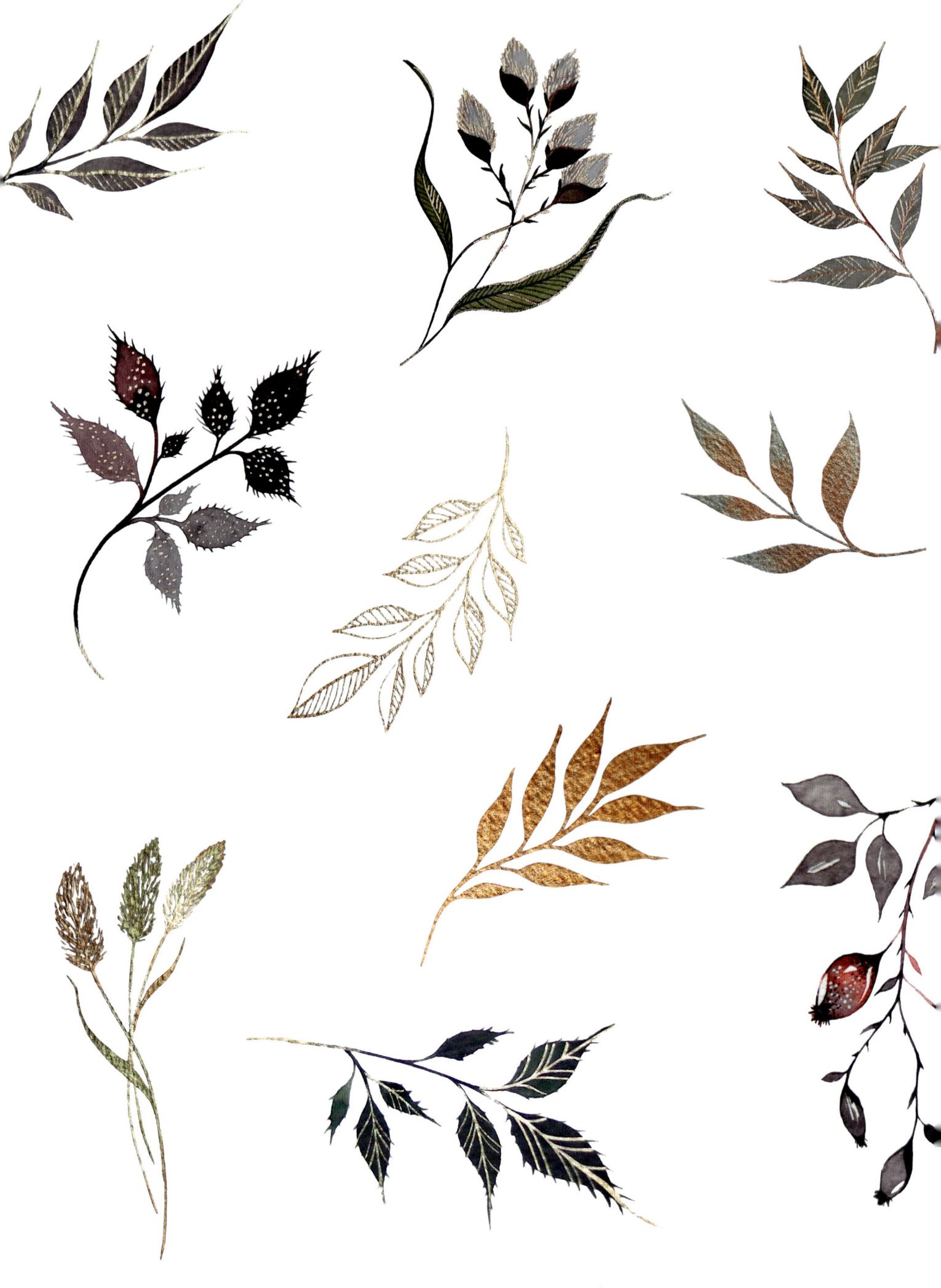